Behind Closed Doors

Behind Closed Doors
Memoirs of an American Call Girl

E. S. Silversmith

ISBN: 979-8-218-62764-5 (paperback)
ISBN: 979-8-230-66789-6 (eBook)
Library of Congress Control Number: 2025904092

Distributed by Ingram Content Group
Copyright © Ingram Book Group LLC
https://www.ingramcontent.com

First Edition

Acknowledgments

To K.,
For encouraging me every step of the way.

To J.,
A wizened wizard with the secrets of the universe.

To all my customers of years past:
Do you think it was easy pretending to be that dumb?
Also, use the soap in the hotel bathrooms.
You know who you are.

Table Of Contents

Introduction ...i

Prologue ...iv

Chapter 1 Bachelor Parties ...1

Chapter 2 Orange Juice ...13

Chapter 3 Stand Up Comedy ...24

Chapter 4 Friendzone ...33

Chapter 5 When No Means Yes ...45

Chapter 6 Plap ...49

Chapter 7 She's A Pirate ...68

Chapter 8 Wasted ...85

Chapter 9 Mycena Subcyanocephala ...100

Chapter 10 Don't Tell ...114

Chapter 11 All Natural ...118

Chapter 12 Oysters ...133

Chapter 13 But Why? ...145

Chapter 14 Plastic Wrap ...163

Chapter 15 Minivan Mistress ...170

Chapter 16 Meat Flap ...186

Chapter 17 Puddles ...203

Chapter 18 You Can Only Go Up ...218

Chapter 19 Dry Mouth ...225

Chapter 20 Unicorn ...235

Chapter 21 Yes, Master ...243

Chapter 22 Bruh ...267

Afterword ...297

About The Author ...300

Introduction

I guess I don't know where to start. The usual thing is my name is E., and this is how my story began. I have two cats, a dog, a white picket fence, and an insatiable thirst for anything but the ordinary. Or maybe I grew up in a trailer park and was molested when I was twelve by some drunken asshole who had nothing better to do.

I could be a single mom with a deadbeat boyfriend who only takes a break from beating me when he is high on heroin. I could be a sex addict who, after losing all self-control, decided to make some money out of it because I'd be out there doing it anyway. A junkie, doing whatever it takes for her next fix. A bored housewife that moonlights in the industry because her husband doesn't pay enough attention to her. Maybe I am a woman who needs to pay off her husband's gambling debts before the cars get repossessed and the mortgage falls into foreclosure. Married, single, newly divorced, widowed, kids, no kids, rich, poor, homeless, young, old.

Honestly, I could be any combination of the stories above, because like the clients we served, we came from all walks of life and in all shapes and sizes. There was no one-size-fits-all reason for being a sex worker; we all had our reasons, and not all of them were tragic or even interesting.

The only common theme I ever saw in all my years as an escort was that we all needed money and didn't have a better way to get it. We each owned our unique, broken piece of the American dream and were doing our best to simply get by. We paid our taxes, living month to month like most other Americans, and were one financial hardship or unexpected medical expense away from becoming destitute. We were, and are, incredibly and overwhelmingly average. But most important of all, and the part that society likes to gloss over the most, we were all people just like you.

Of course, there were differences. Certainly, a normal Tuesday night for you may not consist of stripping nude in a hotel room with a stranger you have never met, and I imagine your business expenses don't consist of fishnet stockings and lipstick. Still, with all things considered, I am not so different from the man walking down the street with a briefcase, rushing off to get to a meeting on time. Anything done professionally becomes a banal task before long, and the adult entertainment industry was no exception. Just like flipping burgers or teaching a classroom of rambunctious kindergartners, it was work, but unlike the latter, it offered a rare glimpse into the raw underbelly of society.

For me, being an escort exposed me to a wealth of experiences I would have normally never been a part of, and I saw a darker side of human nature that few ever get a chance to see. It was gritty and sometimes sad, but it also always held the potential for lighthearted moments of unexpected joy. Each day, and each client for that matter, was a unique opportunity to peek into a window of the most vulnerable, intimate thoughts a person possessed; I was personally privy to the feelings and desires that most people will never share with another living soul and will likely take to their graves. I was both a person and a ghost to my clients, a nobody with no real name or consequence. Because of this, few had problems sharing their secrets and whispering about the desires lingering deep within the far corners of their minds.

The media tells us that sex workers are a certain kind of people. I see on television hookers being murdered by a deranged serial killer, and the fact of the life lost is handled as nothing more than an afterthought needed to advance the story of a criminal drama. No care or consideration was given to the woman who was murdered. In our society, I learned quickly that a sex worker's life is considered less than worthless. Who cares if another prostitute lies dead in the gutter? She is human trash, after all, and the worst of the worst. Women who sell their bodies are viewed as scum, living at the lowest rung of the social ladder as outsiders.

No one I worked with wanted to openly admit that they worked as an escort to anyone outside the industry because of the shame and humiliation it carried; many of us had already been disowned by our families and subsequently treated as if we were already dead. We were forced to live secret, double lives in order to support ourselves and our families. Many of us had small children at home, and many more had boyfriends and husbands.

We were hated by housewives and shunned by the same men who paid top dollar for our services. We were viewed as disgusting, disease-riddled drug addicts or selfish gold diggers too lazy to get real jobs. Yet, despite being considered the wretches of society and denounced by all, there was a never-ending sea of clientele eager for our services time and time again.

I have also seen the media tell a tale of glamour and fast, easy money. Beautiful women living lavish lifestyles, full of admiration while being showered constantly with expensive presents. Women who spent their time sipping cocktails on tropical islands with young, attractive men who are kind, loving, and also great in bed. They are portrayed as completely independent feminists who have conquered the system by taking advantage of the weak-willed nature of man. This woman is depicted as a winner and a girl who is always on the lookout for the ultimate score.

These representations, both wildly different from one another, may help sell movies and television shows but do nothing to reflect the complexity and day-to-day struggle of a real American sex worker. My stories, like the stories of countless others just like me, share a perspective unknown to most. We are mothers, wives, sisters, aunts, and daughters. We are regular people, worthy of both dignity and respect, who exist in a world on the fringes of human experience.

Prologue

"So, you want to tell me how you're feeling today?"

Seated behind a desk in front of me was an older man. His accent, some manner of European I couldn't determine, was syrupy thick and flavored his every word.

I fidgeted in my seat, saying nothing and pulling my body inward in an attempt to make myself as small as possible. I looked at him, this man with his attention half fixed on my medical record as he nonchalantly flipped through each page, stopping only to sign documents placed off to the side.

"I'd like to go home today," I spoke without making eye contact, my voice barely above a whisper.

The man's uncaring eyes flitted up from his paperwork for a moment before returning to his task. He cleared his throat and stared at me again, waiting for me to fill the silence.

"Um, the doctor. I spoke to the doctor today, and she said I was doing better. I've been taking my medication. I feel better. Really," I said as earnestly as I could muster.

In truth, I was in fact not feeling better, and I had only been taking the medication for the past week because the doctor stiffly informed me that I would not be discharged unless I was fully compliant with the treatment plan. So down the hatch they went, pills in the morning and pills at night.

The sound of his pen scratching its way across page after page was the only noise that filled the cramped office space. The abundance of candles and air fresheners filling the room did nothing to cover the lingering stench of stacks of old boxes filled with years of medical documentation.

"Do you have a job?" he asked.

I felt my pulse quicken as a bead of sweat made it down the back of my neck.

"No," I said honestly.

He paused thoughtfully and scribbled something on one of the papers.

"What about school? How is that going? It says here that you have a fairly impressive GPA."

I swallowed hard, feeling my face grow hot. A lump was forming in my throat, and each passing moment made it harder to think, harder to speak.

"I do, I mean, I did," I managed weakly, "before I came here. It was mid-terms, and I missed my exams... and failed my classes."

The man nodded in response, and the sound of ink on paper filled my ears once again.

After a few minutes, he put down his pen and straightened the stack of paperwork neatly in front of him. He pulled a sheet from the bottom of the stack and slid it across the desk towards me.

"Now one more thing," he said, this time looking right at me, "do you have any more thoughts of harming yourself?"

I flinched, the memory of waking up disoriented in the hospital still fresh in my mind.

"N-no," I said quietly, my eyes falling to my feet, "none at all."

The man only sighed in response.

"Sign here, and here, and here."

Robotically, I obeyed. The instructions that followed, concerning which doctor to call and where I would pick up medications sounded almost muffled. I could see his mouth moving, but the words were barely penetrating the dense fog of my mind.

After a few minutes of nodding in the right places and saying *yes* when expected to fill the gaps of conversation, he stood up and walked me out of his office.

In my arms, I held a brown paper bag full of all the belongings I had on me when I was admitted. I clutched the bag close to me as I shuffled silently behind him, thankful to leave the sterility of the hospital after two long weeks. Other patients watched with curiosity and envy as the man led me to the locked double doors that were the only way off the unit. With a simple scan of his badge, a loud clicking sound signaled my freedom.

Outside, the bright glare of the sun blinded me; I had seen nothing but the constant low hum from fluorescents for what seemed like a lifetime. I winced, my eyes struggling to adjust to the natural light. It was mid-day, and the cool autumn breeze brushed against the bare skin poking out of my t-shirt. I looked around, searching the parking lot for my boyfriend's car, but saw nothing but leaves tussling softly in the wind.

He had told the social worker that he would pick me up while they were planning my discharge, but he was nowhere to be seen. I watched the birds in the trees, and slowly the afternoon faded into early evening. Goosebumps covered my body as I shivered, my body fighting as the temperature began to drop. Eventually, I heard the sound of music, far too loud for a hospital campus, roaring into the parking lot.

It was my boyfriend, late as usual.

He rolled down the driver's side window and the smell of marijuana wafted towards me. We had no money since I had lost my job after being admitted to the hospital, and I frowned, wondering how he managed to buy it. He was never one to keep a job, either, but somehow, he always found a way to get high.

He grinned when he saw me and made no effort to apologize for being hours late to pick me up. Once inside the car, the strong stink of weed smacked me in the face and made me gag; it was the scent of my childhood, my father. The smell caused a rush of painful, horrific memories to flood my mind, and my body responded by emptying what remained of my lunch violently out onto the curb.

*

I sat on the couch and slowly lowered my head into my hands. At my feet was a pile of envelopes. I wriggled my toes on the soft carpet, musing at the bits of ash and dirt embedded in the fibers, as a large wet droplet plopped onto the papers. First one, then another, until the ink began to bleed through the paper.

I watched the peaceful swirling black color diffuse across the surface of the envelope as my mind fell deeper into chaos. My boyfriend, my darling lover, had spent all of our money on weed while I was away. Now, with the bank accounts empty, we had no way to pay our bills.

I shut my eyes, letting two soggy tears spill down my cheeks, and reached for my phone. I clung to it, pulling it to my chest with both hands, and stifled a sob.

He had failed to even pay the phone bill, and I anticipated that the service would be shut off at any moment. Seated nearby, he was giggling at the TV while pressing buttons on his video game controller, oblivious to the gravity of the situation.

I knew there was no use trying to argue with him, and that asking him to get a job would be a waste of time. He couldn't pass a drug test, and that was if he even made it that far. As long as I knew him, he was extremely unmotivated; it was challenging just to get him out of bed in the morning or to do his own laundry.

Despite his shortcomings, I couldn't let him go. I had gone back and forth about the relationship so many times and even threatened to break up with him during heated arguments. We would fight, make up, and then make love. He always told me that he loved me and held me late at night when I cried and raged against the injustice of the world. I needed him, and no matter how many mistakes he made, his love made it all worthwhile.

I looked around the room, taking in the dirty, unkempt space. There was laundry strewn about, the sink was full of dishes, and I knew without looking that the cabinets were bare. The furniture was thrifted and in poor shape; the couch had a smell, that despite numerous attempts with a multitude of cleaning agents, could not be gotten rid of. The only chair we owned was close to falling apart, not that we needed it; there was no dining room table, no coffee table. Other than smears of grime and yellow from years of secondhand smoke, the walls were empty. Our shoes were sitting beside the front door, and the sound of the neighbors arguing could be heard through the paper-thin walls.

The weight of my failed suicide attempt began to suffocate me. The pills were not working, and I was worse off now than when I had decided that my life wasn't worth living anymore. I knew that I needed a job, and fast, but my employment history was less than impressive. Try as I might, my mental health kept me from maintaining the predictable schedule employment required. I would get a job, do well for a couple of months at most, and then I would start spiraling downward again after being triggered. I tried my best to navigate an unfriendly world with little patience for a mentally unstable eighteen-year-old girl. I was barely functional and left floundering in a vast sea of uncaring capitalism.

Feeling my blood pressure rising, I breathed in deeply, counting slowly to ten before letting the air out all at once. I could taste my rising anger like acid on my tongue. I continued this way, unsure of how much time had passed, struggling to calm my frayed nerves. Eventually, I swallowed hard and wiped the tears off my reddened face. I was angry, but there were more important matters to attend to.

Money.

I needed money, and fast.

I looked over at my boyfriend, his eyes red and hazy, hopeful for some sign of understanding. Some evidence that beneath his vacant expression, he was also drowning in turmoil, perhaps even remorseful for putting us into this financial predicament.

I watched him closely and felt my stomach drop as he reached into his shirt pocket and pulled out a joint. He was still blindly fixated on the TV, grinning stupidly. He flicked his lighter, and the tip of the joint burned orange-red as he inhaled.

"Seth?" I said timidly.

His eyes, glassy and empty, betrayed no evidence of acknowledgement.

"Seth?" I said again, louder this time, "we need money. What are we going to do?"

He blinked and took another hit on his joint.

"You could try stripping again," he said, holding the smoke in as he spoke.

He then exhaled all at once, filling the room with the stench of weed. I felt my stomach knot as my mouth filled with saliva. Swallowing and fighting back my queasiness, I turned to him, my eyes wide and filling with tears.

"You can't be serious," I choked out, barely able to speak.

Unfazed, he took another long drag.

"I get that you said it bothered you or whatever, but we really need the money."

I leaned forward on the couch, my elbows digging into the tops of my knees. My head sank further into my hands, my fingers lacing themselves through my long, thick hair. I squeezed, letting the sharp pain ground me in the moment. I stared down at the carpet as my fingers gripped tighter, shifting my focus to the pile of envelopes now wilted at my feet. My tears, steady now, continued to pepper the paper one at a time, spreading new splotches of wetness across the already warped surface.

In truth, it had done more than bother me; it downright terrified me. I had tried stripping during a previous bout of financial desperation but failed miserably. Getting the job was easy, as I was blessed with natural beauty, but making it worthwhile was another story. It turned out that there was a lot more to being an exotic dancer than just looking sexy.

I quickly learned that clubs were vicious, competitive battle grounds full of gorgeous women all vying ruthlessly for the same five dollars. A lifetime rife with severe physical and sexual abuse had left me meek and timid, making me no match for the strong, aggressive personalities of the more experienced dancers.

The other issue was the customers themselves; I hated being pawed at by men, and exposing myself for money made me feel more worthless than I had ever felt in my entire life. I had to fight with catty women for the attention of disgusting drunken slobs for dollars at a time, and I simply couldn't hack it. It was barely a month before I quit, and I had promised myself I would never compromise my dignity again for mere money.

I slowly lifted my head up, steadying my breathing as I went. The sensation of my heart, pumping hard and fast, had settled into the forefront of my awareness and was beginning to make me feel dizzy. My palms grew slick, and I closed my eyes, feeling my muscles tighten. I grabbed a nearby t-shirt strewn on the back of the couch and began absently fiddling with it while the cold cotton absorbed sweat from my hands.

"I-I can't," I squeaked, "you know how it was. I just… can't."

Seth had already relaxed in his chair, engrossed once more in his video game. I let the sound of him pressing buttons fill the silence for a few moments before I mustered the courage to speak up.

"Did you hear me?" I said louder this time, "I can't go back to the strip club."

Raising my voice above a whisper was enough to grab his attention. He paused his game, setting the controller down in his lap. Stretching, he leaned all the way back in his seat, letting his arms dangle backwards behind him.

"I didn't want to mention it, but my boy's wife, Tara, she does private shit and makes bank. He told me about it the other day."

I froze.

Private shit?

During my short stint at the club, I learned that there was another type of performer that was paid to go on dates with customers, do private dance shows, and generally offer a more intimate and exclusive experience than a man could get anywhere else. This entertainer was called an escort, and any time the topic was brought up in conversation, the dancers would sneer judgmentally and laugh about how pathetic and trashy escorts were. They would giggle while drinking their martinis and gossip relentlessly about the former employees who were caught with customers after hours. There was a zero-tolerance policy for such behavior, and strippers found selling private shows outside of work were immediately terminated.

The part that made escorts especially taboo was the understanding that they actually offered their clients sex in exchange for money, which was a dramatic leap beyond anything expected of a stripper. For that reason, the dancers viewed themselves as superior; they made money by masterfully performing mesmerizing, athletic displays of brazen sexuality on stage, not by lying flat on their backs.

As I sat on the couch, taking in what my boyfriend had told me, my eyes slowly found their way back to the stack of soggy overdue bills on the carpet. I watched in slow motion as another droplet of salty fluid fell onto the pile and soaked its way through the paper. My body rattled as a heavy sigh left my lungs.

Money.

It was something I didn't have but desperately needed.

My eyes wandered from the waterlogged paper at my feet to the pile of textbooks lying haphazardly in the far corner. Past assignments were scattered nearby, each a painful reminder of my failure.

I had scholarships, I had a chance. I was supposed to be somebody, and people believed in me. But I chose death and failed at that, too. My hands wove themselves through my hair once more as I squeezed my eyes tightly shut.

Money.

I needed money to go back to school. I lost my scholarships and now had to pay out of pocket for my tuition. Minimum wage was far too low to afford the apartment and my classes, and that was if I even had the time to attend after working forty plus hours a week.

I ran the numbers in my mind, once, twice, and knew they didn't add up.

Opening my eyes, I glanced at the corner again and let my gaze rest on scribbles of equations from calculus class. I loved math, and each problem solved felt like a tiny victory to me. I examined the numbers and symbols thoughtfully from a distance, and for the first time in weeks, I felt a shard of happiness blossom within myself.

I loved school. Education had always given my life meaning.

Images of drunken men in dark rooms full of stale cigarette smoke and booze danced in the forefront of my mind, teasing me with their promise. I hated being touched, being grabbed, being used like a piece of meat.

My phone vibrated, breaking me from my internal reverie. I flipped it open and saw a single text message. *Your payment is past due. Please contact us to make payment arrangements to avoid service interruption.*

I gulped and snapped my phone shut.

The sound of frantic button mashing became deafeningly loud as my stomach gurgled. The stench of weed trickled past my nostrils, and saliva began pooling on my tongue. My eyes trailed from the stack of bills at my feet to the textbooks in the corner and then to my boyfriend.

How bad could it be?

CHAPTER ONE
Bachelor Parties

As an escort, a big part of what I did was offer interactive entertainment for gatherings or events. What this actually translated to was that I did an enormous amount of bachelor parties. It could be a birthday, or a retirement, or a guys' weekend away from the wives, but mostly I was involved with pre-wedding celebrations.

Personally, I had mixed feelings about the traditions surrounding bachelor parties and found them crude and disrespectful to the future bride. I harbored serious moral qualms about them, but because of their potential to be quite lucrative, I couldn't refuse the work.

I usually received notice of a group party about a week in advance, and the standard practice was to book multiple women at a time. A two-girl show was by far the most popular choice, but it wasn't unheard of for massive events to reserve three or more dancers.

Even if it was just one other woman for a bachelor party, it caused a lot of anxiety; you could try to argue about feminism or body positivity all you wanted, but the reality of my job was that the skinniest worker with the biggest boobs made the most money.

At these shows, becoming the favorite was everything because it meant you had the best chance of earning the highest tips. When financial resources were finite amongst party goers, which they often were, being the most popular was the difference between eating ramen noodles and filet mignon.

So, when a party was looming on the horizon, it created enormous pressure, even when finances were in the clear. Group parties meant direct competition between other escorts and myself, and clients were not shy about verbalizing physical flaws and making comparisons.

Looks-wise, I was not out of shape or overweight by any means and had natural beauty to spare. In normal circumstances, this would cause me to stand out, but in a group of other women who all made their living off of being sexy, I hardly stood out.

Many of my co-workers went all-in with the escort lifestyle and purchased liposuction and breast implants. Since I was a student, I viewed the job as temporary and had no interest in making more permanent body modifications. I used makeup, styled my hair and wore cute clothes, and the rest was lucky genetics. In a room of model-esque Barbie dolls, I crossed my fingers and hoped that my girl-next-door vibe would be a hit.

As far as weight, the other women were rail-thin while I maintained a slightly shapelier, softer appearance. I wasn't overweight, but unlike my coworkers, my ribs and abs were not visible beneath my skin. Even with my strict diet and exercise regimen, I was never able to achieve the svelte, ultra-lean physiques that I knew were only possible from prolonged starvation or a drug habit.

Half-starved and strung out was certainly a look men drooled over, but it didn't fit with my lifestyle; during the day I had class, and performing well meant nourishing my body adequately to maintain mental focus and clarity.

Even so, if I was aware in advance of a group party, my anxiety resulted in begrudgingly following their cue and starving myself, or at least severely limiting my caloric intake up until the event.

I didn't want an eating disorder, but I couldn't help it; lower body fat correlated to higher tips, and if I was hurting to pay bills or this was the first show I had been booked for in a couple weeks, I couldn't risk it.

Agency-wide dry spells followed by a huge multi-girl party meant competition was fierce. Some of my co-workers were single moms or on the brink of going into heroin withdrawals, and money was especially important. Competing with a mom who needed baby formula was not for the faint of heart, and nine times out of ten, she'd outclass me and leave with everything.

Putting aside the competitive aspect, I dreaded bachelor parties for ethical reasons. I didn't understand why a man would want to get lap dances and be smothered by the tits of a total stranger before he got married. It seemed bizarre and backwards to me; if you found the love of your life, why are you interested in other women? The whole thing felt like a farce.

A party with escorts was as sleazy and underhanded as you could get, and a sure-fire way to sully a union before it was made official. My go-to when it came to those situations was to avoid the groom and focus on the best man instead.

Sure, I regularly facilitated infidelity of all sorts on a semi-regular basis, but seducing another woman's soon-to-be husband at his pre-wedding bash felt grimy. They hadn't even tied the knot, and I was already creating a potential lifelong source of marital strife. I at least wanted to give the wife a chance to stop putting out before I ruined her marriage, so I avoided the groom.

While some of the grooms-to-be were very hands-off and only reluctantly went along with the festivities to please their eager buddies, others were quite the opposite. They would try to suck my nipples and attempt to slip fingers into my vagina as if I wouldn't notice. If they managed it before I slapped them, they would hastily lick off all the juices to get a taste of my pussy, all while making constant eye contact. It was revolting considering that the man pushing my boundaries was days from becoming someone's husband.

What really got on my nerves was when they popped their hard dicks out of their pants during a lap dance and attempted to slide it inside my vagina. It was a brazen act of disrespect, and the logic eluded me. Did he think I would just let him fuck me if he slipped it in while all his friends watched? It was ridiculous and disgusting. What particularly bothered me was that men tried this regularly, and because they were trying to be sneaky, they weren't wearing condoms.

Can you imagine if you got married to your true love, had sex for the first time with him, and he gave you an STD? What a way to start a marriage! Despite these risks, there was no shortage of grooms willing to roll the dice and put their future bride's health in jeopardy.

As the evenings pressed on and partygoers became more aroused, they became more reckless: the groom would solicit me for sex, the group would ask me to give them all blowjobs, or the worst was when all the groomsmen would pool together their cash in a bid to surprise the guest of honor with a sexual encounter as a wedding present.

These were the same people who presumably knew the future bride, actively encouraging the groom to commit premarital acts of infidelity. It was completely disgusting, and I hated every minute of it. Hearing *my girl never swallows, can you show me what it's like before I'm chained down forever?* or *my fiancé said anal is off limits, how much do I have to pay to have it one last time?* from multiple grooms made me lose all faith in the institution of marriage.

There were shows where the future groom would be ballsy enough ask me for my personal phone number. He would tell me how he wanted to meet up with him after the wedding so he could *show me how a real man treats a lady.*

The inappropriate behavior didn't stop at infidelity, either. It was not uncommon to see the drunken party-goers trying hard drugs for the first time. Men doing lines of cocaine off my butt cheeks or sucking down shots as it dribbled off my tit was the norm, and sometimes my co-workers would join in on their recklessness.

Maybe I was a prude, or maybe I wasn't a total idiot. Booing and chiding from the crowds when I wouldn't take a shot or get high was a regular occurrence for me, and apparently driving home safely later was not a valid excuse to abstain.

It was my prerogative to maintain a laser sharp, sober focus while making money. I was not there for fun, and it was not a social event for me; in my free time, there was a whopping zero percent chance I would hang out naked with a bunch of drunken assholes.

I was a socially awkward, self-proclaimed nerd. If I wasn't studying, I was playing video games or building a new *Magic the Gathering* deck. I didn't possess the charisma and drive that the other women had, and I never fully meshed with the more outrageous parties.

Besides, if I wasn't careful, I could end up in someone's trunk. With so much inherent risk, it irked me when a coworker got stoned or partook in party favors. Not only did it put her safety in jeopardy, it also created an unfair financial advantage. The clients tended to favor the fun one who would do lines of coke with them instead of the boring, responsible one, whose casual insistence on sobriety was ruining the vibe for everyone.

Obviously, I can't speak to the priorities of the girls who used the job as an outlet for free drugs and booze. I didn't possess the perspective necessary to understand how it felt to be hopelessly addicted, and I imagine it made it harder to say no. With how broke the drug addicted workers were, I guessed that illicit substances were expensive, and getting any amount for free was a boon.

An hour or two deep into these parties, things would become taxing. Babysitting men as they became increasingly belligerent and handsy was not my definition of a good time and watching someone fall and break a coffee table in half was only *fucking hilarious* the first few times.

After attending countless such gatherings, the ensuing pandemonium became a colossal chore that was full of nothing but trouble. My ass would get constantly smacked until it was beet red, guys would jokingly dump alcohol onto my naked body, and people would start falling down flights of stairs or vomiting into sinks.

Learning to navigate the evolving tangle of inebriation and debauchery while still coming out on top required a certain amount of finesse. After years of keen observation and practice, I learned that the key to maximizing profits was to balance equal parts silly and sexy.

Yes, undoubtedly the men wanted a hot babe with giant tits to grind on their lap and parade around naked, but they also wanted a good time in general; this party was a big deal for them, and they wanted it to be a night they could remember for the rest of their lives.

Being smoking hot and naked was a big piece of that puzzle, but it wasn't enough to make a night truly memorable. Studying veteran dancers and experimenting with my own ideas for a couple of years led me to create a technique that never failed. It could be older men, younger men, foreigners, it didn't matter.

This routine was a hit every time and always got me paid the big bucks without having to drink or otherwise imbibe with the clients. After

5

doing a few lap sexy dances and getting the room riled up, I would shift gears by getting one of the partygoers to take off his belt. Holding it in my hand, I would ask the groomsmen if they thought the guy getting married should be punished, and the group would always explode into laughter and jeers. At that point, I would drag the groom-to-be to the center of the room, have him drop his pants, and then get down on all fours like a dog.

I would start by gently spanking him with my hand at first, yanking down his underwear and exposing his bare bottom. Laughter would then fill the room, and that was my cue to begin whipping with the belt as everyone cheered along with each subsequent smack.

It drove all the men absolutely bananas to see their buddy getting spanked by a hot naked chick, and they loved it when I hit hard enough to leave a mark.

If there were two girls, one of us would be holding a tie around his neck like a dog leash while the other teased him. We would also lay him on the floor and have one of us rub our tits and pussy in his face while the other grinded and danced around on his crotch. Making the groom bark like a dog, wear lipstick, or blindfold him and then have him guess what body part was touching his face was all part of the show.

We would do anything we could get away with, and usually judged how far we could go by the reaction of the crowd. We would even take turns sitting on his back and riding him around like a horse while spanking his bottom with the belt. The name of the game was mild, sexually themed humiliation that just barely pushed the boundaries of everyone involved. It was gentle enough to be harmless, but unique enough to be burned into the minds of the partygoers.

What really helped sell the humor and fun was exaggeration. The more excited I was, the more the room went crazy. It was easy to get them riled up because they were usually drunk out of their minds. Once the party reached the golden tipping point, anything I did, however minor, would cause the room to erupt in howls of laughter.

After the theatrics of the main show were over, it was common to break down into smaller groups. Sometimes we would hang out in a hot tub, play pool, or otherwise fuck around to keep them entertained.

Doing anything topless was usually a big hit with a room of horny drunk men, so it wasn't hard to pass the time.

During these periods, other girls would head into the back room with various men. When a dancer did a private show, the other would hang out with the group and keep an eye on things. Since I didn't do any extras at these events, I was basically the designated hang-out girl.

I never asked what the other women were doing, and they didn't tell. If they wanted to earn extra money by going all the way with a soon-to-be-married man, that was their prerogative. For larger parties, I often made plenty of money from the lap dance show, so I didn't see the need to take things to the next level.

This refusal to do extras came with its own caveats. I would get pouty complaints when the other escort was offering blowjobs or anal in the back room and I *wasn't even doing hand jobs*. Rolling my eyes, my response to these whiney comments usually went along the lines of *I don't do full service, hon,* followed by a seductive wink.

Occasionally, my friendly dismissal caused me to become more of a commodity at the party because I was harder to get. I wouldn't put out, and some men saw this as a challenge. They would try to sweet-talk me or offer me large amounts of money in an attempt to break my solidarity.

Even with ample cash waved in my face, I declined. If the other woman wanted to line them up bukkake style and have them jerk off onto her face for extra cash, cool. I'd watch with objective curiosity, but I wouldn't get involved.

Client Mckinley

One day, with no advanced notice, I got called out to a bachelor party at a motel a little after two in the morning. Seeing how late it was, I assumed we were summoned because the bars had closed, and they weren't ready for the night to be over.

When I arrived, my suspicions were confirmed; the two-story motel building was in the same parking lot as a trashy-looking strip joint. It was a short walk from the strip club to the motel, and I cringed at the

7

implications. I also knew that there was a high probability that the men who called would be a drunken, rowdy mess.

When I got out of my car, my suspicions were confirmed: there was a group hanging around outside in the third story breezeway playing loud music with their motel door wide open. They talked loudly as they walked in and out of the room, smoking cigarettes and drinking beer, and one of them was pissing outdoors on the wall.

I wanted to shrink and sneak away, but it was too late. One of them spotted me, and they all made a loud noise in unison, sort of like a jubilant *hey!*

Even though the other girl hadn't arrived yet, I begrudgingly joined them, knowing they wouldn't stop yelling at me until I came over. It was kind of embarrassing, to be honest, waiting around with them because of how noisy they were; I knew other people were probably sleeping in the same motel, and that these men were a nuisance to literally everyone.

While I stood there waiting for my coworker, they ceaselessly peppered me with stupid questions like *what is your real name?*, *do you have a boyfriend?*, and *does the other girl coming look as good as you?*

It was exhausting maintaining my friendly demeanor while repeatedly dismissing their questions, and I kept reminding the group that we would negotiate our plans after the other woman arrived. I could see erections in some of their pants, and the men kept squeezing themselves uncomfortably close to me. I could smell a layer of sweat and booze on them, and it made my stomach turn.

My patience wore thin as they continually disrespected my personal space, touching me without permission and blowing cigarette smoke in my face. I guessed that since they ordered me from an agency, they assumed they could treat me however they pleased. They would come up behind me and grab my tits, squeeze my ass, and one of them even picked me up and carried me over to one of the beds, plopping me onto it and promptly undoing his pants before I stopped him. It was a real shitshow, and I wished the other woman would hurry the hell up so I could get it over with and leave.

When she finally showed up, we collected the booking fee, gave our recited spiel about how they needed to follow our rules or we would leave with no refunds, and got started.

I repeatedly emphasized that any touching without permission or refusal of our boundaries would result in us leaving immediately with no refund. After they drunkenly nodded in the affirmative, I shrugged, exchanged looks with the other equally enthused entertainer, and started dancing.

Just like the men themselves, the show was a bit of a mess; we tried to give lap dances, but they kept pulling us into positions so they could dry hump us and attempt to remove our clothes. Granted, they were being silly about it and were responsive to our resistance, but it was pushing on my last nerve.

How many times do you playfully smack a man in the face for crossing your boundaries before you start hitting harder? These guys were so drunk that they probably couldn't feel my slaps, anyway. It was grating, fumbling around in the bed with them, and the clock seemed to move at a snail's pace.

We had been going back and forth with them, attempting to dance while simultaneously avoiding being violated in the process, when one of the men got my attention and called me over to him.

At this point, this particular man had already propositioned both of us for sexual favors, which we collectively declined. I wasn't in the mood to keep telling him no, but thankful for any excuse to escape the drunken bed wrestling.

"Hey E., do you like fish?" he asked, beer in hand, with a confident, drunken smile plastered on his face.

I stared at him, unsure of how to respond.

Fish? Like actual fish?

I had heard many, many off-the-wall comments from intoxicated dudes trying to get into my pants, but this one was new even for me.

"Uh... like salmon? I guess I do. Why?" I answered sweetly, unable to mask my confusion.

"Well," and as he said this, he grabbed my hand and started leading me to the bathroom, "I have something to show you."

9

I sighed but allowed him to pull me to the bathroom door. So far, his request seemed harmless, and a break from the shenanigans in bed was welcome. He winked at me one last time and then opened the bathroom door.

Before I could see it, I could smell it: the strong, unmistakable odor of fish. There were fish in the bathtub. Actual no-shit fish. I did a double take, my brain trying to catch up, and sure enough, there was a bathtub full of large fish floating dead in cold, ice-packed water.

On the bathroom floor, I saw several plastic bags that had been ripped open and lazily cast aside. The ice had obviously been purchased from a local convenience store earlier, and the packaging was left stuffed on the floor beside the toilet.

The odor was intense, and the fish looked a bit too dead, like perhaps they were not iced quickly enough. There was a very strong odor saturating the bathroom, and I was surprised the stench hadn't drifted into the rest of the motel room. I glanced down and noticed the wad of towels bunched up against the bottom of the bathroom door, and realized they were the only thing keeping the offensive odor at bay.

Many thoughts race through your mind when you're looking at a motel bathtub full of dead fish at three a.m. Was it a threat? Was he going to chop me up and put me in the tub with the fish if I didn't do what he wanted? Was he a kinky, backwoods weirdo who was about to ask me to shove a fish-head up my cooch for twenty dollars?

I didn't know the answer, and my pulse quickened in response to the possibility of a threat. The smell of fish became unbearable as my senses kicked into high gear, and I barely kept myself from gagging. Even without the smell, the cold, dead eyes of the fish bobbing lifelessly in the grimy tub were enough to turn my stomach.

The man, not paying attention to me, was busy beaming with pride at his catch. After collecting myself, I managed to break the silence.

"Um. What?" I said incredulously.

To be fair, I didn't know what else to say. There are not many life experiences that prepare one for an unexpected bathtub full of dead, stinking fish.

"E., lookie here," he said, drunkenly pointing to the largest fish of the bunch.

He then pulled me in closer, effectively smooshing us together into an awkward, one-sided embrace.

"You see that? We have been out here fishing for two days, TWO DAYS I tell ya, to celebrate my buddy's marriage, and would you take a look at them beauties."

I did look, and I didn't know what was happening.

I was already barely maintaining due to the smell, and the bizarre conversation was pushing it.

I glanced over at the clock, hoping for a polite excuse to leave, but it was still too soon to leave without getting in trouble. Defeated, I decided that all I could do was remain silent, hold my tongue, and let morbid curiosity be my guide.

"I'll tell you what E., if you let me fuck you, and you don't even have to suck my dick or pretend to like it," he said, taking a swig from his beer, "I'll let you take one of them there fishes home with you, maybe even two if yer lucky. Swear to God on my mother's grave."

At this, he crossed himself, and looked me drunkenly in the eye, waiting for my response.

Jesus Christ.

I blinked, stunned. Staring down the drunken idiot barely keeping his balance, it took the concerted effort of every fiber of my being not to snap.

I pinched the bridge of my nose, exasperated. I could see him now, drunk on a shitty pontoon boat with his buddies, rambling on about how *one time I caught a fish SO BIG that I was even able to use it to buy me a hooker, and I swear on my life, it was THIS big!*

For a moment, I weighed the real possibility that perhaps I was on a hidden camera TV show, and it was a bizarre practical joke. But no cameras popped out, and no snarky comedian was telling me *you are on such and such game show and you have won this spectacular prize!*

No, this was real life, and mine was the kind of life where drunken assholes tried to barter with smelly dead fish for access to my lady bits.

With no other explanation available to explain his behavior, I reasoned that the man standing beside me truly thought I was a fucking idiot. He fully expected me to be *delighted* and more than willing to do him a huge favor by helping to clean up the disgusting fish mess. And, of course, I was only privy to such a luxury because I was trading him sex, and I should thank my lucky stars for the opportunity.

I stared at the soggy, lifeless creatures and felt a new wave of anger rise from within; even if I did accept the offer, what was I supposed to wrap the fish in? My panties? It was absurd! The audacity, I tell you. I didn't know whose husband this was, but she needed to come get his ass and take him home.

I remained silent for a few moments, really wanting the client to think for even a second that his little ploy had actually worked, and I was about to fuck him in exchange for one of his stupid fish. I let the pregnant pause fully marinate before laughing in his face.

I told him the time was up, and I had no choice but to decline his offer and leave. That son of a bitch looked baffled that his plan didn't work, and that genuine confusion made me want to kick him in the nuts. Maybe I wasn't the best person in the world, but I sure as hell was worth more than a stinking, dead fish.

The real kicker was that as we were living, he still tried to convince us to haul away some of the fish for him. I could take as much as I wanted, he promised. At that point, I dropped all pleasantries and told him hell no.

My life was not the best, but I bet it was a whole lot better than the woman who was married to a guy who tried to buy a hooker with fish.

CHAPTER TWO
Orange Juice

Client Edmund

Every now and then, I would get called into work at a very strange hour. For someone like me, who was used to being busiest during the wee hours of the night, getting a call at nine in the morning was highly irregular.

When I didn't respond to the text message, my employer called repeatedly until I woke up and acknowledged the job. Apparently, I had been picked from the roster and now had to report to work within the hour. Grumbling, I rolled out of bed, disliking how often I was conspicuously the client favorite at ridiculous hours of the day.

The address was about thirty-five minutes away, so I had very little time to get myself ready. I did what I called a speed shave, where I perched myself in a series of awkward positions in the shower while I shaved all the unwanted hair from every crevice of my body. Shaving was a very boring, routine part of my life, and I hated what a time sink it was.

My hair would grow back to prickles after twenty-four hours, so I shaved on a daily basis. Waxing would have been a lifesaver, keeping my skin soft and hair free for weeks, but it had to grow out in between sessions, which wasn't a possibility due to my schedule. It turns out that when men paid top dollar for female companionship, they didn't want a hairy beaver in their face. The other option was permanent hair removal, but I never followed through with it because it was expensive, and more importantly, I was lazy.

Shaving regularly came with unique challenges as well. Contending with razor burn had become the bane of my existence. If I didn't apply post-shave balm every single time, idiotic clients would see an ingrown hair and think I had herpes.

I had gone through almost every product on the shelf until I found one that actually prevented razor burn, and it was a miracle. It was designed for men of color to use on their faces, but of course worked for all skin types. It was very smooth and creamy and had a pleasant smell. Because it was crucial for my daily routine, whenever I saw it in the store, I would grab every container off the shelf.

The only downside was that I had to be careful not to use too much or my skin would peel. Other than that tiny detail, it was a total godsend. I could shave myself to silky smoothness with a five-blade razor every single day, and no one was the wiser. No redness, no bumps, no nothing.

That morning, after I finished my quick shave and primped myself enough to look cute, I drove out to meet my client. I was chugging an energy drink and listening to whiney girl rock in the car on the way and musing to myself about what kind of weirdo had ordered me at nine in the morning on a weekday. I had received calls like this before, and they were never what I would call 'normal'.

Once, I got called in around eight a.m. for a show and it was one of the most uncomfortable events of my life. I was requested not by the client, but by his at-home care aid, a male nurse. He proceeded to hand me an envelope of cash that had apparently been collected by the family. For clarity, the client himself was older than dirt, wearing a diaper, and half-asleep in bed watching television.

In a bid to be helpful, the care aid told me he could remove the soiled brief and clean him, so that I could get to business without getting dirty. The nurse had zero interest in me personally and spent most of the booking trying to communicate with me on the old man's behalf.

The old guy would repeat *what? what?* over and over because he couldn't hear or understand what we were saying. The nurse used crude hand gestures, repeated things over and over, and even repositioned the bed-bound geriatric such that I would have better access to his genitals.

Let me tell you something; it was a bad time.

I ended up walking out of that nightmare, much to the chagrin of the nurse who kept insisting, *but this is what the family wants!*

Multiple early morning bouts of shenanigans had left me with serious reservations about any booking that occurred before nine o'clock at night.

But back to the morning in question. When I arrived at my booking, I realized it was not a hotel, but a high rise with a waterfront view. The parking was private, and I had to be buzzed in and get a tag from security to avoid being towed. I started wondering if this was a super-rich old man, because who else could conceivably afford to live in a place like this and not be at work in the morning?

I waited by the entry door for my client to let me into the lobby, and was completely flabbergasted when a young, African American man greeted me warmly and thanked me for coming. He wasn't terribly bad-looking and had very good manners. I was already wrong in my assumptions, and it was refreshing.

Once we made our way up to his condo, he asked me to look around and make myself at home. This guy was friendly and politely chattered away about his work and life while I poked around his living space. There was a gorgeous view from the balcony doors that showcased the beauty of the waterfront property. I was very at ease and didn't feel any threatening vibes whatsoever.

The only thing that seemed off out of the entire situation was that he had a large carton of orange juice on the counter with two empty glasses beside it. He was standing there thoughtfully, and I watched curiously as he poured a large glass for himself, proceeded to drink it, and then offered me a glass as well.

"Um... No thanks?" I answered politely, unsure what to say.

I never accepted food or drinks from clients because I was paranoid they might try to drug me. Also, it was orange juice. It was weird.

He frowned a little bit when I said no and offered me water instead. I also declined. He said he had bottled water if I preferred it instead, and I declined again very politely.

At this point, he was opening the fridge and offering me a slew of different liquids, insisting that he would drink some too AND let me pour both glasses. He explained that it was reasonable I would be cautious, but he wanted me to feel okay with having a beverage, because I must be thirsty.

What the actual fuck?

This guy was nice, and he tipped me a few hundred dollars up front when I collected the booking fee the second I walked in the door. I could not figure out what his shtick was. He kept offering me drinks, and the more he did it, the more I felt inclined to refuse.

I was growing concerned that perhaps this man had secretly built up a tolerance to some kind of drug and that he put it in all the drinks, hoping his willingness to consume them with me would trick me into imbibing. I know it sounds far-fetched, but I had seen the movie *The Princess Bride* as a kid and it had a scene of where that kind of thing happens in it, so I always thought it was a lurking possibility.

After we went back and forth about not accepting a drink for a bit, I told him I was going into the bathroom to get changed. This guy was weird, but he was also nice, so I still wanted to show him a good time. I walked over to the bathroom, shut the door, and started to get changed. When I lifted the toilet seat, he immediately started banging on the door.

"Hello? Are you okay in there?" he said nervously.

"Um... Yes. Just getting changed. Be out in a minute," I answered, digging for my can of mace.

I could see the shadows of his feet under the door frame as he kept knocking and asking me if I needed anything. He wasn't leaving me alone, and it was making me anxious. I had the door locked, and even though he was jiggling the door handle, he wasn't able to get in.

Strangely, I didn't feel in danger and told him to give me minute and that I would be right out. I thought to myself that maybe this guy was afraid I was going to rifle through his medicine cabinet and steal something. That I could understand, especially considering his overall demeanor, so I did my best not to let his fervent attempts to gain access to the bathroom bother me.

When I came out of the bathroom, he was indeed standing right in front of the door. He looked a little distraught.

"Here I am," I said expectantly.

He stood there, his head hung low.

"Are you okay?" I asked.

"Yes," he said, pausing for a moment, "but, did you pee while you were in there?"

I always peed in the bathroom when getting changed into my dance outfit, as it was very hard to stop mid-show to go potty. Something about urinating was off-putting to the clients, so I made sure I was capable of entertaining for the whole hour without having to stop in between to empty my bladder. I remember I had just flushed the toilet with no problems, so it couldn't be an embarrassing plumbing issue.

"Yes, I did," I answered, unsure, "is that okay with you?"

Crestfallen, he shuffled away and plopped down on the couch. He appeared lost in thought and a bit melancholic. Looking down at his feet while fidgeting with his fingers, he spilled the beans.

"The reason I called you here... Well, it started when I was a kid."

I had heard many stories from clients at this point, so I knew what to do. I joined him on the couch and buckled up for an adventure. These tender moments of self-reflection and openness were rarely what I would call heartwarming.

"When I was a kid, my parents got me a babysitter. You know, so I wouldn't be alone all the time while they were at work."

He paused, taking a breath, perhaps readying himself mentally for whatever he was about to tell me.

"So, she didn't want to leave me alone, 'cause you know, I was a little kid. So, she would take me into the bathroom with her when she had to pee. And I would watch."

He paused again, this time looking me square in the eyes.

"And... I liked it. I liked watching her pee," he finished, looking relieved.

Ah.

The constant, pressured offerings of beverages suddenly made sense and thankfully were fairly harmless. He was just a regular, run-of-the-mill weirdo. His insistence on entering the bathroom also fit with his story; he wasn't trying to kill me, he just wanted to watch me pee.

Being a true professional, I wanted to accommodate him, but I had already relieved myself, and I wasn't about to drink anything I didn't walk in with. Reasonable story or not, I didn't know this man from Adam, and I didn't trust him not to drug me.

"I really wish you would have told me when I got here," I explained, "I already used the bathroom while I was getting changed."

"I know, that is why I was trying to get in. Do you think you could go again?"

The sadness from moments ago on the couch had faded and was replaced with excitement; his eyes sparkled with delight at the prospect of actually getting to fulfill his fantasy. Before I could answer, he scurried over to the kitchen and started pulling out drinks from the fridge. Grinning, he playfully shook the container of orange juice at me.

"You want some OJ?" he teased, "I just had some, and it's actually pretty good."

I want to make something clear. I am not the type to shame others for their kinky desires. I love exploring sexually, and I think all people should be free to do so if it doesn't cause harm to others. While unusual, there were issues with this man's desires, other than his need for me to consume beverages in his home. I had heard too many stories, true or not, about women being drugged and then subjected to terrible, sometimes deadly outcomes.

I wanted to be that cool girl who would make all his fantasies come true. In truth, I had zero qualms about him watching me pee, and I really did wish he had told me the second I walked in the door. Knowing I wouldn't be able to go again anytime soon, I felt bad. Not bad enough to give him back his money, but you know, bad.

As delicately as I could, I explained to him that it was against company policy to eat or drink while working (a lie), and that I was unable to help him out. He was disappointed, but in keeping with his general pleasantness, he verbalized understanding and admitted that it was a good policy to keep people like me safe.

Honestly, the guy was great. He was friendly, respectful, and overall, an easy person to be around. I offered him a nude lap dance show, which he declined, so I left.

On the drive home, I was at odds with myself, wondering if I had made the right choice; it was a harmless kink, and I could have made more money if I had only obliged him. Was it right to refuse the drinks? He was so insistent about it, which made me more hesitant than I would normally have been. I was deep in thought, mulling it over, when the phone rang.

Strangely, it was my boss.

I frowned. What did she want from me? I checked out on time via text, as was the standard, and I collected the booking fee for them.

"Hello?" I answered hesitantly.

"E., the client just called complaining about you."

My boss did not sound amused, and I was genuinely surprised. I very rarely got any complaints, and when I did, they were usually by angry, drunk men I wouldn't have sex with them.

"He said you wouldn't agree to pee on him, which he was willing to pay you to do, and that you wouldn't take any of his drinks."

I thought for a moment. This wasn't exactly the truth, but it was close enough. Correcting my boss would do me no good, plus it was irrelevant. I was not being contacted to go over the details of some random person's sexual preferences.

"Okay, and...?" I asked.

I wasn't sure if my boss was going to issue a refund, but I wasn't about to head back to that dude's house to give him money. Especially since he had the nerve to complain about me after pretending to be so nice.

"He said you didn't give him back his money," she added impatiently.

Here we go.

"Yes, that's true. He paid me up front for my usual stuff, and then didn't want it. It's not my fault he wanted extras. When he didn't want what he paid for, I left."

I was matter of fact and did my best to not sound bitchy and annoyed, even though I hated these stupid conversations. Clients were dicks. They lied.

"Oh. That isn't what he said," she said, her tone shifting back to her normal bubbly friendliness.

"Yeah, and he kept trying to get me to drink things when I kept saying no. He was a total dick about it. Fuck that guy."

"Hmm... okay. Yeah, fuck em. Are you available for the rest of the day?" her tone was more relaxed, and as expected, she took my side after hearing some details.

It is important to note that in the business, we operated under the assumption that the clients were always lying about everything. Sometimes they would pay you, you would do your thing, and then they would call and try to get their money back.

Buyer's remorse was big when it came to post-nut clarity, but that wasn't our problem. For some of the clients, it hit pretty hard, and then we would get threats from people demanding their money back. It happened all the time, and since there was no shortage of clients, we told them to fuck off.

While I had never personally seen it myself, I knew that my employer kept a list of clients that we no longer served; be it by name or address, there were some places we simply would not go.

I had heard from another girl during a booking once about a wild experience they had that resulted in a new addition to the ban list. They were called out to a dumpy, run down motel and the person who made the reservation was a pimp, trying to recruit new women to work for him.

Apparently, he told her that he would love her, treat her right, and give her everything she ever dreamed of. He even had a girl who used to work for the company beside him, newly ravaged by hard drugs, explain how nice it was having a pimp and how much she loved him.

Crazy, right? Luckily, she got the hell out of there safely. After that little experience, the address was put on the infamous list. I was actually told by my boss, too, that if I ever had a client try to convince me to go to the aforementioned address, that I needed to run away and let them know immediately.

There were other ways a potential client could end up on the list, too. If someone repeatedly called and then never answered the door, that was a problem, since we couldn't collect the booking fee. Without the booking fee, the worker didn't get compensated for traveling, and the boss didn't make any money, either. This wasted time was especially impactful on the busier nights of the week, so the company didn't take any chances with unreliable clients. Something I experienced, which did result in a ban with our company, was a bit more unusual.

Client Keegan

I received information about a show a couple cities over, which wasn't too far of a drive, in the middle of the night. The client lived in a run down apartment complex in a less than desirable part of town.

When I got there, I noticed that the building was nestled between tall trees, which cast an eerie shadow from the dim glow of nearby traffic lights. Some of the light fixtures on the building itself were partially broken, and the flickering light caused a seriously creepy, scary-movie vibe. Despite the inherent spookiness of the building, I didn't see any hobos sleeping in the parking lot, or small groups of people clustered around a transformer-made-table using drugs.

The apartment building itself was organized like this: two levels, with two units directly across from each other on each floor. The breezeways were open air, and so were the stairs leading to the second floor. There were four units total, but only one car other than mine in the parking lot even though it was the middle of the night.

I scoped out the building a little and noted that my client's unit was on the second floor. After a little trepidation, I decided that I already drove all the way out there, and I might as well at least try. You never know, and sometimes you get lucky.

Climbing the steps, I stepped lightly, trying to avoid as many creaks as possible. I liked being quiet in situations where I was unsure, because you could potentially hear people talking before they knew you were listening. Being sneaky like this held the possibility of giving me the edge in an otherwise completely unknown situation.

21

When I got to the door, I paused, listening for any signs of activity inside, but heard nothing. I frowned, hoping for a clue about what was going on, and knocked. No answer. I waited a few moments and then knocked again, this time louder and longer, in case my client was asleep in his room. I waited, paying close attention for any signs that indicated a person was stirring around inside. I waited, but all I heard was silence.

Frustrated, I grabbed my phone and called my boss. Whenever we had a booking where the client didn't answer the door, the boss would call them.

After several attempts to get ahold of the person inside, my boss called me to let me know that there was no answer. We were discussing this when I heard a voice behind me.

"Hello..." the voice said, barely above a whisper.

I spun around, my boss still on the phone, and saw that the door across the hall was cracked open, and what looked like a teenaged boy was peeking out and staring at me. He couldn't have been a day over twenty, and that was being generous. He looked nervous, and his eyes were extremely bloodshot. The stink of weed smoke drifted in my direction from inside his apartment.

I looked him up and down, said nothing, and turned back around, ignoring him. I went back to knocking on the door of my would-be client, not wanting to engage with his neighbor. Discretion was one of our company values, and I took it seriously. The young man behind me spoke again.

"I'm a producer... Have you ever thought about being in a porno?"

After this, it clicked. The empty parking lot. The lack of noise from inside the unit. I had been called here by this dumbass kid, who intentionally gave my boss the address of the presumably vacant unit across from his.

I told my boss I had to go and hung up the phone. I turned around and looked at the kid standing in the doorway across the hall. I couldn't believe the gall of this little shit, waking me up at two in the fucking morning to play games like this.

Did he really think his plan would work? That an escort would show up, not be able to find who she was looking for, and agree to fuck him on a whim while he videotaped it?

I gritted my teeth, wanting to cuss him out, but controlled myself. Instead, I walked down the steps towards my car. As I walked away, I could hear him saying, *hey, wait, I'm a producer!* in a vain attempt to get me to turn around and entertain his plight. After I explained this to my boss, the phone number and the address were both put onto the do-not-book list.

CHAPTER THREE
Stand Up Comedy

Client Toby

Ah, the trailer park. A wondrous place full of magic and whimsey, a
curiosity to all those who gaze upon it from the safety of the outside.
There were multiple such places within my city, but one in particular
outshone them all. The inner happenings of said trailer park remained
shrouded in mystery for those who didn't reside there, myself included.
Since I was never sent there for work, and didn't have a personal reason
to enter the property limits, I had never been inside.

I had heard fascinating tales of baby mommas and fourteen-year-
old alcoholics inhabiting the place, but I considered these nothing more
than urban legends, perhaps even perpetuated by the people who lived
there as a lark. There was a rumor circulating that a local stripper was
drugged and dumped into a ditch there by one of her regulars, and stories
like that spread like wildfire and made the location an absolutely
scandalous place.

Personally, I had no tangible evidence to support the numerous
claims of debauchery aside from the lingering bad reputation. My nature
was to question everything and believe little, so I doubted the veracity of
some of the more dubious happenings.

I did note that some of the wilder stories were substantiated by a
few of my coworkers who lived there. It seemed that the place could not
escape the damning image of a hillbilly hellhole where drugs ran rampant,
and stepfathers regularly molested their teenaged daughters.

Still, when my daily wanderings had me driving by, and I couldn't help but gaze inside. My clients offered me no opportunity to explore such a place; I was a bit on the expensive side, and my base hourly rate without tips priced me out of most budgets. I was a luxury experience, and seemingly one that could not be afforded by people who resided in the trailer park. One night, however, I got a text from my boss informing me that I had finally been booked at the notorious establishment.

It was my chance, my golden opportunity to find out for myself if all the rumors were true. I was simultaneously terrified and elated; I would soon step foot into the modern-day Wild West that lurked in my city's backyard.

Based on the years of gossip, I knew this was the kind of place you didn't want to visit in the daytime, and definitely not after dark. For a moment, I debated refusing the booking, mildly afraid of whatever unscrupulous person had reserved me. Fishing out my can of mace, I resolved to face the proverbial lion's den and not let stories of crime and taboo thrills scare me off.

Driving through the threshold and into the park was like walking through the doors to Narnia, and I felt goosebumps as I crept through the neighborhood. I turned my lights off, not wanting to disturb sleeping residents, and crawled through the winding roads of cramped housing.

When I arrived at my client's address, it was pretty much exactly what I had been picturing in my mind: a dilapidated, filthy, trash-riddled dump. Definitely not the worst in the park by a long shot, but not the best either. The neighbors' homes were hardly an improvement, and it appeared that the entire neighborhood was one windy day away from becoming condemned.

Taking a closer look, the property looked like the ungodly lovechild of an indie documentary and an eighties slasher flick. The yard was full of a wide assortment of garbage and metallic debris; car parts, literal broken open bags of trash, half-destroyed lawn ornaments, and scattered collections of sun-bleached children's toys were everywhere.

The only thing the yard didn't have was decent grass. Weeds, and lots of them, had cropped up around all the miscellaneous piles of junk in lieu of any other greenery. It was as if the rust and debris were the best kind of fertilizer on the market, because the weeds had an uncontested botanic monopoly over the entire area.

There were also numerous broken-down cars, all in various stages of disrepair. I spotted what I presumed was my client's daily driver right away; unlike the other cars on the property, it was the only vehicle with all its doors, tires, and hood still attached. Even so, the windshield was cracked, the paint chipped and rusted, and one of the windows busted out and patched up with cardboard and duct tape. I was unsure, wondering if I could be mistaken and the client wasn't home, but the mud and tire tracks leading to the car suggested regular use.

As I finished being nosy and shifted my focus to the booking itself, my eyes took notice of the sharp metallic fragments lying around and the strangely discolored patches of soil. I was growing very uncomfortable and terrified at the possibility of accidentally brushing up against rusted metal on my way to the door.

The accumulated masses of rotting food waste also instilled the fear of being attacked by a family of territorial raccoons. I was convinced that this festering rummage pit had to be an environmental health hazard, growing by the day and leaching God only knows what into the soil.

Ready to get the booking over with, I took a deep breath, clutched my taser, and got out of my vehicle. I froze next to the car door, eyes squeezed shut in anticipation, awaiting the impending doom of being violently stabbed by a gang of trailer park crazies or eaten alive by a swarm of feral rats.

After a few moments of not being accosted, I hesitantly opened my eyes and glanced around nervously. The night was quiet, and all I could hear was the gentle sound of insects and frogs croaking in the distance. Yes, it was dirty and run down, but on all accounts, it was a very quiet neighborhood. I didn't even hear the sound of barking dogs.

Okay, maybe it's not as bad as I thought.

Calming down, I took another, more rational look at the property, and put my misgivings aside. For a hotbed of crime and sin, the entire neighborhood didn't make a peep after midnight. Feeling foolish, I shook off my jitters and located the steps leading up to the trailer door, determined to see the booking through.

Standing beside the car, I frowned at the daintily painted toes poking out the front of my open-toed shoes. Wearing heels had been a very, very poor choice. I was worried that on my way to the trailer's steps, I might cut myself on a piece of glass or filthy debris. Taking my time, I planned each step strategically, avoiding even the tiniest of potential hazards. Tetanus or hepatitis A was not the kind of bonus tip I wanted from this show.

When I finally made it to the front entrance, I frowned; the door was barely functional and rigged to the frame with a couple of bungee cords. It was crude, but it worked, so I shrugged and pulled it open.

My foot brushed against something lumpy, and I shrieked, recoiling instinctively as my heart jumped out of my chest. At the doorstep was a large pile of waterlogged, crumbling newspapers, and I had inadvertently poked my foot right into them. My toes, now uncomfortably moist against my shoes, were covered in bits of old pulpy mush.

I hadn't considered that the person who lived in a place like this cared about current events, and felt embarrassed that I, a university student, didn't even have a subscription. Pulling a napkin from my purse, I dried off my foot one toe at a time, and started to feel guilty about being so judgmental.

I had yet to see a petty crime or even hear a wayward gunshot in the distance. In my own neighborhood, the periodic booming of gunshots had become merely background noise, so I was beginning to seriously question the validity of rumors that pervaded the area.

Now came the moment of truth. I stood on the doorstep, quietly waging war with myself about whether or not I should knock on the door. There was a real chance I could get away with just leaving and claiming the client didn't come to the door, but not even *trying* to knock on the door was a bad idea.

Whenever a client didn't answer the door, the boss would put in a concerted effort to get verbal confirmation that they cancelled. If I walked away, I risked being sent right back to a client who was now irritable about me being late.

After a moment of psyching myself up, I decided that getting things over with was the fastest way to safely be on my way back home to

27

the sterility and comforts of my own space. Cockroaches or not, I had to go inside and at least try to offer the base show or I'd get a verbal lashing from my boss.

Based on the state of the property, I expected the booking to be a total bust and had long since accepted the reality of not getting tipped. Looking around the property once more, I reframed my perspective and became skeptical about even collecting the booking fee.

When I finally built up the courage and knocked, an older white guy answered the door. He looked like a very grizzled, possibly mid-forties man who had done way too much hard living. While he definitely looked younger than fifty, his skin was creased with deep wrinkles from years of working outdoors. His hands were caked with what looked like flecks of dried paint and plaster, giving him away as a laborer. His clothes looked no better and were covered in various stained blotches from what I presumed was earlier that day. He was also missing some teeth and had a scraggly bush of greying facial hair speckled with more paint.

In one hand, he was clutching a dented soda can, functionally serving as a make-shift crack pipe, and in the other hand a lighter. He reeked of the unmistakable odor of crack cocaine, a smell that I was unfortunately familiar with from other clients.

As a non-drug user, I always wondered why crack cocaine users consistently chose to use a can. Was it some kind of unspoken rule? Like *okay, I'm going to smoke crack and be a crackhead now, time to bust out the ceremonial dented aluminum beer can.*

While I reflected on this, the client fiddled with some ash, nestling it perfectly at the bottom of the blackened, dented hole, and lit up. I sighed, resigned to yet another night of bullshit.

I watched the ragged man lean against his door frame, a person clearly lost in the throes of drug addiction. He paid little attention to me, and I waited impatiently in the summer air for him to invite me inside. He coughed, sputtered, and lit up again. I glowered, annoyed at the lack of common courtesy and blatant drug use.

He was dirty, he was vile, and I was stuck with him for the next hour. I rolled my eyes, amused at my own lack of foresight. What was I expecting to find in a place like this? Prince Charming? I had to make the best with the hand I was dealt, and currently that hand was getting high with a soda can.

Reluctantly, I nudged him indoors, following close in tow and hating every second of it. Inside, the lights were dim, and as far as I could tell in the darkness, the furniture was sparse. Vaguely, I discerned boxes and trash taking up the majority of the floor space, and for that reason, the room felt claustrophobic. I had to walk along a narrow path to avoid bumping into things, barely able to see.

Eventually, I settled onto his couch, exasperated and mentally out of gas. The client leaned on a desk directly across from me, picking at his pipe merrily. He hummed and fidgeted, lost in thought and seemingly indifferent to my presence. I sighed deeply, not caring about my audible displeasure, because all this client cared about was getting high.

I sank into the couch, bored, and took a better look around. The only light present in the room was from the stray beams of moonlight pouring through a tiny window on the far wall. Occasionally, I would hear the characteristic sound of him flicking his lighter, followed by a brief flash of fire that illuminated the dark space, uncovering a new detail of his slovenly ways each time.

Slowly, as my eyes adjusted to the dim surroundings, I realized that something was scattered all over the floor. I narrowed my eyes, trying to focus; it looked like a huge mess of rectangular-shaped pieces of paper had been carelessly thrown about the room. As I studied the floor, trying to catch the fleeting details each time he sparked his lighter, my eyes adapted to the darkness.

At once, it dawned on me that the floor, the couch, and even the desk he was sitting on were covered in cash. Every denomination was strewn about the place in a big, disorganized mess, and as a whole, there was money *everywhere*.

I froze, realizing I was surrounded by the type of wealth I had only ever witnessed in the movies.

My mind raced, suddenly acutely aware and interested in my surroundings. It would have been very easy to scoop a huge handful off the floor and run out the door, but I had principles, and one of them was that I did not steal. Besides, he was clearly high out of his mind, and trying to bolt out might incite a violent reaction.

So, there I sat, studying the bumbling fool fiddling away with his crack pipe, trying to make heads or tails of what was happening. The incessant drug use now made sense; he could afford mountains of crack with this kind of dough and was probably knee-deep in a binger.

Being that the client had all the makings of a general laborer and lived in a dump, the vast amount of money lying about was suspicious. Did he rob a bank? Kill someone? Sell drugs?

I seriously doubt he got the money from painting houses, so I automatically assumed the only explanation had to be ill-gotten gains. Trying to rationalize legal scenarios where a person kept gobs of cash lying around wasn't helpful, either, because nothing felt sensible. Staring at the dragon's hoard of treasure in front of me, I remembered how dangerous of an area this was. The gears in my head turned, and I began to ponder how such an absentminded fool had so much cash lying around and had not been robbed by locals.

At this, my attitude shifted from bewildered to terrified; there was a real possibility that this bumbling crackhead was a murderous, drug dealing kingpin. Movies like *Scarface* taught me that drug lords were insane and liable to go berserk at any moment.

I was shaking in fear, too afraid to speak, when the client broke the silence.

"Hey girl, come here," he said, not looking up from his task.

Knees weak, I did nothing and instead watched nervously as he continued to fiddle with his pipe.

Seeing my hesitation, he reached down, pulled open a drawer on the desk, and pulled out a crisp one-hundred-dollar bill. I stared at him, unsure and unwilling to take it from him.

He smiled pleasantly at me and then extended the crisp note, encouraging me to grab it. From the couch, I could see that the drawer was also overflowing with cash. It was madness.

When I finally stood up to take the money from his hand, he started giggling uncontrollably, like it was the funniest thing he had ever seen in his life. Puzzled, I watched as he became lost in peals of uncontrollable laughter. Out of context, it was incredibly disturbing to watch a stranger laugh hysterically. His ribs continued to shake as he laughed and laughed, and as creepy as it was, this was still a hell of a lot easier than most of the other stuff I did at work.

After a moment, still giggling, he extended another hundred-dollar bill in my direction and asked me politely to sit down. I took the money and complied, and he instantly broke into another uncontrollable bout of laughter. He was laughing so hard that tears were coming out of his eyes while I sat there doing my best not to have a panic attack.

Not sure what to do, I spent what felt like a very long time sitting down and standing up while he laughed his brains out. Oddly, he could not get enough of paying me to do such a simple task. The game would only be interrupted when he stopped for a moment to smoke crack, and then it would resume, the room once again filling with booming laughter.

In between standing and sitting, I had plenty of time to reflect on what was happening. I speculated that perhaps it was some manner of power trip for him. Maybe in his daily life, he was constantly turned down by women, and now that he had money, he was taking his new power to the extreme.

Why this was so unbelievably humorous to him, I could not say. It was hard to imagine what he was thinking, or if he was thinking at all. He had been smoking crack nonstop since I arrived, and it wasn't a stretch to assume he had been doing it before, too.

I spent what felt like an eternity playing his game and collecting one-hundred-dollar bills. When I had received enough money to take an entire month off work, I politely informed him that my time was up and that I had to go.

Granted, I probably could have stayed there all night and made a small fortune, but I wasn't greedy and honestly just wanted to get the hell out of there.

Now, he was absolutely creepy, especially with the laughing, but also sweet in his own way; I could tell he wasn't ready to be alone and felt bad for him. After a brief chat with my boss, I informed him that another girl would soon arrive to visit with him. He was still rolling in giggles and smoking when I walked out the door, and that was fine with me.

I can't say what the next girl did to him, or what became of the bizarre small fortune in that trailer, but I went to bed that night completely relaxed and happy with the knowledge that I didn't have to work for an entire month.

CHAPTER FOUR
Friendzone

The town I worked out of was adjacent to several larger cities and created a reasonable drive to multiple burgeoning areas of economic growth and development. This was great, because it meant a huge population of permanent and traveling clientele. However, it also meant occasionally facing a hefty commute.

I was personally responsible for arranging transportation to and from each call, and the travel times varied substantially. Most calls were at hotels, which had a fairly predictable rotation of hot spots whose addresses I knew by heart, but some bookings were at private residences.

This is where things got tricky; some of the higher-end residential areas were quite a distance away from the main city, which meant a huge commitment of road hours. For any booking that required more than an hour of drive time, the company policy was that the client paid a larger booking fee up front to ensure the cost of travel for the escort was covered.

Getting sent out to a client living hours away was taking a huge chance; even if they prepaid all the fees, the company needed a signed credit card slip or the charge could be disputed. The client could fall asleep or even change their mind before I managed to arrive, and if that happened, I had to eat the cost entirely on my own.

The other negative was that all bookings carried the same odds of being lucrative, and being farther away didn't necessarily equate to more money. There was nothing more frustrating than traveling for hours to meet a client, only to find out that he was broke and a complete waste of

33

time. In those scenarios, not only did I not get a tip to compensate me for my time, but I also paid a substantial opportunity cost; if I spent hours on the road traveling, those were hours I couldn't spend entertaining other clients closer in town.

Once in a blue moon, I would get booked for a location three or more hours away and scream internally. This meant I was committed to spending an entire night driving and couldn't sleep in between seeing clients. My normal practice was to go home after each booking and nap until the next one, which made going to school during the day possible.

I spent most of the day awake in class or studying, so those overnight naps were crucial for my safety on the road. Even if I was tired, getting there was often O.K., with caffeine and pure, unadulterated hatred fueling most of the trip, but making my way home was a different story. The adrenaline and anxiety that kept me alert during the show itself would fade rapidly, and all that was left was grogginess as my body demanded rest.

Often, I was operating on four or less of sleep and struggling to keep my eyes open. My vision would lag, and staying awake became a constant challenge. No amount of coffee or loud music was enough to compensate for my lack of sleep, and when it got so bad that my vision blurred while I was nodding off behind the wheel, my only option was to pull off of the interstate and sleep for a couple of hours at a rest stop. This was incredibly dangerous and something I tried to avoid as much as possible.

Client Nelson

One evening, after driving three and a half hours, I arrived at a secluded, gated community. Unlike some of the other posh neighborhoods I had been in, this one was the real deal; I had to wait for my boss to wake the client up and inform the security guard to let me in. The community boasted twenty-four-hour security, with only one way in and out that was manned by a guard at all times. I appreciated the privacy this offered but hated the hassle it created for me to gain access to the property.

The guard was insistent on knowing who I was, who I was visiting, and why. I refused to provide my driver's license or personal address for their logbook, and this was a problem. The guard proceeded to take photos of my license plates and re-verified that I was allowed access to the premises. I was growing increasingly paranoid, terrified that my anonymity was in jeopardy. None of my clients knew my real name, where I lived, or even my phone number. I shrouded my identity from clients in a cleverly crafted veil of lies and intrigue, and now there was an overly zealous rent-a-cop threatening my privacy.

I didn't want the client to request copies of the logbook entry and use the data to stalk me, so I began bickering with the guard, demanding that my information be erased. I argued back and forth, pleading my case as best I could while being extremely vague about why I was there in the first place, but the guard didn't budge. Eventually, I gave up my fruitless efforts with the security booth and accepted my fate; some of my details had been recorded, and I could do nothing about it. Instead of sulking, I shifted my focus to the community itself.

After driving through the gate, I couldn't help becoming enchanted by the opulent splendor contained within the community walls; for a person that had grown up in crippling poverty, it was like stepping into a fairytale. Lush, tasteful landscaping blanketed every inch of the common space, giving the sprawling slice of suburbia a forested touch. The properties themselves were as beautiful as they were intimidating, easily within the multi-million-dollar price bracket. It was obvious that the people who lived there resided within a world I had never known, and it was fascinating.

As a person who frequently worried about making my rent on time or having enough money to buy groceries, I couldn't fathom living in such luxury. I imagined that beautiful people lived inside the beautiful houses, enjoying comfortable lives of ease and indulgence in a way completely foreign to me.

Early in my career, seeing places that flaunted enormous wealth felt enchanting and romantic. I was still naive enough to entertain the girlish daydream of meeting a rich client and falling madly in love with him against all the odds. In those fantasies, the customer was handsome and kind, and swept me off my feet. I imagined long, intimate eye contact and hot, steamy sex. I would travel the world with my rich Mr. Right, leaving no stone of finery unturned. I reveled in the idea of living a life of ease while my respectable, considerate lover footed the bill.

Driving through the sleepy community that night, my daydreams faded as I began to feel painfully out of place; while the residents were nestled cozily in bed, I was sneaking through their neighborhood to meet someone for money. As I crept along, the pristine nature of my surroundings only added to my crushing feelings of wrongness. I did not belong and couldn't shake the nagging feeling of violating some unspoken rule by simply being there.

A sense of sad resignation consumed me; as I searched for the client's address, I remembered my place in the world. I was an escort, and romance was not part of the job. Men didn't call me to woo me, they called me to entertain them and offer them companionship that regular women scoffed at.

I sighed, defeated, and focused my mental wanderings instead on what kind of man my client would be. I assumed he would be an older, grey-haired fellow who probably spent most of his days in a golf cart cat-calling women his granddaughter's age. I was willing to wager that he drank a lot of whiskey on the rocks and spritzed too much cologne on his polo shirts. As I pictured what my evening would likely look like, I sighed again and took a swig of my energy drink. I hated creepy old men, especially creepy old rich men who didn't understand the meaning of the word *no*.

Navigating the winding roads and beautifully maintained common areas, I turned a lakeside corner and finally found what I was looking for: a handsome home overlooking the water that boasted a large, masterfully maintained frontage. I pulled over, stopping my car across the street against the curb, and verified the address on my phone. There was an expensive, brand-new car in the driveway parked right beside a golf cart.

Ah fuck.

As my eyes adjusted to the light, I jumped when I realized the client was not only standing outside on his driveway, but staring intently at me. I steeled my rattled nerves from the unexpected shock and immediately replaced my grumpy frown with a placid smile. He could see me, and that meant I was in work mode. I told myself that his presence outdoors wasn't as creepy as it seemed because the security guard had called him multiple times to verify that I was a guest.

Of course he would be waiting outside for me, I told myself repeatedly, *this isn't weird at all.*

As my eyes adjusted, it dawned on me that I had completely missed the mark in terms of his appearance. He was in his early thirties, tall, potbellied, and looked like he desperately needed a shower. He looked every bit like the kind of guy at the comic book shop who hated clipping his toenails and disregarded most personal hygiene in general. He was the embodiment of the classic nerd, and I immediately hated how his appearance reinforced the stereotype that men who liked computers and video games were disgusting creeps. Even through my car window, I could easily make out a crop of greasy, unwashed hair peppered white with flakes of poorly controlled dandruff.

I struggled to maintain my fake smile as I sighed a third time and wished for the standard rich old fart I had been expecting instead. At least that kind of man bathed regularly and changed his clothes. I hated being pawed at by old lechers, but anything would have been an improvement over the greaseball waiting for me in his driveway.

Once I was able to compose myself, I grabbed my bag and got out of the car. The energy drink I chugged on the way over was doing nothing for the long drive and lack of sleep, so I pinched myself hard until the pain made me more alert. I was struggling but put on a sleepy smile, determined to make the hours on the road worth my while.

As I made my way to the driveway, the wind blew and wafted his body odor into the depths of my soul. He didn't just look like he didn't take showers, he smelled like it, too.

Suppressing the urge to gag, I counted each step as I walked up the driveway, forcing my brain to focus on anything but the smell. Once I got close enough, his long, gangly limbs reached out and embraced me awkwardly. He pulled my tiny body into his tall frame, squeezing me far too tight for my liking. I could feel his hot, stinking breath on my scalp as

37

he smelled my hair, making no effort to hide the sound of himself inhaling deeply. A chill ran down my spine, and my body became rigid as the creepy, gross man took another painfully obvious whiff.

As politely as I could manage, I disentangled myself from him, putting a comfortable arms-length distance between us. I disguised this intentionally as a way to introduce myself formally, and he took the bait. I shook his hand and introduced myself as officially as possible, standing straight and tall and sounding strictly business.

He was far too familiar and friendly, and my plan was to remind him that I was here for money and did not instantly become his girlfriend after simply showing up.

He regarded me with a crooked smile, exposing a mouth of yellowing teeth, and my lip quivered as I barely kept up my façade. Years of playing collectible card games at my local comic shop on game night had taught me what kind of guy this was, and I was not amused. My hometown shop had even gone as far as putting up a sign saying, *we reserve the right to ask people with an unpleasant body odor to leave*, and this was the kind of man it applied to.

I stood grinning, shifting my weight uneasily as he finished smoking his cigarette in silence. After what felt like a lifetime's worth of forced, awkward small talk about the weather, we walked up the driveway towards the entrance to his massive home. He tried to reach down to hold my hand, and I shot him a look that said *are you fucking kidding me right now?* as I snatched it away. He stiffened up, fumbled his hand into his pocket, and led me into his house without making further eye contact.

I wasn't trying to be a frigid bitch, but I couldn't exactly play girlfriend and boyfriend with him, either. Trying to hold my hand seemed like such an invasion of my personal space and was honestly too intimate of a physical exchange to share with a virtual stranger. Aside from the social taboo, he hadn't paid me, and the luxury of physically touching any part of my body did not come cheap.

After we entered his home, I was baffled. Based on where this guy lived, he was clearly loaded, but the inside of his home reminded me more of a guy living in his mom's basement. The interior of his home, much like his physical appearance, had all the likeness and charm of a

38

greasy garbage dump. Furniture was sparse, and it made the large, lavish rooms look vast and empty, like a trash-filled tomb with extravagant crown molding.

Some of the rooms were filled with boxes, and the boxes themselves were filled with *something*. Based on the stains on the outside of the boxes, and the unusual smells permeating the spaces they occupied, I was afraid to ask because frankly, I did not want to know. Looking at the client, it could have reasonably been his long forgotten thirty-day-old groceries left rotting in the bag, or laundry he packed up into boxes simply to avoid washing it. There was no getting around it, the guy was gross in every conceivable way.

The client struck me as the kind of person who didn't wash their hands after using the bathroom, and I was terrified. I began to clutch the hand sanitizer in my bag obsessively, afraid to touch exposed surfaces and doorknobs. I didn't know when the last time he had cleaned his house was, but it could have been never. I didn't understand why he didn't at least hire a housekeeper, because the neighborhood he lived in suggested that he could have easily afforded it.

Eventually, we made our way to a large bedroom at the back of the house with an attached bathroom. He must have liked this room in particular because it was set up like a makeshift studio apartment; there was a queen-sized bed, a couch, a few bookshelves, a cheap plastic poker table, and some blankets on the floor serving as rugs. The bookshelves were full of manga and Western style comic books, figurines, and board games.

Some of the manga were on the floor, and I recognized a few of the titles. He had generic taste, and there was a good bit of hentai type of stuff mixed in. I giggled when I saw an impressive collection of *Love Hina* nestled neatly on the top shelf with signs of heavy reading on the spines. Having enjoyed the series myself when I was younger, I ascertained that this guy must have had a harem fantasy.

Once he had settled down on the couch, I got him to sign the credit card slip for the booking fee and went to the restroom to change into my sexy dance/lingerie outfit. Much like the rest of the house, the bathroom was filthy and looked like it belonged to a teenaged boy. Empty

39

canisters of potent body spray were piled up on the counter, and the shower only contained a single bar of hand soap. When I came out, I noticed something I had missed on my first pass of the room: a plastic milk crate covered in a sheet was beside the couch, and the items on its surface were familiar to me.

"…are those *Magic the Gathering* cards?" I asked, unable to mask my excitement.

Hearing my words, the client stopped what he was doing and turned to face me.

"Yes, they are. Do you play?" he said smoothly, cool as a cucumber.

His little nerd heart must have been beating right out of his chest because he suddenly looked ten times more excited than when he saw me walk out of the bathroom in revealing lingerie.

"Yeah, I used to play a lot," I said, genuinely interested.

This was, in fact, not a lie. Magic the Gathering is a strategic card game where players collect cards and build decks to play against opponents in a variety of formats. When I was younger, I used to build mediocre decks and spend my Friday nights playing against other enthusiasts at the local card shop. While I was never the best player, especially since I didn't have the money to buy the more expensive cards, I loved it, and seeing the cards filled me with a welcome sense of nostalgia.

I asked to take a look, and I peered through his deck. I saw many cards I remembered playing with myself and became completely lost in what I was doing; I forgot that I was standing in a stranger's home, dressed in skimpy lingerie and there for work. Leafing through the cards, I relaxed and engaged with him casually about the game. We talked back and forth like old friends, discussing the various nuances of the game and chatting about which colors we liked playing best. After a little while, I remembered the true purpose of my visit and refocused my attention back to his wallet.

The world is a mysterious place, and often full of surprises. Somehow, instead of the usual ilk, I managed to talk my client into paying three hundred dollars an hour to play cards with me in my underwear.

So, we sat, for about four hours, playing cards with anime playing in the background, eating junk food, and goofing around. Because I was an anime fan myself, I was able to enjoy the shows we were watching and overall use the experience to my benefit.

I was playing the part of the perfect, sexy nerd girl of his dreams, and it wasn't even much of a stretch; I truly enjoyed eating Cheetos and playing cards while we watched anime together. For once, my job didn't feel like work, and my irritability from driving for hours faded away.

Through all the playful banter, I could tell he wanted to take things to the next level. It was clear from his suggestive, crude jokes that he wanted to fuck me, or even simply to reach out and touch me. Unfortunately for him, he was crippled by his shy and socially awkward nature. He lacked the marbles to make the first move, and I knew it. I decided that feeding into his lewd comments, but keeping just enough figurative distance to keep him in the dark about whether or not it was okay to touch me, was my best move.

To be fair, I was indeed having an absolute blast spending time with him, and I was getting paid handsomely for it, too. Even with how well we seemed to get along personality-wise, there was just no way I would let him dip his slimy, greasy weenie inside my body. He was too unkempt and smelly to even consider it as an option, no matter what he was willing to pay me.

At some point, perhaps in an attempt to nonverbally communicate his desire to move things in a more sexual direction, he took his pants off. He stood there, in the middle of the room, staring at me silently as if the gesture spoke for itself. Being a true asshole, I nodded in approval but casually returned my focus to the playing cards as if nothing had happened.

He was wearing stained tightey-whities that were too big around the leg holes, and the bagginess somehow made them look worse. Seeing his long, hairy legs protruding out of the ill-fitting underwear was a glaring reminder of the stark contrast that existed between my client and the neighborhood he lived in. I couldn't believe this was the same guy's house; he was a complete mess in every conceivable aspect. I mean, he couldn't even pick out a proper fitting pair of undergarments, for fuck's sake.

He cleared his throat and smiled at me, hoping I would pick up on the hint, but I wasn't letting him off the hook so easily. Instead of reciprocating sexual interest by undressing myself, I clasped my hands together and playfully asked him if he was going to give me a striptease. He looked a little defeated, but weakly smiled back and obliged my request by performing the worst rendition of an erotic dance I had ever seen in my life. It was awful in that way that made it glorious, and I couldn't look away. He coaxed me, flopping his dong as he went, trying desperately to get me to engage with him.

But, no matter what he did, I carefully maintained an air of utter obliviousness, keeping the pressure on him to make the first move. He kept trying to make subtle advances towards me, which I repeatedly pretended not to notice. He was far too timid and unsure of himself to initiate anything directly, or to confront me for avoiding him. I could see the internal struggle playing out in front of me; my client clearly wanted more but lacked the social skills to follow through with his desires, even with a person whom he had paid to spend time with him for this very reason.

In what I considered an act of growing exasperation, he offered me an extra five-hundred-dollar tip, which I accepted without explanation or discussion about what it was for. I knew he meant for this to be a non-direct way of communicating to me that he was ready to do the deed, but I continued to play the fool. Instead of giving him what he wanted, I chose to play up my deliberate obliviousness even harder and found that he was too much of a 'nice guy' to call me out for it.

What I found especially amusing about his lack of confidence was that he didn't know what to do with his hands; he would lean in towards me, obviously moving in to touch me, but get paralyzed by anxiety and bail halfway through. His hand would stay frozen in midair while he deliberated on following through, and I did nothing to reassure him. Far from helping him, I pretended not to notice his repeated foibles and instead redirected his attention to the anime playing on the television or a book sitting on his shelf.

This tactic worked to my benefit. Despite how sexually frustrated he was, he couldn't resist the urge to rant about a comic book character or correct me about something I had purposefully mispronounced or explained wrong. I would ask him a question, carefully crafting it in a way that I knew was deliciously wrong, and watch him implode. This continued for *hours*.

Eventually, he mustered up the courage to directly request a striptease, which, to my credit, I did. I was amazed he had mustered the mental fortitude to ask me at all, so I had no problem doing it for him.

What I didn't do, however, was let him touch me. I sat him down on the couch and danced in front of him roughly five paces away. The floor was filthy, so I had to lay down a blanket on the floor to protect myself while I did my floor routine. I took my time, slowly removing my lingerie piece by piece, until I was gyrating nude on the blanketed floor before him. The more excited he got by my erotic display, the more I played up being a total airhead.

My usual practice with clients was to use my lap dance/floor show as a tool to seduce them and squeeze more tips out of them. I took enormous pride in my ability to utilize my languid dancing to increase my financial gains. With this client in particular, I felt no such compulsion to impress him, having already earned enough by doing nothing.

Since I already had the money I needed to pay my bills, I decided to make a game out of turning down every one of his advances as awkwardly as possible. I'm sure it was cruel and quite possibly traumatizing for a person struggling with social anxiety, but I didn't care. I didn't want anything to do with him sexually and wasn't interested in earning a regular that lived hours away.

Around the fifth hour, when my time was finally almost up, I decided to take my psychological torment to the next level; I needed to be sure he wouldn't call me again, so I had to play extra dirty. I had already observed that he was too much of a vagina to argue with me, so I used my lifetime's experience around nerdy men to say the perfectly wrong words. I gushed about what a *fun, cool friend* he was and how he was *so different from all the others* and how *I wish there were more nice guys like him*.

Even though I had intended for these statements to be the definitive nail in the coffin that pushed him over the edge, they were not.

He blushed in response to my words and began to playfully refuse what he thought were legitimate compliments. He tittered and stammered while I stared back dumbfounded and grew red in the face myself. By

43

trying to be a bitch, I had inadvertently done the opposite of what I intended and encouraged him instead.

Emboldened by my kind words, he reached out and bear-hugged me, squeezing my tiny frame into his chest while my skin crawled. He felt and smelled just as bad as he looked, and it was everything I could do not to scream when a flake of his dandruff landed on my face.

I drove off in a state of frozen terror. Once he was out of sight, I pulled over my car and hyperventilated as I frantically brushed every speck of his dandruff from my body. The security guard frowned at me as he saw me driving out of the complex in nothing but my underwear, rubbing my breasts vigorously with hand sanitizer. I felt like his stink was lingering on me, and I thought every minute sensation on my skin was more dandruff. I was past the point of caring, and no number of shrewd looks from an uptight rent-a-cop was going to change that.

CHAPTER FIVE

When No Means Yes

Client Carson

One night, my naive delusions of invincibility were shattered when I was raped at work. You might think, *can a sex worker be raped?* Just as a wife can be violated by her husband, the answer is *yes, of course*. In fact, most of the work I did was not sex acts, and instead simply lewd erotic displays. If I did sleep with a client, it was because I wanted to, and I had determined my personal risks, legal and otherwise, to be low.

Money was exchanged for my company only, and whatever happened after that was strictly between two consenting adults. For clarity, I was never under any actual obligation to sleep with anyone, and this was made clear to the clients. The extent of the 'good time' they paid for and what that entailed was entirely up to them. If they treated me like crap, I would leave.

I was at a fairly routine booking for a heavier client, wherein nothing extra had been discussed, when he pushed me onto the bed and forced himself on me. He was a lot stronger than me, and I didn't want to get beaten up for resisting, so I resigned myself to silence and let him do his thing.

It was terrifying and awful, but fortunately, it ended very quickly since I didn't fight back. It was strange, in a detached sort of way, when

45

he climbed off of me afterwards and tossed a few hundred-dollar bills beside me.

I sat on the bed, staring at the money for what felt like an eternity, before I grabbed it and rushed out of the client's home. For years I had operated under the illusion that I was in control, and though clients pushed boundaries, no one had ever truly violated them.

Driving home that night, reality sank in. I kept reliving what happened, oscillating between anger and bitter sadness. Certainly, a crime had been committed, but I didn't know what to do; the police weren't an option, because there was a real possibility I would be arrested regardless of what happened to my perpetrator.

My throat felt hot and tight as it dawned on me that I couldn't count on the legal system to help me. In our society, I was at the bottom of the barrel. No one would listen to me or believe me purely because of my profession. Sex workers were discriminated against and looked down upon by virtually everyone, clients included.

This was not news to me, and I was well aware of it long before I was ever raped. It was only an interesting, philosophical concept before I was actually experiencing it, and I hadn't grasped how isolating and damning it felt until I needed help.

Tears dribbled down my cheek as I considered whether or not to go to the hospital. I definitely needed an STD test, and prophylactic treatment to be on the safe side, but I didn't have health insurance. Medical costs were, and still are, incredibly high in the United States. Besides that, I would have to lie. They would ask questions, and I wasn't ready to give them real answers, which might keep me from getting the treatment; I needed medical care for a rape but couldn't ask for it without revealing myself.

There was also the looming threat of facing potential legal consequences if I told anyone about what happened in order to get proper care, and I was terrified that the hospital would tell the police.

Another factor, perhaps miniscule compared to the others, was the fear of judgment. I knew that if I told the truth, I would be treated like human garbage, judged and dismissed, and never treated fairly or with any modicum of decency. Society preaches about treating all people with

46

dignity and respect, but in practice, that isn't what I experienced at all. In essence, I felt totally and completely helpless.

When I got home that night, I explained to my boyfriend what had happened. At first, he was livid, but he quickly switched gears when I told him I was afraid to go back to work and that he needed to get a job.

Suddenly, he told me that I had no choice but to go back to work because we needed the money; without my job, we would be evicted and become destitute. To him, every monetary obligation associated with our day-to-day life was my responsibility and mine alone.

He argued that expecting him to work a minimum wage position was selfish because I could make a month's wages in one day. Expecting him to spend eight hours a day working for pennies was insulting and unfair, and he vehemently refused.

The rape, having only happened a couple hours ago, was still fresh while he argued his position. I had not even taken a shower yet, and he was insisting that I return to work. Instead of comforting me, he turned the focus to his selfish anger, cloistering himself away in the back room while he got high until I apologized.

Crying alone in the shower that night, I remembered that I lived in the real world, and the real world was a dark place. For people like me, life was not a fairy tale, and my kind of stories didn't have happy endings. No prince was coming to rescue me, and no proverbial white knight was waiting to whisk me away from all my troubles.

The next day, I returned to work, numb. For the first time in a long time, I was afraid. My confidence had been scoured away, and all that remained was an eerie awareness of the futility of my situation.

The everyday comforts of my life had turned into shackles overnight, trapping me in a dangerous situation. I had no family to lean on, no formal training for gainful employment, and nowhere else to go.

Overnight, my outlook on the job changed; I became more cautious, and the rose-colored glasses that easy money had glued over my eyes were lost forever. What I did was dangerous, and I had little recourse if something went terribly wrong.

The stories of serial killers, and how many victims were prostitutes, filled me with unspeakable terror. It disturbed me how little empathy existed for the sex workers in these tragic tales; no one cared that they had been brutalized or even considered their deaths as a loss to society. The emphasis was on catching the killer because *regular* people were at risk. It was sickening.

Wasn't I more than just a sex worker? Didn't I have a life, a story, a future worth living? I felt like my existence was less than worthless. Based on the true crime I read, people would be glad if I was killed since my profession was viewed with disgust. I couldn't bring myself to read the comment sections on YouTube videos or news articles, as the stringent hatred was too much to bear.

For several months following the rape, I dissolved into panic whenever I received a text for work. What if I was murdered? What if I was raped again? What if I got HIV?

I would sit in my car, taking deep breaths to calm myself, in order to muster the willpower to knock on the door. I needed to keep up the persona of a fun party girl, or I would make zilch. No one wanted to pay for the company of a party-pooper, so maintaining a cheerful, pleasant demeanor was crucial. I balanced fear with the need to survive and suppressed my anxiety in order to work. Debbie downers didn't get tips. Debbie downers couldn't pay their bills.

Emotionally, it was exhausting keeping up the façade. Before, it was only about lying well to not get caught while racking up tips. Now, after the rape, it was about clinging to my mental health with a smile.

CHAPTER SIX
Plap

My company had more to offer its clients than one-on-one experiences with a beautiful woman. Before I worked in the industry, the media had led me to believe that it was a man's ultimate fantasy to have two women at once. In practice, however, this is not something I saw to be true at all. In fact, the only customers I ever knew of reserving multiple women at once were larger group events, such as bachelor parties or college fraternities. Ordinarily, this meant reserving two women of contrasting looks for the same show.

For the most part, I didn't have any issues with working with other escorts; the other women in my profession were mostly friendly, and since we all had shared the common goal of maximizing our profits, we easily adopted an 'us-vs-them' mindset at most shows. Unless it was explicitly stated, we split the tips evenly and collected them up front, so there was no direct competition.

Working in teams also offered an element of safety that otherwise was nonexistent; we would arrive together and leave together, no exceptions. At times, it could be frustrating if a dancer was late, but for the most part, it kept us far safer than if we were working alone. One person could keep an eye on drinks while the other performed, and we could provide backup if a drunk got too handsy.

Even with these benefits, it wasn't all cupcakes and rainbows. There were some hiccups that made the multi-girl shows a tad less straightforward than a one-on-one private booking. For starters, each escort had her own unique set of governing rules she abided by, and a mismatch in this area was an unavoidable part of working with others. Since it was standard practice before every show started to give a spiel about what the rules were, and the consequences of breaking said rules, candid discussions were required.

Generally, we would talk to each other about tipping fees and what behaviors were acceptable as a group while getting changed in the bathroom. If things were copacetic, we all agreed to charge the same thing for base services and (mostly) worked as a team to hustle the room for extra cash. In this regard, I got along better with some girls than others, and the boss did her best to pair together escorts that operated on similar principles and generated more repeat clientele.

Since not all of us agreed on what our job actually entailed, it created a little conflict. The reality was that not every escort possessed enough dancing skills or guile to make tips entertaining, so their only schtick was selling sex. Sometimes, finding common ground with women like that was impossible, and bookings became a total drag. I couldn't get away with selling a three-hundred-dollar lap dance show if the person standing beside me was offering bareback blowjobs for fifty bucks a pop. Regardless of what the other woman looked like, the choice was an easy one for most drunk, excessively horny men to make, and in those circumstances, I made nothing.

The financial drawbacks of working with others extended to the booking fee as well. Since reservation fees were part of how the agency got paid, any reductions to that spilled over onto the escort. The company offered a discount when booking two or more women at once, which meant that the dancer's share of the fee barely covered the cost of gas to get there. If tips weren't made, going to a multi-girl show meant operating at a loss.

Sometimes, customers were unprepared or unable to tip up front, which meant even more financial strain on the workers. It was common for customers who were limited on funds or hesitant to drop several hundred dollars up front to adopt a 'pay as you go' approach, and in that circumstance, being the group favorite was paramount to making any money. At times, the men were looking for a statue-esque, prissy model type, and at others they seemed more inclined towards a husky woman with tattoos with a mouth like a sailor. It was impossible to predict, and we all hoped that we would be the one chosen by the group.

Another variable essential to making money at large parties was catching the attention of the man with the deepest pockets. Typically, he was the one with the credit card that was already comfortable spending money, and the one who was likely bankrolling the cost of entertainment.

It was common for clients to request enough girls so each man present could have an escort to himself, and for them to take turns picking which girl they wanted. Whoever was paying for the experience was generally the guy who picked first.

It was a bit nerve-wracking when it came to the picking; I was never the last girl picked, but I wasn't always the first, either. We all wanted to be chosen by the man who paid for everything, and not his broke-ass friend who was just lucky to be there. Like it goes in regular day to day life, sometimes you win, and sometimes you lose. It was the way in went in the business, and I accepted it for what it was.

I knew that it was statistically impossible to always be the favorite, especially with such a wide variety of personal tastes that dictated what attractive was. My boss liked to employ women who fit a popular visual niche, so any client could get a close resemblance to the female stereotype he wanted.

This overarching constant potential for fierce competition with the other women created a lot of psychological problems for me. In simple terms, I was not a socially aggressive person, and a huge part of why I detested working in strip clubs was the constant cut-throat, catty behavior it required to be successful; if you wanted to make any money, you had to be okay with stepping on the heads of everyone around you, and that just wasn't me.

I did not like going to work thinking that I had to be wittier and/or sexier than someone else in order to pay my bills on time. In fact, just knowing in advance that a large multi-girl party was looming on the horizon filled me with serious anxiety; I would be directly compared with the other dancers, and it meant I had to look my best.

I would get my nails done, painstakingly style my hair, and fuss over which outfit suited my curves best. All the small details mattered when appealing to the male fantasy, and you never knew which detail would make you stand out to the right person.

Part of my anxiety also included drastically altering my dietary intake. Feminism and body positivity are wonderful, but it was undeniable that when it came to work, men greatly preferred rail-thin women without an ounce of unwanted body fat. The last thing I wanted was to lose out on making any tips because I ate too much for a couple of weeks in a row.

To stay on the safe side, I ate almost nothing whenever a large party was coming up, and if I did eat, I usually ended up making myself vomit on purpose afterward. It was awful and debilitating, being so afraid to consume anything in fear of jeopardizing my finances, and it plagued me with guilt whether or not I ate.

Occasionally, when the party was booked several weeks in advance, this effect was exacerbated, and I would become weak and frail. I would barely eat, and by the time I got to the event, I usually had lost between five and ten pounds. I was thin and athletic to begin with, so I didn't have much to lose. Even though I knew this logically, I was incapable of looking at myself in the mirror without becoming hyper-fixated on my appearance. I couldn't eat without falling into a depressive spiral if a party was the following week and end-of-the-month bills were fast approaching.

Other times, my personal issues working with other women were more… complicated. The industry attracted a lot of strong, colorful personalities, and at times, they didn't mesh well and caused unexpected friction while dealing with clients.

Worker Peaches

One evening, I was informed that I had been chosen for a double booking, a term we sometimes used to signify a reservation of two women at once, with an escort I had never met before. I had been working with my agency for years by that point, so I knew all the veteran dancers. Newer women would pop in and out at the agency with predictable regularity, but they seldom lasted long enough for me to even learn their names.

This particular dancer had been with the company for years, but strangely, I had never encountered her before. I wasn't thrilled at the prospect of unraveling that mystery, but I couldn't refuse, either. I had already agreed to go, and quitting now meant annoying my employer and losing out on potential work in the future due to being unreliable. I grumbled, preparing myself for work with less than the usual alacrity, and rolled my eyes as I walked out the door.

Pulling out my phone, I double-checked the address and groaned; the motel I was headed to was in the part of town where vagrants begged at every corner and used drugs openly in the street. Seeing people passed out on the sidewalk with drug paraphernalia was both depressing and frightening, so I went back inside and changed into shoes better suited for running.

The motel itself, uniquely awful in its own right, brought an additional panoply of problems to the table. Black mold-infested bathrooms, leaky plumbing, and roaches climbing on the walls were just some of the many amenities available. The last time I was there, I ended up throwing out everything I brought with me, terrified I would bring bugs into my house.

Knowing ahead of time that the client chose the shittiest motel in the worst part of town was a bit of a wildcard. It could be that my soon-to-be client was experienced with escorts and was saving as much money as possible for tips. It wasn't unusual for clients familiar with our agency to choose the cheapest lodgings possible to have more financial bargaining power with the woman they ordered. More likely was that my future client was a total cheapskate or simply broke.

First-time customers or men without deep pockets often called the agency with high hopes that the booking fee was all-inclusive. The fee itself was very affordable, and even a person making minimum wage could have conceivably paid it. The only thing the booking fee covered, however, was a single strip-to-nude lap dance show, which lasted about fifteen minutes max, and anything that happened afterwards was between the dancer, the client's wallet, and God.

Men who were trying to pull a fast one would spend upwards of thirty minutes trying to convince me that my employer promised them

53

that the booking fee was all-inclusive, claiming I owed them sex, or whatever else they demanded. What the clients didn't realize was that I knew for a fact exactly what my boss told people over the phone and knew verbatim the words used to describe the services we provided. Because the work was legally grey, we had to walk a fine line to avoid getting into trouble, and this meant not making any promises about sex for money or offering services beyond the basic show over the phone.

Men pressed, too, trying to determine what their booking fee would get them. Every time, no matter how insistent, my employer repeated the same vague response that neither confirmed nor denied anything illegal and made it clear the company was not familiar with the practices of the individual entertainers.

The clients, being oblivious to my depth of knowledge, had zero moral qualms boldly lying to my face, demanding that I have sex with them while insisting my boss promised an all-inclusive experience. They would go as far as threatening to call my boss *right now* and *get me in trouble*, but that they were willing to let my behavior slide *just this once* if I gave them a blowjob.

These little power trips, where the client would attempt to leverage fear as a way to bully me into sex acts, were despicable and made me burst into laughter. Their reaction to my lack of concern made me laugh even harder and resulted in a very confused, uncomfortable looking client. I always found it fascinating when the clients believed I would cave to any request on their word alone, especially when it was wrapped into a coercive statement involving my employer.

I didn't bother arguing back and forth with them. They were liars and would say anything to manipulate me into free services. Instead of entertaining their bullshit, I would watch their faces turn white as I called their bluff and called the agency on speaker phone.

My boss, a woman who used to work as an escort herself, would calmly and firmly tell customers to fuck off and bicker back and forth with them. As long as I collected the booking fee, she didn't care about the customer if they were being argumentative shits. I had established myself as a reliable, strictly business-focused worker without a drug habit, and my employer didn't want me to switch to another company. I also only called with legitimate issues, so she took all of my on-the-job calls seriously.

It was amusing watching a customer pass through the stages of grief as the lies blew up in their face. Being that my employer herself facilitated the booking, blaming their misunderstanding on another phone operator wasn't an option. There was no manager to talk to, and no obligation on our part to make them happy. They would go from angry, to reluctantly apologetic, to pleading, and then back to angry again. It was difficult watching a man argue with a third party for unfettered access to your body, as if you had no say in the matter.

When the clients persisted, we always reminded them of the agency policy regarding poor client conduct and that no refunds would be issued. After angry, aggressive demands that they be allowed to fuck me ultimately failed, the client would laugh it off and tell me something along the lines of *well, you can't blame me for trying.*

This behavior was pathetic and disgusting, and echoed the 'customer is always right' mentality prevalent in the United States. It baffled me how naïve clients could be regarding the agency, and that they actually believed we weren't working in tandem against them to make a profit.

But back to the booking: When I arrived that night at the run down, shit hole of a motel, I saw a slightly pudgy woman, somewhere between thirty-five and forty-five years of age, leaning up against an older model convertible with a cigarette hanging loosely from her mouth.

Pulling into a space, I suspected it was the other escort, but hoped it wasn't; the woman was the spitting image of everything that was wrong with how Hollywood portrays prostitutes. She had curly, voluminous red hair, over-done, garish makeup poorly concealing years of too much time spent in the sun, a skin-tight cheetah print mini dress cinched tight around her waist with an oversized, black leather belt, and pair of over-the-knee patent leather boots.

I inhaled sharply, nodding to myself as the puzzle pieces clicked into place. Of course I hadn't met her before, we were different types of entertainers. I did mostly bachelor parties and dance shows, and I had a sneaking suspicion she made her bread and butter off something else entirely.

I stared at her, frowning, and my mind began to wander. She was unbothered, staring at her phone and letting it all hang out. I felt like I could smell her just by looking at her. Questions began to populate in my mind and demanded answers.

Why did she choose to wear clothing that accentuated her protruding tummy?

Why did she choose to apply a shade of concealer that didn't match her skin tone?

Why did she dress in a way that gave off the impression that her pussy looked like a pair of used up mud flaps on an eighteen-wheeler?

Everything about her image seemed to scream *hey world, I fuck for money*. She was the most unattractive person I had ever seen in my entire life. Imagine a redheaded, fatter, uglier version of Fran Dresser that was on the wrong side of thirty and nursing a crack habit.

If I hadn't known any better, I would have assumed she had wandered into the parking lot directly off the street corner. I could easily picture her approaching cars at stoplights in a shitty part of town with a pimp watching possessively nearby.

I couldn't wrap my head around why a person would make such a conscious decision to look like a walking, talking personification of a negative stereotype, but there she was in all her glory, smoking like a chimney while flicking her cigarette carelessly into the grass.

She saw me standing by my car in the parking lot and waved both arms enthusiastically in the air. I shrunk in my seat, wishing I could turn invisible or pretend to be lost. Sighing deeply, I accepted my fate and reluctantly joined her in the parking lot.

If her looks weren't enough of a slap in the face, her voice and attitude took things to the next level. She didn't just look vulgar, she was; her grating, raspy voice carried the unmistakable lilt of a raging cunt, and her deliberate choice of language was... colorful. After chatting with her briefly in the parking lot, I felt an urge to go home and shower off the grime.

While coming to terms with my co-worker, two eager men began cat-calling us from the second story breezeway of the motel. They were holding beers in the air and cheering obnoxiously, advertising their obvious inebriation for the world to see.

My co-worker, seeing the men, waved back and matched their overzealous energy, effectively letting them know that the entertainment had arrived. The men, smoking cigarettes and stumbling around their hotel door, started hooting even louder.

I sighed deeply.

Fully committed to an evening of bullshit, I decided I wanted to at least collect the booking fee before I found an excuse to bail. I carefully walked towards the building, kicking trash and broken glass aside with each step, and made my way to the outdoor stairwell. The area smelled strongly of urine, and a shoeless man was sleeping hunched over beneath the stairwell with a burnt piece of tin foil in his lap. I cringed, freezing in place until I verified he was truly asleep and hadn't noticed me, before cautiously making my way to the concrete steps.

Clutching my canister of mace, my heart raced with each step. I was terrified of being attacked, stabbed, or raped at any moment. For all I knew, the whole call was a ruse to get fresh victims on the property to mug, and a gang of deranged vagrants would jump out from behind a dumpster wielding broken glass bottles of Mad Dog 20/20.

My fear was exacerbated by the evening air, which was hot, humid, and sticky in the worst of ways. The warm heat intermingled with the dumpiness of the local area, causing an unpleasant odor to linger heavily in the air. The wet stink clung to me with each successive step, leaving me uncomfortably moist as I feared for my life. I could hear the loud clacking of my co-worker's boots on the concrete behind me, her heaving breaths nasally as years of smoking left her no match for the stairs.

When we finally reached the men, the unrelenting humidity and city odor had eaten away what little patience I had left. The clients wanted to finish smoking their cigarettes before heading inside, and before I could say anything, my co-worker loudly agreed, pulling out a fresh smoke as she caught her breath from climbing the stairs.

I sighed again, joining them against the railing as the two men made sloppy, overzealous discord with the other woman. Remaining silent, I observed the men closely, analyzing their clothing, shoes, and haircuts. I listened to the drunken banter, and began slipping in gentle probing questions when I could, thankful for any chance to uncover details of their professional lives. I carefully led the conversation, expertly targeting the flow of small talk to size up their wallets and determine how readily they might part with their hard-earned cash.

Judging by the uniformity of their matching side-faded haircuts and clean-shaven faces, they looked like a couple of military guys. This was no problem at all to me; military men meant military pay, which in my experience meant credit cards. My patience and expectations, which were quite low up until this point, perked up a bit. There was a real chance the men on the balcony had money to spare, and if I was lucky, they were leaving on a deployment soon and would be willing to blow every dollar they had on a last hurrah. I cleared my throat, ready to layer on the charm, but before I could get a word out, the other woman spoke.

"Maaaan is it HOT. It ain't even good FUCKING weather out here, am I right or WHAT?"

Stunned, I stared at her, not quite believing my ears.

Laughter peppered her candid speech, and I struggled to keep my jaw from dropping open. I gripped the steel railing, casting my attention to a cluster of seagulls fighting over garbage, hoping to distract myself from the nasally sound of her voice. The drunken men, however, were unbothered and appeared delighted for any reason to turn the subject matter towards sex. They laughed along with her, and one of them lifted his shorts to show how his balls were stuck to the side of his leg from the humidity.

I sighed again, crestfallen, realizing that the booking would be a complete waste of time. My coworker was connecting with the clients in a way I never could, and they were eating it up. They laughed and smoked, cheerful in each other's company, while I was the odd one out. My pride felt wounded to be bested by such an appallingly hideous creature, and I expected to be undercut out of any tips by rock bottom prices for bareback anal.

Bored, I passed the time watching my contemporary do her thing. The men were far too intoxicated to notice my keen observation and carried on while I astutely took mental notes.

Her method of hustling was so very different from my own, and it dawned on me that perhaps this woman was a seasoned veteran and knew *exactly* what she was doing. Her words were vulgar, yet specific. There was a chance she was foreshadowing her inability to offer legitimate sex and clueing the clients in that she would only be giving handies or blowjobs. If she was on her period, it was a clever maneuver that primed the men mentally, even if they didn't realize it, for a specific type of sex act.

Her choice of attire and attitude also made it very clear that she fucked for money, and this probably saved her a lot of time; if a man was interested in what she had to offer, there would be no beating around the bush. She definitely wasn't the kind of woman you would find dancing on stage or giving a lap dance, and she gave me the impression that she made her living gurgling semen.

Our interactions, though brief, did little to retract from this assumption. While crude, I had to admire her game; a client knowing up front they were getting a piece of ass likely increased the odds of spending whatever was in their pocket. This was certainly to her advantage when being paired with someone like me, who was not as easy to read.

I was deliberating the possible complex psychological motives behind her choice of manner and dress when she loudly cleared her throat and hawked a huge loogy out onto an unsuspecting pigeon below. The group, sans me, erupted into wild fits of laughter before taking turns trying to hit the other birds in the parking lot.

I blinked, slowly nodded to myself, and began accepting the situation for what it was without ascribing higher meaning to it. She farted loudly, lifting her leg as she did so, and made no apologies. Watching her hack up large wads of mucous over the balcony, I realized there was a real chance that she was, in fact, just a dirty old hooker after all.

When we went into the motel room, my hunch about her possible motives seemed right; the more inebriated of the two gentlemen chose her immediately and was very verbal about how horny he was. I was selected by the more bashful client, who became visibly nervous by me simply touching his arm. There was quite a personality discrepancy between the two, and I wagered it had not been my customer's idea to call us.

Once we had collected the booking fee, my client and I made our way to one of the queen-sized beds on the far side of the motel room while the other pair headed into the bathroom. It was an odd choice, but who was I to judge. I figured with a body like hers, having a little privacy probably made her feel more comfortable in her own skin.

I managed to get a one-hundred-dollar tip from my client and had a decent time chatting while performing a few on-the-bed lap dances. He was very nice, and polite even when touching me, and overall treated me with dignity and respect. We were joking around about how gross the motel room was, and about what a scary part of town we were in.

He was a nice guy, and honestly seemed like someone I could have seen myself dating or at least having a fun time with if the circumstances were different. He asked me if I knew the other girl, and I responded in the negative. His face implied he had the same impression of her that I did, and we shared a knowing look.

After finishing my dance routine, I was ready to pack up and go. I grabbed my things, got dressed, and even gave my client a hug. Even though I was finished working, policy dictated that both entertainers left at the same time. After I explained this to the guy I was with, we collectively decided to step outside and smoke cigarettes in the breezeway to pass the time. On the way out, we walked by the bathroom door, which was left wide open.

Without thinking, I glanced inside, and it was a mistake. The guy was leaning against the bathroom counter with his pants and underwear hanging around his ankles. One hand was raised in the air trying to keep his beer from spilling, while the other was in a fist, firmly clutching a fistful of her hair. She was on her knees in front of him, her acrylics clacking against the linoleum, giving him a sloppy blowjob. I could see her head bobbing back and forth along his shaft and could tell there was no condom. She was just going for it, raw dogging that hot dog with everything she had.

Shocked, I found myself unable to look away; it was like watching a train wreck, and I stared stupidly, struck simultaneously by both terror and awe. The sickly, thick aroma of sex wafted towards me, suffocating me with the pungent scent of exertion and body fluids.

The man's drunken hooting while she went down on him served as a humorous counterpoint to the revolting sight in front of me. He struggled to remain upright due to how inebriated he was, and as a result, he periodically steadied himself with the hand tightly clenching a fistful of hair.

She would gag and struggle in response to being used for balance, the unexpected weight forcing her uncomfortably deep onto his penis. Judging by the rate that she was bobbing her head, coupled with the feverish stroking of his erection, I could tell she was trying to speed things along. I was mesmerized by her concerted efforts, and knowing how drunk guys could last a long time, I felt bad for her.

The guy walking out the door with me saw this, too. He froze, slack-jawed and bug eyed, and I wondered for a moment if he had ever seen his friend naked, yet alone drunkenly getting a blowjob from nasty hooker. Judging by his expression, my guess was a resounding *no*.

So, we stood in silence in the motel breezeway, looking out into the barren parking lot, waiting patiently for them to finish up. We both knew what was happening a few meager feet away from us, and the poorly constructed walls did little to conceal the noise, but neither of us would openly acknowledge it. I think in that moment we were both processing what we had witnessed; he was probably wondering how well he really knew his friend, and I was lost deep in thought, hoping I'd never end up desperate enough to become the woman in the bathroom. Whatever the reason, we stood in solemn introspection for what felt like an eternity.

When they finally came out, her makeup was smeared all over her face, and her hair was a mess. Her flushed face was covered in a thin layer of saliva and sweat, her exertion plainly visible as a stray glob of white goo dotted her cheek. Even her eyes were still watering from the ordeal, and I could smell the faint odor of cock and semen on her breath. There was no doubt about it, she had really gone the distance to finish the job.

61

Disgusting or not, I had to hand it to her; it was a marathon effort, and she pulled it off.

In contrast, the guy who came out alongside her looked happy, relaxed, and completely refreshed. In a loud, obnoxious voice that boomed across the parking lot, "HEY, DID YOU GET YOUR DICK SUCKED, TOO?".

Mortified, his friend shook his head with a deliberate slowness. I guess he wasn't ready for such a comment after what he had seen. What a guy.

On the way home that night, I took a serious mental inventory of my life. That night was the first time in my career that I had witnessed firsthand how awful things could become. I was terrified of making the wrong choices and ending up like her, reminding myself that she didn't get where she was in one day. Sobered at the thought of being forced to survive that way, that night I promised myself I would never compromise my core values for money, no matter what.

Worker Veronica

Per the usual way, I got a text one evening about a group show a couple of cities over. I was being paired with someone I had never met before, so I experienced my normal pang of anxiety. I wasn't in the mood for any shenanigans, so I was hopeful that this other woman would be a normal, drug free, friendly individual who wouldn't cause me problems by merely existing in the same room.

Knowing I had competition, I took my time getting ready for the booking, making sure I looked especially cute. Once I was satisfied with my appearance, I spritzed myself with my favorite fruit scented body spray and drove to the hotel.

I took great care to arrive on time, timing my drive and rushing at the gas station, only for the other entertainer to be late. Tardiness was one of my pet peeves, and the other escorts had an annoying habit of being anything but punctual. I would always get an outlandish, ridiculous excuse as to why a person was late: my washing machine blew up, my car caught fire, my ex-boyfriend tied me to the bed and forgot about me... I had heard it all before and didn't believe a single word of it. The only excuse I would accept without question was something along the lines of *my drug dealer was late, and I had to use to avoid going into withdrawals*, not that any of coworkers would admit to that.

Brooding, I waited in my car, soaking in a sea of negative thoughts and boredom for twenty long minutes. Before I axed my nicotine habit, I would spend my time waiting smoking cigarettes and playing silly games on my cell phone. Sometimes, I would read books or doodle pictures on a piece of mail lying around.

On the busier nights of the week, another employee's lack of punctuality affected my earnings. The sooner I finished a booking, the sooner I could be available to take another one, and wasting an hour sitting in my car was costly. It wasn't uncommon on Friday and Saturday nights to do back-to-back shows, receiving details for one booking as I checked out of another. It only took one good show to make the entire night worthwhile, and getting that client came down to luck. If you weren't available, you lost out.

When the other dancer finally arrived, I met her in the lobby and took a brief inventory of my competition: She was not bad-looking at all and had a naturally athletic build. She was a little shorter than me but fatter in all the right places. She gave no hints of being a bottom-of-the-barrel drug addict and instead gave off girl-next-door vibes. I realized she was not only attractive, but also sporting a head of flowing locks that reached her mid-back.

Fuck.

I paused, fighting back sudden anxiety; this woman was not only beautiful, but she also had the same hair color as me. Having the same hair color made direct comparisons by clients much more likely, and physically, I was no match. When there were multiple women, men generally selected their entertainer based on blonde vs brunette vs redhead. This tendency was so predictable and ingrained in the male client base that our agency presented women on the phone by hair color first, followed by a physical description.

I frowned, realizing she was more classically beautiful and likely had the advantage. For her looks, she strangely came off as timid and unsure, which was puzzling. This was a gorgeous woman who was in the perfect business to take advantage of her favorable genetics, so her lack of confidence was odd.

Once we got upstairs, two men were waiting for us in the hotel room. The room itself was nothing impressive, boasting two queen-sized beds placed fairly close to one another along with all the other standard hotel room accoutrements. A desk, a lamp, a nightstand, etc. The only things that were out of the ordinary were two oversized duffle bags full of hockey gear.

The men, casually chatting back and forth like an old married couple, gave every indication of being old friends and also very drunk. They weren't just into their cups and floundering, they were actively drinking still. They sat, leaning against the headboards of each respective queen-sized bed, roaring at each other's jokes while spilling booze onto the sheets. Their obnoxious, inebriated behavior was annoying, but it also meant that if we left half an hour early, they would be none the wiser.

Much to my delight, each man immediately preferred one girl over the other, so neither was left with an entertainer he didn't like. My concerns about making zilch vanished, and my confidence returned. Once we collected our flat fee for a lap dance show, we put on some music and got started.

The standard routine for in-bed lap dances was laying the client against the headboard in a semi-reclined position, propped up on pillows with his legs spread apart. Commonly, the clients would start out fully dressed, and we would incorporate 'sexily' removing their belts, pants, shoes, etc., as part of the dance routine. Stripping a man down to his boxers was something I did regularly, and the men went gaga over it.

Entranced, they watched as I teased off each sock, slid off their pants, and lightly ran my fingers over freshly exposed flesh. The trick was over-dramatizing each movement, prolonging the tease and building the tension as much as possible. The men loved being undressed by a beautiful woman, and I loved running down the clock.

These men in particular had paid extra for non-stop nude lap dances with the ability to touch us anywhere except our genitals. This was pretty standard, and overall felt like just another mundane experience with a couple of drunks. The clients selected the same stereotypical songs for us to dance to, and like every other client, we got the ...*oh my gawd, you're going to LOVE this music...* spiel. Between the piercing, awful music and obnoxious drunken rambling, it was hard to get a word in without yelling.

I was lost in thought, wondering idly if the eggs in my fridge were fresh enough to use for a quiche, when I felt a hard slap on my left butt cheek. Slurring his words, my client was attempting to flirt with me while sloppily groping my ass. This was par for the course, so I brushed his hand aside and pretended to flirt back, going through the motions while waiting for my timer to go off.

It was then, while I was grinding away mindlessly on the client's lap, that I happened to glance over at the other dancer. She was standing on the bed with the other guy lying between her legs while dreamily looking up at her crotch. She was shaking her hips seductively and using her hands to slowly loosen the strings holding up her bottoms. At this point, her bare breasts were already exposed and fully on display, but the client was focused on what her hands were doing. Smooth as butter, she turned around, bent over, and slid off her underwear. When she shimmied back around, that's when I saw it.

Her vagina.

It was... special. Everything about it looked textbook, except for one not-so-tiny, glaring detail: her clitoris. It protruded from between her labia like a long, droopy finger, beckoning the client with each hypnotic sway of her hips. My dancing slowed to a halt as I did a double take; I could hardly believe what I was seeing, and the wandering hands of my client faded into the background. Her clitoris dangled freely in the air, a testament to the strength of the untold feminine form.

I wanted to remain professional, but I couldn't help myself. As I danced, my gaze kept finding its way back to her crotch; it was so different, so unique. It was almost like a tiny little female penis was poking out of her pussy lips, completely free and not taking no for an answer. I pictured the other woman on a seaside cliff, wearing a flowy skirt with no panties, lifting her leg and peeing boldly into the salty spray of the ocean. In my mind, she was courageous. She was feminine. She was saying *fuck you* to people in public, asserting her femininity and staring down any passerby that dared to look her way, as if to say *what?*

While staring, I started to wonder if her sexual partners sucked on it in a way similar to fellating a man, or if when she masturbated, she ran her fingers up and down its length like a penis. Did it firm up when she got highly aroused? I had so many questions, and zero answers.

As I reflected on the oddity before me, her lack of confidence in the lobby suddenly made sense. I flushed, embarrassed at my lack of consideration, and quickly averted my eyes. For all I knew, she had no choice but to keep this job, and based on the kind of clients who frequented the agency, she likely had to tolerate the savage roasting of her roast beef on a regular basis.

Everything was going smoothly until I lost my cool and started giggling; she was mid-dance and gyrating mere inches from his face when the clit-penis-finger-thingy *plopped* onto his cheek and slowly slid across it.

It was like it happened in slow motion. I could see her protruding genitalia flush against his visage, sticking slightly to his sweat moistened skin as it went. Whether I heard the distinctive 'plap' sound of it colliding with his flesh or I imagined it, I could not say. I was so lost in the moment. And it didn't just happen once, either. She kept doing it again and again, assaulting him senselessly with her lady dick as he drunkenly grappled with gravity.

Each plap of pseudo cock against his ruddy cheeks pushed me further to the edge; I had long since given up dancing and was now entirely focused on the spectacle before me. When it stuck to his skin, and she had to wiggle to get it free, I lost all composure and erupted into an uncontrollable fit of giggles. Each time it made contact with his skin, I chortled, unable to stifle my laughter. As I watched, I saw her clitoris looming towards him like an unrelenting, meaty pendulum of doom.

Plap. Plap. Plap.

I was shaking, both hands clasped firmly over my mouth, when my coworker finally connected the dots. She looked at me with a hurt, knowing expression, fighting back tears as she stormed off to the bathroom. The men, still drunk and oblivious, hardly noticed anything was amiss and didn't complain when I followed her.

I know what you're thinking, *wow, you're a real piece of shit.* And you wouldn't be wrong, but I still stand by my opinion that she partly brought it upon herself.

For one, she knowingly possessed a unique attribute in a business where physical appearance was paramount. Aside from that, and the main point here, is that she had no business forcing her lady bits onto his face. Clearly intoxicated, the client was arguably unable to consent. He could barely walk in a straight line, let alone tell her to stop rubbing her dangly lady dick all over his face. Perhaps I was wrong for laughing, but she definitely owned some part of what happened.

CHAPTER SEVEN

She's A Pirate

Working as a call girl meant regular exposure to a range of questionable behaviors most people would find unacceptable: men crying on my shoulder expecting sympathy for being caught cheating, dudes masturbating into socks, or even getting smacked so hard on my butt that it left a clearly delineated hand-shaped mark.

But after doing it for years, being subjected to mild abuse and being demeaned was such a normal part of my life that it became boring and unremarkable. Who cared if some man called me a filthy whore while throwing cash in my face, or if another guy tried to 'surprise' me by aiming his ejaculate at me. It had become such a banal aspect of my life that I didn't even raise an eyebrow.

Another man in a hotel room asking me to watch while he jerked off? Meh.

Insert your eyeglasses into my vagina so you can have something to remember me by for tomorrow? Been there, done that.

Choke a guy until he almost passes out while he cums on a photo of a parakeet? Whatever.

I disliked admitting it because I liked to think that I was too intelligent to be so affected by my work, but the job had left me bored and jaded. The result was that I viewed most traditionally sexual things as not sexy at all. A job was a job after all, and to me, mine was about as exciting as watching paint dry or alphabetizing a five-foot stack of paperwork.

The day-in and day-out was incredibly dull, and over time, it took more and more for something to actually register as exciting or inappropriate on my radar. Certainly, every new client brought their own unique sexual desires to the table, but to me, they were all uninspired.

Sometimes, a client would spend most of the hour-long booking with me simply working up the mental nerve to share their deepest, darkest fantasy. The hard part was acting surprised, or even interested, when it was something painfully vanilla that I had heard dozens of times before.

Of course, there were times when regardless of what a client was willing to pay, I drew a hard line and said *no*. Usually, this was because a client's attitude rubbed me the wrong way or gave me the impression that something was just not right about them beneath the surface. Following my intuition was a big part of what kept me safe. Even if it seemed unfair or unwarranted, if I got bad vibes from a customer, I refused to do anything but the base agency requirement of a nude lap dance.

One such client was one of my 'regulars', a frequent customer who requested me specifically on a fairly reliable basis. Generally, getting and keeping a regular customer was a good sign as an escort, and meant that you were doing well. The idea was to get as many high-paying regular customers as possible to stabilize your cash flow.

Having a regular would have been a boon, except for this case in particular. I hated this client with a passion and always begged my boss to send anyone else. He would call and request me all the time, and since he paid good money to spend time with me (and only me), my boss wasn't keen on losing that kind of income. My pleas for another worker were ignored, and I always found myself gritting my teeth and grumbling during my drive to his house, a drive which I had begrudgingly memorized from having to visit so often.

The guy wasn't the worst customer I had ever had, per se, and in fact was far from it. He never tried to beat me up, or threaten me, or even trap me inside his house. My issue with him was that he refused to respect my boundaries, no matter how many times I was mean to him or demanded it. That and he was a sleazy crackhead that fostered an unhealthy, bizarre infatuation with me.

He would book me for multiple hours at a time, knowing full well it was against company policy to leave before my time was up. Being a long-term customer, he was well-versed in company policy and exploited it. My hours-long bookings would be stretched out to the very last minute, and if I did happen to leave early, he would complain. I hated being forced to spend so much time cooped up in his house while having to tolerate his bullshit.

What exactly do you do for three-plus hours stuck inside with a crackhead who sits on his kitchen counter singing to himself and followed by bouts of nonsensical philosophical rambling?

I didn't know, either.

Without being high myself, his profound revelations were not nearly as interesting to me as they were to him, and I couldn't stand listening to his bullshit. Sure, he was paying me, but it wasn't enough. Nothing was enough for spending hours in your underwear babysitting a crazy person. Whenever I was with him, time dragged on for what seemed like ages, and all I wanted to do was leave.

With other clients booked for the normal one-hour time slot, I spent the first fifteen minutes or so explaining the agency's rules and getting changed in the bathroom. Then I would negotiate higher tips followed by providing entertainment for about thirty-ish minutes tops. Finally, I would cut things short at the forty-five minute mark, saying I had to get dressed in the bathroom and gather my things.

It was no secret to the clients that my timer started the very moment I walked in the door, and much to my advantage, this made the actual amount of work I had very small. For a standard booking, I spent significantly less than an hour entertaining them and often employed time-wasting tactics to burn down the clock. I would re-apply lipstick, intentionally strike up conversations that the client was too polite to interrupt, or skillfully probe at psychological wounds that would cause my clients to spend most of their hour talking to me about their feelings.

With multi-hour shows, however, this was not the case; I couldn't bullshit away most of the booking getting changed in the bathroom or making pointless small talk. I had to provide actual entertainment for literal *hours*. It was exhausting maintaining a fake persona for hours at a time, and it wore me down tremendously.

While I was fantastic at providing brief, fun experiences, the challenges of longer shows put my entertainment skills to the test. There was only so much grinding in someone's lap to the top forty pop hits before it got dull for everyone, and the onus was on me to keep things fun. Finding creative ways to keep a client engaged was not fun for me, and since everyone was an individual, it meant thinking on my feet to come up with something that suited the personality of each client.

So, when I got booked at my regular's house, I died a little inside. I knew I would be stuck there all night and had no real way to cheat the clock. I couldn't piddle away the hours because he knew all the spiel and was acquainted with my made-up persona already. He would cut me off and rush through the formalities as quickly as possible when I walked in the door and immediately get started on his bullshit.

I was a captive audience for his crazy, drug-induced garbage, and he knew it. He also knew that whenever my time was up and I said I had to go, he could call my employer and request more time until my shift was up, effectively trapping me while my mind melted from boredom. He abused our system, and I hated him for it.

What made matters worse was that he was always trying to push drugs on me. I would arrive and he would have a large pile of (what he claimed was) cocaine on the dresser, or pills, or something I didn't even recognize, and tell me it was for me.

He would also try to get me to smoke crack or marijuana with him, or drink alcoholic drinks he prepared specifically for me. I didn't have a drug or alcohol habit, and even if I did, I was no fool; I never accepted anything he offered me for fear I would end up in his trunk or chained to a radiator.

To me, declining party favors was common sense. How stupid could you be to ingest mystery drugs and take a client on his word that a drink wasn't laced? As far as trusted sources to get illicit substances from, I figured in my mind that a person trying to buy sex from you was the last person on the planet you could place faith in. And I was right; I heard my fair share of stories about women facing terrible destinies after trusting a client they thought was their friend, and I wasn't about to let it happen to me.

There was also legal risk. I knew the police would never believe an escort who denied culpability, and I would end up in prison for possession even after passing drug testing. I knew my social status wasn't the best when it came to dealing with the law, and I didn't want to put that to the test over something as serious as drugs. I was constantly paranoid about police bursting into his house and arresting us both because of the things he kept in his house. Whenever I left his residence, I would always double-check my belongings and make sure he didn't slip anything into my bag. I couldn't risk getting in trouble because he wanted to do me a 'favor'.

At the time, I was a cigarette smoker, so whenever he did try to push drugs on me, I would use smoking as an excuse to politely decline his offerings. I would hem and haw, saying I needed to smoke a cigarette first while I thought about it.

Like a goldfish, he would forget what he asked and circle back around to it later, and I would push things off using the same method repeatedly. It turned out that I smoked a lot of cigarettes at his house.

The final thing that was positively maddening for me about this client was that no matter how rude, annoying, uninterested, or downright mean I was to him, he always booked me again.

Some nights I had zero patience and would be as much of a bitch as I possibly could, being sure that I crossed the line and finally pissed him off enough that he would forget about me, but I was wrong. I could not shake his interest, and my boss wouldn't let me drop him as a client. I couldn't wrap my head around his seeming obsession with me, and I hated being forced into tolerating his bullshit for hours on end. He wasn't able to afford to tip me, either, because he spent all his money on the hourly agency fee. Since my boss made a killing on the hourly rate, I had no choice but to go.

Client Tom

One night, I had an important exam the next day, so I made doubly sure I was off the work schedule. I wanted to study until I couldn't read anymore and then get a full night's sleep. School was important to me, and doing well in school was even more so. Getting good grades gave me an identity beyond pushup bras and strip teases, so I clung to it and protected it fiercely.

When my boss called me in for a five-hour show with my regular, I was livid. Apparently, he had negotiated with my boss and paid extra per hour to book me since he was told that I was off schedule, and my boss, not wanting to miss out, agreed for the extra fee.

I was furious, but she told me to suck it up and get dressed. I knew better than to get on her bad side, so I angrily hung up the phone and reluctantly went to the bathroom to get ready. I cursed under my breath as I shaved my legs, and then my vagina, making sure not one spec of hair remained.

What was I supposed to do for *five hours*? All I wanted to do was study and sleep, and I wasn't even supposed to be working. It was late at night, and I had hours left of brutal cramming before I could snuggle up in bed. My brain was already scrambled eggs from studying all day, and I knew I didn't possess the mental energy needed to handle the client.

The last thing I wanted to do was deal with a rambling crackhead. He had a track record of singing badly at the top of his lungs followed by abrupt sessions of staring off into space in complete silence for up to forty-five minutes at a time. I grit my teeth, seething in anger that this was about to occupy the rest of my evening.

Since I hadn't expected to work, I didn't take my typical nap during the day, and as a result, I was grumpier than usual. I fantasized about telling my boss off and quitting, leaving the world of escorting behind, but that was all it was.

Fantasy.

The reality was that I didn't have much of a choice, and if I refused the booking and made my boss lose out on a big payday, I would have hell to pay and surely regret it later. Begrudgingly, I followed orders and got myself ready for the client.

While getting dressed, I couldn't help but fixate on just how much I hated his guts; he was always dragging me into his idiotic drug binges, not tipping, and generally being a colossal pain in the ass to deal with. I was fed up with his crap, and this time I was determined to leave a lasting impression.

This time, I told myself, *will be the last time.*

I chuckled darkly, all at once realizing that perhaps there was indeed a way to get rid of him once and for all. Wasting no time, I rummaged through my nightstand looking for a certain something to help make the night a little more interesting. After rifling through my cluttered collection of various sex toys, I found exactly what I was searching for: a large, pink, vibrating dildo. Grinning devilishly, I stuffed it into my dance bag along with some restraints and headed out the door.

My planned mischief had turned me from sour to elated in moments. I spent the entire drive fantasizing about what I would do to my client and how he would think twice before ever calling me again. I had high hopes for my plan because I knew from experience that he was all too agreeable to anything I asked of him, especially if it was vaguely sexual in nature. He was like putty in my hands if I said even one mildly suggestive word to him, and I intended to take full advantage. He wanted a good time, and he was about to get one he would never forget.

When I arrived at his house, I could tell the moment the door opened that he was high and drunk. The foul, stagnant stench of crack smoke and booze on his breath made me want to hurl. He wasn't just disgusting, he was utterly repulsive, and I felt my stomach do tiny flips as my energy drink threatened to fight its way back up.

Even more than a decade after moving on to better things, the mere smell of alcohol blended with cigarette smoke makes my skin crawl. All of my least favorite clients boasted the same pungent odor and shared the same hazy-eyed lustiness. They would breathe heavily from their mouths and talk loudly, spewing their stink all over you. Before becoming a call girl, I was never one for drinking, and the experiences I had only amplified this disinterest.

While still working, I accepted that dealing with drunken assholes was just part of the job, because by the time I got there, almost every single client was at least intoxicated with alcohol. Outside of work, however, it was a different story.

Because of my strong negative associations with the smell of alcohol, I was unable to go to a bar or even simply have a drink with a friend without thinking about work; the smell was inescapable, and even the slightest hint of it sent my body into overdrive.

All I could imagine were handsy men who gave me a hard time and demanded too much for too little. These were the kind of men that would attempt to slip fingers into your pussy, thinking you wouldn't notice, and the kind of men you had to literally slap in the face to get them to pay attention to the word *no*. My body would involuntarily tense up in response, whether I liked it or not, and this reaction caused me to abruptly leave many outings with friends.

I would start fidgeting and images of my most reviled clients would start popping into my head. Nausea and anxiety would wash over me in waves, and eventually the suffocating feeling would become too much to bear, and I would be forced to politely excuse myself. It wasn't as if I could explain my situation, either, as the true nature of my job was basically a secret to everyone.

I wasn't shy about my disdain for drunken men, either. God help the man who tried to hit on me while out with friends if he had even the smallest trace of alcohol on his breath. I was normally hard to get, but mostly agreeable since I liked to fuck, but when I smelled booze their chances of getting into my pants dropped instantly to zero. All pleasantries were dropped, and I became a raging cunt.

It was as if all the hatred I had for my clients poured from me like a faucet directed towards the poor, innocent men who happened to bump into me in public. Looking back, I feel kind of bad about it. I was mean, cruel, and enjoyed rejecting these hopeful lovers in the most damaging ways possible.

But back to my story. That night at work, my client's eyes were red, and he had a sleepy expression that transformed into a friendly smile the second he saw me. It was obvious that he was crazy about me, which only made me hate him more. He warmly welcomed me inside and offered me a drink, not even bothering to shut the door behind me.

He never bothered peering out the door to see if a pimp was with me, or locking the door behind me to ensure no one would rush inside to rob him. New clients were always a bit cautious at first, but not my regular. Because I had been here so many times, he seemed completely at ease in my presence and trusted me completely; he knew from experience that I didn't steal, and that I always came alone.

He treated me like an old friend and dropped all the pretenses that normally dictate polite social interaction. Without a word, he meandered over to the kitchen area and sat up on the counter, beginning his usual ritual of smoking his crack and singing to himself in giddy elation. He would bang his legs on the cupboards beneath him in time to his off-key warbling while picking at his crack pipe and mixing ash with his drug.

Watching him so peaceful and happy on the counter filled me with nothing but fury; I was utterly exhausted and had an exam first thing in the morning. I was booked for *five fucking hours* and would likely spend every moment listening to hair-brained conspiracy theories or his awful singing. I was seething, but like every other time I had seen him, he didn't care.

I scowled at him, but he didn't care. He continued picking at his pipe, seemingly lost in his own world. He was never phased by my bitchy attitude or snappy comments; no matter what I said or did, he just smiled and looked absolutely tickled that I was even talking to him in the first place. In this regard, he reminded me very much of a golden retriever puppy, always bounding full-speed back to its owner like it was the best day of its life.

It could have been that I looked like his ex-wife or a girlfriend he had when he was in high school, or perhaps I was reminiscent of a one-night stand that he remembered fondly. I had certainly run into that situation before, and every time I did, it was creepy.

I learned over time, based on the photos of ex-lovers that my clients often felt inclined to show me, that it was a common thing for a man to seek out companionship that reminded him of a past flame. Occasionally, and much to my disgust, some of my clients even sought me out because I looked like their daughters, biological or otherwise. It was disturbing, but turning down good money was a luxury I couldn't afford.

For this client in particular, I had no idea where his odd fascination with me stemmed from. He never once showed me a photo of another woman or blubbered on ceaselessly about the proverbial one that got away. Sure, I had seen plenty of porno mags lying around his house that depicted women that looked similar to me, but it could have been a coincidence. I wasn't exactly unique looking; I was conventionally attractive for the type of work I did, and in my opinion, somewhat plain compared to my co-workers.

I never asked where the odd fascination with me came from because with how often he called me to his house, I didn't want to know. The second I started asking questions with genuine interest, I risked viewing a client as a person instead of a source of income. I didn't need guilt stopping me from getting paid; compassion for clients was not something that bode well in the industry. The men I saw were not my friends, my boyfriends, or even casual acquaintances: they were paychecks, and nothing more.

Another reason I avoided asking too many personal questions was because I risked the client thinking that we had developed a legitimate personal connection. The moment a client thought they were 'special' was the same moment that they would try to exploit that status for all it was worth. They would expect special treatment from me, usually in the form of sexual favors or the expectation that I would be okay with meeting them outside of work. I had zero interest in either of those things, so I learned early on the importance of keeping my clients at an arms distance. The real trick was balancing personal mystery and intrigue with just enough familiarity to get them to max out their credit cards.

Standing in the kitchen and holding onto my bag, I suddenly remembered what I had brought with me. My lips curled into a mischievous grin as I stared intently at the man who had forced me to waste my precious study time. He was lost in thought, not even aware of the sudden shift in my demeanor, still singing badly and staring off into space.

"Do you want to come upstairs with me?" I said, batting my eyelashes.

He blinked, seeming unsure of me for the briefest moment, before taking the bait. He gingerly hopped off the counter, scooped up his various drug paraphernalia, and followed me obediently upstairs to the master bedroom without question. Each step we took up towards his room filled me with more sadistic glee; I was so close to finally putting an end to dealing with his shit, and the promise of freedom and revenge was intoxicating. My heart was pounding as I reached the top of the stairs, letting myself into his room before making my way over to his bed.

I turned to face him, smiling sweetly, and patted the bed with my palm, beckoning him. He paused again, traces of reason eeking through his clouded judgment, before happily complying with my request and sloppily planting himself beside me. He eyed me suspiciously but couldn't hide his delight; I was alone with him in his bedroom, probably like he had imagined hundreds of times while jerking off.

With my soon-to-be victim exactly where I wanted him, I looked around the room and then suddenly exhaled through my teeth. On the dresser, there was a sizable pile of white powder with a loosely rolled up one-dollar bill, crusted at the edges from overuse, beside it. I could see the dried white powder clinging to rolled paper mixed with traces of blood. It was disgusting, and not the first time I had seen drugs lying around at his house.

"What the hell is this?" I demanded, pointing to the pile of powder on the dresser.

"Oh... For you. I know you like it," he said sleepily, seeming pleased with himself as he relaxed back onto the bed, "go ahead, try some. It's good."

I could feel my blood pressure rising as I brought a hand to my face, pinching the bridge of my nose. I was not in the mood for his bullshit and offering me drugs was one of the ways he liked to push my buttons.

I grit my teeth, feeling my anger swell up deep inside me, but caught myself before boiling over; since I knew I wasn't coming back to his house, I didn't have to be nice. I marched over to the dresser, and in one sweeping motion, I quickly swiped the entire pile of fine powder onto the carpeted floor.

"Oopsie," I giggled, his eyes growing wide as saucers.

I watched him, pleased with myself for pissing him off, and curious to see if he would snap. If he did go nuts and try to harm me, at least it would be an excuse to leave early and go home. But instead of freaking out, all he did was thoughtfully take another hit off his crack pipe.

His lack of reaction annoyed me, and I decided it was time to cut to the chase and stop wasting time. I was on a mission, and it was time to focus and get things done.

I took off my top, revealing the sexy lingerie cupping my breasts underneath, effectively diverting his attention back to me from his drug use. Using the momentum I had created with my tits, I languidly asked if he had ever been tied up before and then winked before sweetly asking if he wanted to have some fun.

Yes, *fun*.

Looking back, maybe this was a bit unfair; he had been calling me for a very long time and had been probably waiting for ages for me to show the slightest hint of sexual interest. At that moment, I suppose I finally seemed willing, so he immediately agreed to let me tie him up.

I giggled again, pleased that he had taken so little convincing, knowing that I was now one step closer to finally being done with him for good.

While I was busy adjusting knots and checking for proper circulation, he had the bright idea to ask about a safe word. He had been rambling about nonsense the entire time I was working, and I snapped out of my groove by the relevant, intelligent question.

Even though I knew I was about to brutalize him, I had to acknowledge his question; it was legitimate and always part of the discussion whenever one person gives complete power to another. At least in safe, healthy kink circles, that is.

"Hmm... Safe word? How about banana?" I answered pleasantly.

He nodded in agreement, and with that final contract cemented between us, I stuffed a dirty sock that I had picked up off the floor into his mouth and then duct-taped it shut.

Playtime was over.

After making sure he could breathe safely, and rechecking the restraint to ensure he couldn't escape, I walked over to the dresser and started digging through my dance bag. He watched, bug-eyed and completely confused, as I pulled a large pink dildo from the bag.

He connected the dots immediately, and right away started frantically fighting against his restraints while aggressively shaking his head *no*. I only smiled in response and then nodded darkly that yes indeed this was happening.

As far as I could tell, he didn't say banana, or anything that *sounded* like banana, so I ignored him. Plenty of people liked to pretend to resist and got a real sexual thrill out of it, so as far as I knew, this was no different. I let him struggle for a few minutes, enjoying his helplessness while I practically cackled with glee.

I wanted to let the weight of his incapacitation take root deep within his heart and soul, and let anxiety tear him apart. He had made me suffer more times than I could count, and now it was his turn.

Now, I won't lie. I loved it. Maybe because I was angry that he dragged me out to his house on an exam night, or maybe it was because part of me couldn't deny how raw and sexual it was rendering someone I hated completely helpless, but I was having a blast. Watching him squirm and struggle made me feel powerful, and honestly, a little turned on. He was at my mercy for a change, and it was intoxicating; I was drunk on my ill-gotten power, and even the tiniest bit of fear and uncertainty in his eyes filled my glass to overflowing. I savored every moment of his fruitless thrashing and sat there watching him, prolonging the sweet, sweet taste of victory.

Once I could tell his spirit was thoroughly broken, I approached the bed. Since the struggling stopped, and it was clear he had accepted his fate, I ventured to ask him if he had lube anywhere in the room. I heard a deep, muffled sigh through the sock gag, and then he used his head to motion towards a bedside drawer.

I took my time digging through his things, seeing valuables and pulling them out while saying things like, *ooo, this looks expensive, should I steal it?* or *this doesn't look important, do you want me to throw this away for you?*

Naturally, I had no intentions of stealing anything from him, or throwing away his valuables, but it tickled me how acutely distressed he was. He panicked as I systematically examined and then tossed his prized possessions carelessly onto the floor, laughing the whole while.

I even found a thick wad of money, which I proceeded to wave around in his face while saying, *oh my, what is this? is this for me?* He started flexing as hard as he could against the binds, desperate not to let me take his money. I didn't know if it was for his mortgage or taxes or what, but he was hysterical.

Satisfied with how upset he was, I slapped him in the face with the money a few times, teasing him and reminding him of his utter powerlessness. Once I had my fun smacking him with it, I threw it aside, scattering the bills into a huge mess all over the floor.

Ethically, I was against theft, but I wasn't one hundred percent positive he knew this. Sure, I had never stolen from him before in all the countless times I had visited him, but my over-the-top behavior had pushed him into the throes of a minor panic attack. He was breathing rapidly, sweating, and watching my every move like a hawk.

Bored of tormenting him with the prospect of losing all his valuables, I grabbed the lube from the back of the drawer and squeezed a copious amount onto the tip of the dildo. Using my hands, I took care to ensure that the shaft was lubricated thoroughly. I know what you are thinking: *if you hate this man and want to make him suffer, why are you taking such an intentional step to avoid causing him harm?*

The answer to that question is a little complicated, but essentially it boils down to that while I wanted to cause him suffering, I had no desire to inflict any lasting physical damage. I did not want to risk getting in legal trouble for taking things too far, so I was doing my best not to get carried away. In my mind, there was a fine line between an acceptable amount of sadism at my client's expense and ending up behind bars.

It was my goal to teach him a lesson while still taking the appropriate steps to keep the cops out of it. Which, to be fair, was pretty unlikely since escorts were already a legal grey area as is, and no one wanted to involve law enforcement for fear of getting arrested just for having one inside their home.

After I lubed up the dildo, I cast my eyes on my helpless client tied down in the bed. He looked like a mess; digging through his valuables and throwing his money around had really done a number on him, and he did not look like he was having fun anymore. He looked nervous and afraid.

"Are you ready for some fun?" I asked as I stood in front of him, showcasing the dildo in all its glory.

He shook his head fervently *no* in response, so I kicked him in the ribs, then asked him again. This time, he nodded profusely until I permitted him to stop. I then moved his thighs aside and spread his ass cheeks apart as well as I could manage. Though all the hair, I couldn't quite make out where his butthole was. It was a disgusting task, and I hated having to touch his genitals, but I considered it a necessary evil to rid myself of his presence once and for all.

By that point, his whole body was shaking, and he was whimpering slightly. I ignored it and told him to shut the fuck up. The pitiful blubbering stopped, but the shaking only increased exponentially.

Looking at the fear in his eyes one last time, I giggled sadistically before thrusting the dildo up his ass. There was less resistance than I would have expected, and it slid inside him easily with the lube. I frowned, confused, unsure why it had easily slipped in without issues.

The clear lack of inflicted discomfort only made me angrier. This obviously wasn't his first rodeo, and it only spurred me to be rougher and more aggressive. I knew then that the mere act of shoving a dildo up his butt wouldn't be enough to scare him off, so I had to take things to the next level. He had been acting so afraid this whole time, while apparently being no stranger to taking it up the rear. Knowing this, I fucked him as savagely as I could manage until both of my arms gave out.

Hot and sweaty, I cursed at him, struggling to continue to torment him, when he ejaculated. Seeing his gross penis quiver and vomit out spurts of white sludge caused me to lose what little control I had left. All my efforts to make him miserable had failed spectacularly, and he loved every second of it. His whimpers, his resistance, all a show. I had fallen right into his plans, and I knew it.

"What the fuck is this?!" I yelled as he stared back at me with an unapologetic, pleased look plastered on his face.

Angry at my failure, I roughly ripped the duct tape off his mouth. Right away, he spat out the dirty sock, and that's when I saw my chance. Before he could say anything, I pulled the shit-covered dildo out of his ass and rammed straight into his mouth.

"How does that taste, you filthy fuck?!" I screamed, jamming it as far back as it would go.

He was gagging now, and wanting to make him suffer more, I scooped up the cum from his belly with my free hand and smeared it all over his face. Some of his ejaculate even got into his mouth, causing him to gag even more.

Finally seeing legitimate suffering, I felt inspired. I forced the nasty, poopy dildo as deep down his throat as it would go, pumping it up and down all the while. He choked, shook his head from side to side, and even vomited a few times, but I didn't stop. I hated him, and I hated how he had actually gotten off.

Because of the restraints, he had no choice but to endure the brutal face fucking I had given him and looked like hell because of it. He was dripping with sweat, with smears of shit and viscous saliva smattered all over his face. He looked gross, and smelled like it, too. Thoroughly spent, I dropped the dildo, letting it fall right beside his cheek, and hopped off the bed.

I was ready to leave, and at that point, I didn't care that I would be skipping out on hours' worth of booked time. I was done, whether he liked it or not. Glancing over my shoulder, I could see that he looked like a pathetic mess and was not making any efforts to try and escape. I wandered over lazily, inspected him briefly, and verified that he was breathing normally and not actively bleeding from any orifice.

Satisfied that he was not bruised up enough to call the police, I grabbed the scissors from my dance bag and cut one of his arms free. He was still in a daze as I left the bedroom, but I knew he would sober up before long and could get out just fine on his own.

*

The next morning, I woke up and saw no notifications from my boss. I was in the clear; he didn't call to complain after I left early, and I felt a mixture of pride and relief wash over me. I had finally asserted dominance over that annoying crackhead, and would *finally* be free of his bullshit. No more bookings where I had to listen to him sing and ramble for hours. It was a real victory, and I smiled as I got myself dressed and ready for class that day.

Days went by, and I received a call from my employer regarding that client. When she mentioned him, I was more than ready to be reprimanded and fully prepared to accept whatever verbal lashing she had in store for me.

So, imagine my surprise when she started gushing about how my client had such an amazing time. He wanted me to come back again that night and was willing to pay even more than last time to reserve me on my day off.

Fuck.

CHAPTER EIGHT

Wasted

After countless fumbles, I learned that you can never assume a client's level of intelligence based on appearances alone. In my job, making snap-judgments was a huge part of being successful, so as bad as it sounds, applying some learned stereotypes helped me determine which clients were worth my time and energy, and which weren't.

This was especially true at a private party with multiple women present; you would want to focus on charming a guy that would be a good investment of your time. This usually meant not choosing the best-friend who wasn't paying for anything, or the guy who was so drunk that he couldn't sign his name on a credit card slip. It also definitely meant avoiding the 'nice guy' who wouldn't participate in the usual sense, keeping his figurative distance and refusing to spend money because he disagreed with it ethically.

This kind guy was always the literal worst because he would try to relate to you on a personal level in an attempt to separate himself from the other men. He would ask personal questions like *what is your real name* and *so what do you really do for fun?*, before trying to get a free lap dance out of you because *I don't normally do this kind of thing, but I guess I'll let you if you want to.*

In my experience, all of this bullshit always translated into wanting free services from you and/or trying to get you to meet them somewhere during your non-working hours *for free*. It was pathetic, a total waste of time and effort, and whenever I realized I was talking to this type of guy at a group party, I would walk away and not waste another second with him. I went to these parties and events to make money, not to scout potential boyfriends for dates or hook-ups. Why a guy would think someone like me would be willing to meet him off the clock to have sex with him was beyond me.

Because different types of guys had vastly different earning potential, it was really important to be familiar with them to maximize your profits. Stereotypes are often wrong and can be damaging, and I won't deny this. But it does need to be said that when you create these beliefs solely from your personal experience over the years, they hold a little weight when making a snap decision. Giving someone the benefit of the doubt is always the best policy, but it doesn't mean you should completely ignore your instincts and forego experience.

Some trends over the years helped me sift through which men were worth hustling, and which were not. You could be the sexiest dancer alive and do everything by the book, but the bottom line was his bank account. Making a guy fall in love with you was worthless if he had empty pockets.

I learned over time that men who wore a lot of designer brands and heavy cologne didn't have much money, or if they did, they weren't willing to spend it. If I saw a guy with a big, gaudy wristwatch and/or jewelry at a bachelor party or a booking, I would avoid him.

Another common characteristic was the chin strap beard style. I saw this usually on white-trashy Caucasian men, and it made them look like they spent their free time yelling at their mothers or punching holes through drywall. If I saw this intentional aesthetic choice on a man, it was a huge red flag, and my guard shot way up.

In my experience, these guys were very grabby and had little respect for boundaries or limits. They expected everything for nothing, and tended to argue when you wouldn't give them special treatment. If they did have money, they would always make a huge show of pulling a wad of cash out of their pockets and waving it in front of your face, as if just seeing the money would make you amenable to their demands.

Naturally, if you told them they had to pay up front for a service, like a lap dance for example, the cash wad would disappear.

This type wanted you to prove yourself to them or insisted that you trust them in leu of payment up front. Commonly, this manifested as requests for free services in order to prove you were the *real deal* and *not playing games*.

With how often men tried to pull this bullshit, I imagined it worked with the newer girls. As a seasoned escort, I knew the angle was bogus and that this type of client never had any intention of paying you. It was a scam, and a scummy one at that; if a girl performed free services and he told her to kick rocks, she couldn't exactly pursue him legally for what was owed.

I heard firsthand from battered co-workers that if this type convinced you to compromise, it was all downhill from there. He wouldn't stop and would become aggressive if you tried to reestablish boundaries. I had heard too many awful stories from other women about those kinds of seedy men, and my blood boiled whenever I came across them.

A different, less irritating trend I observed was the significance of men wearing casual, unbranded clothing with no logos or designs on them. These guys had clean shaven faces, not much of a cologne smell, and seldom wore any kind of accessories that would signify they had money. Their shoes were clean, and they carried themselves with a relaxed, friendly demeanor.

In my experience, these were the guys you wanted as clients. They were well off, treated you respectfully, and had no qualms compensating handsomely. The real tip off was the shoes; conspicuously casual attire that was coupled with high-quality footwear meant big money.

But, like I said, looks can be deceiving, and you never *really* know what someone will be like until you feel them out a little. Knowing which type of guy to avoid was mostly helpful, and I was rarely wrong in my assumptions.

There were also some special circumstances though, where no matter what, I knew one hundred percent that I was about to be knee deep in bullshit. You might be wondering, *how could you be so sure if it's a total stranger?*

The answer, it turns out, is simple: hard drugs.

I knew plenty of people that used hard drugs, and their lives looked fucking awful. Fumbling for dirty needles, vomiting, not eating for days, and nervously picking invisible bugs off your body? No thanks.

Despite the overwhelming list of negatives, many people were addicted to hard drugs. Even as a non-user, I understood that these people didn't start out entrenched in addiction. A crippling, all-consuming habit didn't happen overnight; it took time. A couple of my co-workers were hopelessly ensnared, and it made them desperate.

They couldn't practice discretion when selecting their clients because they had to use, or else. It was really sad. I didn't know what it was like to take it up the ass for twenty bucks to avoid going into drug withdrawals, and didn't want to find out. This awful reality was so commonplace within my work life that it terrified me and kept me from ever wanting to use any drugs.

Now, clients using was a wholly different beast. Yes, I regularly saw intoxicated men, especially at bachelor parties when the groom was intent on having their last hurrah before being shackled by marriage. These types of clients could be very annoying but were mild-mannered and harmless. They were regular people with regular lives, only looking for a fleeting moment of fun.

Marijuana was a popular choice, and it didn't bother me at all. Potheads were happy, mellow, extremely polite, and unwilling to involve themselves in any conflict whatsoever. I had no qualms with a smiley, giggly guy who wanted to eat jellybeans out of my belly button or take bong hits while I pranced around in my underwear. These men could be funny, and a few of them wanted to simply 'hang out' and watch TV with me naked once they were stoned. They were a delight, and some of my favorite shows involved men partaking in the devil's lettuce.

Much to my benefit, marijuana use frequently caused low-level paranoia. Stoners did not want any problems and shied away from drama. I loved this. They were clearly afraid of being caught by law enforcement for using an illegal drug and for calling an escort.

Because of their fear, if I wanted to leave, I could do it without a fuss. If I put forth even a minor amount of resistance, they would back down immediately. There were no refunds, and no complaints, either. This flexibility was ideal, but entirely unique to marijuana users. Some clients had a taste for the harder stuff, and that came with a slew of challenges.

This was the kind of person that went balls to the wall, holding nothing back as they threw caution to the wind. I am talking about the type of person that got a wild hair up their ass one day, tried some hard drugs for shits and gigs, and then decided that calling a hooker is the next logical step.

Why?

Because firstly, they got super horny once the high set in, and secondly, that's what everyone does in the movies.

Group Party Shinkansen

One evening, I was hanging out at home, relaxing in my underwear, when I got booked for a hotel party. My experience told me that the words 'group party' and 'hotel room' signaled that tolerating drugged up, inebriated men had a place in my near future. I groaned, not wanting to go.

I was feeling bloated and kind of icky because I had started my period two days prior and wasn't thrilled at the prospect of a bunch of dudes manhandling my tender tits. My period itself did not stop me from working, because using a tampon instead of a pad meant no one would be the wiser. In practice, I changed into a fresh tampon in the bathroom while donning my lingerie and focused on lap dances. Even while nude, no one could tell if I tucked the tampon string deep inside my vagina.

When I got to the hotel, I took my time locating the room so I could approach it quietly. I wanted a chance to listen outside the door for any clues about what was happening inside. Ear pressed to the door, I could make out hushed talking in another language and occasional laughter.

I knocked and rolled my eyes when the talking came to a halt, followed by urgent whispers and poorly concealed footsteps. One of the men was trying to spy on me through the peephole without me knowing.

89

His attempt was so obvious that I decided to cover the hole with my finger just to fuck with him.

I heard more hushed, frantic whispering inside when he couldn't see me, so I knocked more loudly and called out *hello* in my sweetest voice.

I had barely taken my hand off the door when it quickly jerked open, and the dark eyes of a stranger eyed me suspiciously. The door was cracked just enough to get a good look at me and to glance around to ensure I was alone. I was used to such behavior and thought nothing of it.

Once the dark eyes verified that I was indeed alone, I was invited inside by a middle-aged Asian man in a black suit.

It dawned on me that 'group party' had been a gross understatement. The hotel room was average-sized, with a king-sized bed and dresser/TV combo taking up a good chunk of the space, and there were at least ten other men cramped into the space. They seemed to share a common nationality, and every single one of them, including the man who let me in, were wearing the same business attire.

Eleven sets of wary eyes examined me, looking me up and down with clinical precision. The group was silent but was otherwise positively brimming with energy and agitation.

Oh boy.

On the hotel dresser were all the telltale signs of cocaine use, and I sighed. Reluctantly, I collected the booking fee and excused myself to get changed.

It is probably worth mentioning, before I go any further, that at this time in my career, I still had a deadbeat boyfriend. He insisted on riding with me to and from bookings in case I needed 'protection', which was adamantly implied on his part but never explained; he was a scrawny coward and possessed nothing that garnered him the ability to protect anyone from anything. To be frank, he was dead weight, and the only reason I let him tag along was because he would whine and pout if I didn't. Getting an endless barrage of argumentative text messages throughout my shift was a stress I didn't need, so I normally caved.

He also used the fact that he was driving me (with my car, mind you) to and from bookings as an excuse to demand part of my profits; he said it was his job being my driver and security, which entitled him to a cut.

Now, I want to be very clear, and I hope that any working girl who reads this and finds herself in a similar situation listens to my words of wisdom: do not pay him one red cent. The only reimbursement he received was in the form of not shattering his delusions.

If he didn't want to keep a job, fine. If he wanted to insist that he was a required piece of the puzzle that let me do my job, I wasn't going to stop him. I even listened without objection while he obnoxiously bragged to anyone who would listen how he ran security detail for a private company. What I didn't do was give him cash or access to my bank account. I figured that letting him live in my apartment and smoke weed was payment enough, and honestly, it felt like too much.

With that being said, on that particular night my boyfriend was waiting in the car for me while I was working. I was in the bathroom, frantically trying to use baby wipes to clean myself off because my flow was heavy. I was taking much longer than normal due to the mess, and the coked-out group of men in the hotel room were getting antsy.

I heard disgruntled murmurs sweep through the room, and one of them impatiently knocked on the door. It had been about ten minutes, and I was still fruitlessly trying to wipe away any evidence of blood. The men, growing more restless by the minute, began arguing amongst themselves. I listened, feeling tense as I realized my flow was too heavy, and I couldn't possibly dance without smearing red on people like a deranged snail.

While deliberating my options, they started banging on the door. My heart began racing as I stuffed all my belongings into my dance bag and pulled my street clothes over the lingerie. I didn't see a place to throw away my used tampon, and I couldn't just leave it on the counter, all bloody and nasty. If I flushed, I ran the risk of clogging the toilet, and that would be a whole other can of worms. I didn't know what to do, and I started to freak out.

Between the banging on the door and inability to clean myself, I concluded that there was no time to explain myself; they were angry, horny, and coked out of their minds. I wanted to run to the door, but the whole group was waiting just outside the bathroom.

In a moment of panic, I remembered that I could call for help. He was no white knight in shining armor, but he was the best option I had. Before I sent my S.O.S., a tiny part of me weighed the real possibility that my idiot boyfriend would actually make things worse. I hesitated, picturing how easily that idiot could turn things into a total disaster, but I had to take the chance.

Things were already bad, and judging by the now rattling doorknob, they were about to get a lot worse. Holding my breath, I sent the text, then clutched my trusty can of mace in both hands, anticipating the worst.

Now, don't get me wrong, my boyfriend was certainly a loser, but to his credit, he was outside the hotel room door making a ruckus within minutes. Yes, it was admittedly terrible execution as far as a rescue goes, but it was better than nothing.

The new threat of a male stranger causing a commotion in the hallway only aggravated the situation, and the group started yelling at me through the door, demanding to know if I knew who was outside.

Afraid, I lied.

Eventually, perhaps to avoid bringing too much attention to themselves, one of the clients opened the door and allowed my boyfriend to enter. It was astonishing that they let him in at all, considering the circumstances. It could have been that they were afraid of police being called, or that the drugs had turned their better judgment to shit. I did not know, but I breathed a sigh of relief that I was no longer alone.

When I heard my boyfriend's voice, I ran out of the bathroom and darted straight towards the hotel door, which he had stupidly shut behind him. Now, instead of making a speedy exit, we were sandwiched in between the closed hotel room door and a mob of angry men.

Despite their growing anger and confusion, men in the group still periodically stepped away to do lines of coke. It was a real mess, and the drugs were only making it worse.

One of them was accusing us of trying to steal their money and demanding we give it back in choppy, broken English. Hearing him explain things from their point of view, I couldn't fault them for thinking that this was indeed an elaborate ruse to rob them. Honestly, considering things objectively, it was hard *not* to see it that way.

I nodded in agreement, eager to return the money to put an end to the drama. I had just pulled the money out of my purse, amiably ready to return it to a tangibly more relaxed group, when my idiot boyfriend pulled out a stun gun.

Raising it above his head, he flickered it off and on a few times, filling the room with loud, electrical crackles. Frozen, I stared at him in disbelief. He brandished the stun gun towards the men, threatening to zap them if they came any closer, then snatched the money from my hands and stuffed it back into my purse.

Undaunted, they responded to the threat by literally striking karate poses like it was a real-life kung-fu movie showdown. I think the intent was to be intimidating, but it was anything but; they looked completely ridiculous, and I stared slack-jawed, mentally trying to catch up. As silly as it was, I could tell by their determined expressions that they really meant business.

While I was deliberating my next move, one of the men let out a loud cry and did an air kick mere inches from my face. I flinched, a mixture of bemusement and terror swirling through me, frozen in place by indecision.

The mob rallied behind him, emboldened by his display, and grew immediately more restless. Their eyes had taken on the glint of a wild, rabid animal, and we were the prey. I could see them shifting uneasily, waiting for the right moment to launch things into total chaos. I gulped, the tension becoming too much, and decided today was not the day to fuck around and find out with a drugged-up version of Bruce Lee.

My idiot boyfriend, bless his heart, was only making matters worse by constantly instigating things with the stun gun. Each time one of the men stepped forward, he would thrust out the stun gun and activate it, filling the otherwise quiet room with electrical snarls.

I glared at him, first angry at him and then at myself; he was never much help, and most of the time just made things worse.

Watching him grin and enjoy taunting the group of highly agitated, drugged out men was making me nervous. I knew if I waited any longer, things would escalate into physical violence. We were outnumbered and physically outclassed, and besides that, I was not a fighter. Since my boyfriend was useless, I knew I needed to plan an escape on my own.

I saw my opportunity when one of the clients pushed through the crowd on his way to the dresser to do another line of coke. The movement discombobulated the group, and this was all the distraction I needed.

I quickly got the door open and ran out before they could stop us. Terrified, I didn't look back until we had managed to exit the hotel. I was out of breath, my central nervous system still catching up to the sudden slew of changes.

Driving away, I was glad no one chased us and reflected on the irony; they had been so afraid of being robbed that they effectively caused the very thing they were afraid of in the first place.

But cocaine wasn't the king when it came to turning mild-mannered men into legitimate crazy people. In fact, there were pleasant bookings that went off without a hitch where people were using cocaine. When it came to methamphetamine, however, it was a completely different story.

Client Todd

In all my years as an escort, I couldn't remember a single encounter involving a methamphetamine addict that wasn't completely awful. *A guy pulled a gun on me and threatened to kill me?* Meth. *A group jumps out and tries to rob me at a booking?* Meth.

Early on, I learned to recognize the physical signs that someone was high on meth to avoid imminent danger. The money was never worth putting my life on the line, and while some risk was always involved being an escort, it was easily doubled when it came to meth.

One night, I went to a booking that forever changed my perspective on hard drug use. When I first got the call, nothing about the booking seemed out of the ordinary, and my boss didn't make any comments about any weird behavior on the phone. It was just another call, on just another boring night.

When I arrived, the house looked well-maintained and beautifully landscaped, and there was even a nice car in the driveway. Eyeing the tasteful frontage, I expected a harmless older guy with money, possibly a recent widower. I felt at ease and confidently strolled up the walkway and knocked without a second thought.

How very wrong I was.

The person who answered the door was not a portly, gentile older man, but instead a bug-eyed, middle-aged lunatic who looked absolutely crazed. He had the appearance of someone who had not slept in a couple of days and was sweaty, unkempt, and jittery. There were sores on his face from where he had been picking at his skin, and he wasn't wearing any clothing aside from a pair of tube socks and obviously soiled underwear.

He was speaking so quickly and erratically that I could barely understand him. I happened to have my boyfriend present with me on this booking as well, and he was standing beside me, equally startled at the sight of captain crazy.

Without missing a beat, the client shoved a wad of cash into my boyfriend's hands, grabbed my arm, and aggressively tried to pull me inside. I was clawing frantically at the doorframe, holding on with all my strength to avoid being dragged into the house. My boyfriend wrapped his arms around my waist and barked that I wasn't going anywhere.

It was an intense situation, and no one expected that the drug addict could be reasoned with, so imagine our surprise when he actually let me go. We were so stunned by the unexpected compliance that we stood there looking at each other, dumbfounded.

The confused silence gave way to the realization that things had indeed escalated, but in a very unexpected way. The man was now grabbing his genitals through his underwear, squeezing his nuts so hard that his knuckles were turning white. His mouth was open, his nostrils flared, and I wasn't even sure he was blinking. His face turned red from unseen exertion, and his breathing quickened. I could see veins bulging through his skin, and I became aware of a multitude of small, bloody marks all over his face. His eyes, wide as saucers, possessed the eerie quality of a wild animal.

In a flash, crazy-meth-guy grabs a gun from God only knows where and points it at us. My mind, still scrambled eggs from almost being yoked indoors, went blank at the sight of a deadly weapon.

My boyfriend, being the absolute gem that he was, offered the man threatening our lives *half* his money back if he would let us go without any trouble.

That's right, half.

When I heard this, I wanted to grab the gun myself and pistol whip the shit out of him. How stupid can you be?

Upon hearing the offer, the man let loose a guttural, shrieking sound and grabbed his nuts even harder, all without ever breaking eye contact. As a scare tactic, it worked; the bizarre behavior was incredibly unnerving and rendered me stupefied.

Unable to act, I made peace with the fact that I was likely about to die, or at least be badly maimed. The haze of my mind shifted from abject terror to numb curiosity.

The druggie had yet to release the death grip on his testicles, and I wondered just how much brute force was required for one to rupture. I could see it clear as day, the crazed meth head inadvertently popping one of his own testicles and falling to the ground, screaming in agony.

While I was lost in thought, contemplating the durability of the average testicle, my boyfriend chucked the handful of cash through the doorway. Green paper littered the air, falling like feathers in all directions. Seeing the money, the guy snapped out of his trance and blindly turned to grab it, forgetting all about us.

Without looking back, we bolted off the porch and ran towards the car as fast as we could. As we sped off, the meth-head was still fumbling around on his hands and knees in the doorway, picking up dollar bills. It is worth mentioning that we were incredibly lucky and that when it came to men on drugs, escaping wasn't always so easy.

Client Jessie

One evening, I walked into a booking at an upscale hotel, the kind with ample security and a registered guest list, and immediately spotted a silver tray on the table with a wide assortment of pills. They were displayed neatly in a row, in different colors and sizes. I didn't recognize any of them, but based on the shifty-eyed expression of the young man staring at me, I guessed they were not the kind you got from the pharmacist.

The fidgety client on the bed and the tray of mystery drugs were a bad sign. I sighed and reluctantly collected the booking fee, nonplused. The agency's plan for that particular show was to collect the money, make up any excuse to dip out, and leave the client high and dry. I didn't ask questions and intended to do what I was told. The problem was that he was already high, and I suspected his cash would not go without a fight.

I didn't bother getting changed, and instead made conversation with him for a few minutes, trying to gauge how fucked up he was. Was he the kind of intoxicated that would passively accept his financial loss, and hope to do better next time? Or the kind where he would howl loudly and try to peel off my skin?

He was very reserved and didn't give much away. He watched me suspiciously, never letting down his guard as I peppered him with friendly small talk. While I was busy chattering away, the fire alarm went off.

Ah, fuck.

Well aware of the plan, I knew it was my dirtbag boyfriend's way of creating an out for me. He had done this in the past when the agency made similar requests, and it was how he justified me leaving the room if I was taking too long.

When I heard the noise, I started panicking, doing my best to pretend to be worried about a fire. The client bought the fire alarm ruse, but what I hadn't anticipated was that he would decide to follow me. I picked up my pace, but he followed suit, not willing to give up his hard-earned cash so easily.

So, there I was, trying to lose a man in a hotel hallway, but failing miserably. Out of ideas, I decided to make this clingy customer my boyfriend's problem; he liked to act big and tough and tell everyone how he was my muscle, so I was going to let him shine.

When I calmly walked up to the car in the parking garage with the breathless customer in tow, my boyfriend's eyes nearly bugged out of his head.

"Hi, this guy wants to talk to you about the money," I said casually, stepping aside and letting the client approach him.

He flashed me a look that said *are you insane?!* while gesturing for me to get in the car.

He entertained conversation with the customer while I made my way around the car and got into the passenger seat. Once I was safely buckled, he shoved the man backward, making him fall on his ass, and shot the car into reverse.

Of course, it wouldn't be that easy.

Unfazed, the client ran up to the driver's side window and started banging on it, demanding his money back. To be fair, we did kind of screw him over, but in our defense, it's what our boss *told* us to do.

We didn't wake up in the morning and say *hey, I wanna fuck over a crazy crackhead and see what happens!*, we had no choice.

I was panicking, afraid the client would punch through the window, but my boyfriend ignored him, and started driving faster. The client, not giving up, kept pace with the limited speed a parking garage allowed.

He followed us for about half a floor before he pulled himself onto the hood of the car and started hammering his fist into the windshield. I was begging my boyfriend to stop, terrified of the man falling off and getting run over, but he ignored me. Instead, he turned on the wipers and sprayed the client with windshield wiper fluid.

Perhaps it was the drugs, or maybe it was how we pulled a fast one and took his money, because this guy just wouldn't give up; after the client got sprayed, he climbed from the hood and onto the roof of the car.

He was hanging on, his fingers visible through the windows as he gripped tightly, screaming at the top of his lungs for us to hand over the money. To me, it was money, and I had no problem making more, but for some reason, my boyfriend wouldn't hand it over. He cranked up the music and drove down four levels with the man screaming on top. Once we made it to the ground floor, we encountered security. The tubby guard saw what was happening and jumped up from his stool, but kept his distance, clearly not paid enough to deal with it.

Not bothering to stop, my boyfriend drove through the exit gate and hit the roundabout that separated hotel goers from the public street. My boyfriend drove in the tight circle, speeding up as much as he could until centrifugal force flung the client off the roof of the car and into the bushes.

Don't do drugs, kids.

CHAPTER NINE

Mycena Subcyanocephala

Client Stephen

I was in bed when I got the text. As usual, it was an address, a name, and an amount of money. The only thing out of the ordinary for this booking was the time of day; it was eleven in the morning on a weekday and the vast majority of requests for me occurred between the evening hours of ten and three. The location was also a hotel notorious for being a hotspot for drug dealers and petty crime, so I was less than thrilled about the arrangement. I didn't have much of a say in the matter, so I shrugged and climbed out of bed. After I let my boss know that I received the text, I checked the address on my phone's GPS and saw that I easily had thirty minutes available to get ready.

After being an escort for so long, getting ready for calls was boring and routine. I showered, shaved my downstairs, and applied makeup. My pre-show getting ready routine meant spending a few moments touching up my hair, spraying on some fruity body spray, and applying lotion to my legs, breasts, and butt. I found that men loved caressing a woman's naked body, so I needed to be enticingly smooth and soft whenever I was at work. Selecting the right outfit was another step in my routine, which ended with double-checking that nothing was missing from my dance bag on my way out the door.

Lingerie, credit card slips, a pen, perfume, tampons, baby wipes, mace, stun gun. Each item was essential, so ensuring I had everything with me before I left the house was of utmost importance. I learned the hard way what could happen if you realized your period started while getting changed in the bathroom, and having the baby wipes handy made removing any stray bits of toilet paper or underwear lint from my vagina a breeze. Since men would literally stare at my pussy from inches away, it had to look and smell perfect. I was a fantasy, after all, and the industry demanded perfection. I also didn't have the option of leaving until my time was up, so making sure everything was neatly tucked into my bag was the last step before going into a booking.

That particular day, I decided on my hot-pink and black striped string bikini set coupled with a pair of fishnet thigh-high stockings. I had recently picked up the ensemble from the local sex shop, and it was my new favorite. It was hastily shoved into my bag with everything else, along with a backup outfit in case it became unexpectedly soiled. I wasn't wearing heels, either, so dressing my legs up with fishnets was essential to sexualize my legs. Men loved the look of a pair of long, slender legs in a pair of heels, so I did my best to offer something comparable since I seldom wore them.

Sometimes, guys would ask me to take off my thigh-highs. They wanted to feel my bare legs rubbing against their body while I danced or to caress me without a layer of fabric in the way. It was a fairly reasonable request, but I didn't always say yes. Thigh highs were my secret weapon when it came to being in a hurry; if I didn't have time to shave my legs, wearing them would camouflage any prickly stubble and no one would be the wiser.

But back to that morning.

When I was in my car and ready to set up the GPS, I rechecked my phone. The name struck me as one made up by someone very bad at coming up with fake names: Mr. Stephen Stevens. A client using a fake name when booking an escort was not unusual per se, and I suspected that the only time we ever got real names was when the customer was using their credit card to pay for it. When men were using cash and provided terrible aliases, I expected them to give me a hard time or ask for bizarre, kinky things that I didn't do. It was as if their perceived sense of anonymity was a potent potion that turned even the nicest of men into raging assholes.

Rolling my eyes and grumbling the whole way, I drove to the booking with my expectations fairly low. The hotel Mr. 'Stephen Stevens' chose was undoubtedly the cheapest, sleaziest one in the area. I had been there before, and it was hard to forget the gross carpeting covered in stains and the overabundance of ten-year-old coupon pamphlets in the front lobby. When it came to hotels, if the clerk at the front desk was sitting there, ignoring you completely while smoking a cigarette, it was a bad sign.

But I do want to add that a dumpy hotel wasn't necessarily a bad thing; it could very well mean he was saving all his cash to spend on me. I had been surprised before by a well-dressed, affable man with deep pockets choosing a less-than-reputable establishment for his rendezvous. It was unlikely, but staying optimistic was all I had.

Of course, choosing the cheapest, grossest hotel in the area could also mean that the guy waiting for me was a cheap asshole and that getting any tips from him would be like pulling teeth. I frowned, aware that it was likely the latter, and wished again I could be back in bed under the covers. Like the rest of my bookings with men I hadn't seen before, I had no way of knowing ahead of time what kind of guy I would get.

When I arrived, I groaned, muttering complaints under my breath as I double-checked the contents of my dance bag and parked my car. Thankfully, no shady characters were lazing about the front entrance, so at least that was a relief. Wasting no time, I walked straight past the lobby and directly to the elevators. The front desk person tried to say something to me, but I ignored him. The thing is, I didn't bother with the front desk people and honestly found them annoying.

No, I don't have a room. No, I don't have a reservation. I am a guest. No, you don't need to call the room to let them know I'm here. I can find my own way, thank you very much.

At the posher places, this sort of behavior was understandable; offering privacy and security was part of the premium guests paid top dollar for. But here, at a run-down dump with paint peeling off the walls, the front desk person was being nosy and needed to mind their own fucking business.

I glanced through my phone in the elevator and located the text with the booking details. I silently mouthed the room number, wanting to remember it so I wouldn't have to repeatedly reference my phone. I felt like constantly checking my phone while standing in front of doors made me look out of place and suspicious, and part of what the clients paid for was discretion. I took this to heart and actively took steps to avoid making it obvious I was a call girl.

I found that the hardest part was deciphering the way each particular hotel chose to organize its room numbers; I would often stand in front of the signs when I stepped out of the elevator, trying to discern whether I was going left or right. It wasn't always straightforward, and I wished more than once that there was a universally adopted system for organizing rooms within a building.

On my way to the room, I grew more curious about what manner of man was waiting for me. Whoever he was, he wasn't at work during normal business hours during a weekday, which was strange. Hopefully, it wasn't because the man in question was recently laid off from work, and he had taken up residence in this hovel masquerading as a hotel. Eventually, I found the room I was looking for and took a breath while I stood silently in front of the hotel door, hesitating.

Knocking on the door was nerve-wracking because it was the last moment where whatever was on the other side was still unknown. Facing uncertainty was hard, and even after doing it for years, I still paused. The client would often glance through the peephole to get a look at me, and this was pivotal; if he didn't like the way I looked, he wouldn't open the door, and my drive would have been for nothing. The agency didn't reimburse me for travel costs if I didn't collect the booking fee, so making sure the customer opened the door was crucial.

Even though I never had a client turn me away before, I always felt a bit of nervous tension building while waiting to see if I would be rejected. My insecurities refused to let me feel any other way, and I did my best to look appealing through the peephole. My practice during this process was to take a step back from the door and make myself more visible. I would then strike a sexy pose or very conspicuously re-apply my lipstick using a pocket mirror. I would do whatever I could to appear like a sexy minx and hope for the best.

When the door finally eased open, I saw that staring at me from behind a half-opened door was a boxy, middle-aged Asian man wearing nothing but a towel. His neck was thick, and he was chubby all over, which gave him an odd, rectangular appearance. He had glasses and shortly cropped black hair framing his reddened face. Overall, my immediate impression was that he was one of the least intimidating people I had ever seen in my life, so I relaxed and smiled at him.

While he watched me nervously, I intentionally brought a finger to my mouth in a playful, suggestive manner. Bringing focus to my mouth was a clever trick to get men looking at my lips, and when men looked at my lips, they thought of what I could do with them.

He seemed slightly tense and uncertain, as they all do initially, so I decided to make the first move to get things started.

"John?" I purred while smiling sweetly.

I was layering on the charm, hoping to calm his jitters and get him to open the door all the way. My efforts must have been enough because he visibly relaxed and opened the door completely.

"Hi, you must be E.. You look just like your pictures. Come in."

Our agency listed all of its available women on a website that was complete with photos, brief bios detailing entirely fictional information about our hobbies and interests, and a base hourly reservation fee. My agency did not believe in the old 'bait-and-switch' that some other companies used, so all the photos on my profile page were actually of me. When I first started, I had to get professional boudoir-style photographs done to be listed, and once the photos were up, I had a seemingly never-ending supply of interested clients.

Now that my client felt comfortable letting me inside, I followed him into the room and was greeted by the standard setup: a king-sized bed, a nightstand with a phone and a hotel directory, a chair beside a desk, and a large flat-screen TV. There was a coupon booklet on the nightstand offering discounts on local cuisine, and I could see a neatly folded pile of what I presumed to be the client's clothing stacked on the chair.

The room was painted a brighter pale blue, which I thought was lovely, and there were a few generic art pieces decorating the walls. I thought the room was pleasant, which was not what I was expecting after my last visit to this hellish dump. I wondered idly for a moment if management had done some remodeling for my last visit, or if they selectively gave the shittier rooms to people they didn't like.

Not wasting any time, I went straight into my introductory spiel of *needing to collect the booking fee so I could check in with my boss*. Whenever I got to a booking, the first thing I did was collect the reservation fee and then send a text to my boss letting them know I had the money and had arrived safely. This was also the start of my standard one-hour-timer, which was how long I was reserved for unless the client paid extra in advance.

I always made sure to place heavy emphasis on the check-in bit, making it very clear to the client that another human being was keeping track of my whereabouts. Whether or not this actually offered me any safety, I did not know. At the very least, I felt a little better with the knowledge that someone, somewhere, knew where I was and when I was supposed to be leaving. If things went awry, my disappearance would be noted relatively quickly, and the police could be contacted right away to investigate.

After collecting the fee and stashing it in my bag, I let him know that I needed to get changed in the bathroom and that I would be right out. My client nodded in approval and walked over to sit on the edge of the hotel bed facing the television. He picked up the remote and started fiddling with it as I walked away.

In the bathroom, I could tell he had taken a shower recently because the floor mats were used and wet. I smiled as I noted that the hand soap was opened and showed evidence of being used, which meant this guy washed his hands. It was super gross, but extremely common that the men I met at work would not wash their hands after they used the bathroom. How did I know? The soaps were bone dry, and sometimes they didn't even bother making the effort to remove the soap out of the plastic packet. I never knew if they thought I couldn't put two-and-two together, or if they were gross slobs and simply didn't care. I always assumed that it was because I was a woman the clients didn't need to impress; I was paid to be there, and it was my job to pretend to like the client, no matter what.

After changing into my cute pink and black striped outfit and liberally spritzing myself with some body spray to cover any lingering urine smell from the elevator, I stepped out to see what exactly 'Stephen' was doing calling someone like me in the middle of the afternoon on a weekday.

He was still seated at the foot of the bed, so I sat down beside him. The bed was comfy and squishy, and not very firm. The client's weight caused him to sink slightly into it, and when I joined him, I sunk in beside him until I was leaning sideways against him. I hated the feeling of a client's moist skin on mine and bit my inner cheek to distract myself.

Instead of acknowledging my presence, the client was silently staring at the television. Looking at the screen, I realized he had been playing pornography on mute the entire time. The porn itself wasn't anything special; it was a blonde lady getting absolutely railed by a group of tatted-up dudes with huge dongs. Still clad in only his towel, he was holding the remote and gazing at the TV more thoughtfully than I would consider normal for a person watching a skanky blonde chick get gang-banged.

I let the silence go on for a few minutes while he watched his show before deciding to try my hand at striking up some conversation. I was there to make money, after all, and I needed to engage with him to do that.

"You like that kind of thing?" I asked him, sounding both mildly curious and deliberately unfazed.

I wanted to sound as nonchalant as possible; if he thought I had an issue with him watching porn, as many women do, it might turn him off from tipping me extra money for my company. I had to be the 'fun' and 'open-minded' girl, ready to roll with whatever he wanted to do. There was no room for putting down kinks or sexual proclivities if I wanted to make a paycheck.

Instead of answering verbally, he only nodded at me, keeping his eyes glued to the screen. Having watched plenty of porn with men at bookings before, I made no effort to rush him or get him to turn it off. Instead, I played into one of my better qualities that served me well in the profession: I read his mood carefully and instead of being overtly sexual, I adopted a kind, non-judgmental disposition and proceeded to thoughtfully engage with him in low-pressure conversation.

In my experience, this approach was what most men preferred. Yes, the idea of some sex-crazed porn star sounds fun conceptually, and it was what the majority of people picture when you mention a high-end escort or sex worker. The ultimate fantasy was seemingly a person who was a willing plaything for a man's every whim, and whose sole focus was on satisfying his most carnal desires. In truth, some men did indeed like that sort of thing. More often than not, though, my clientele were more interested in an intimate experience that involved being understood and accepted for who they were, kinks and bizarre sexual deviance included.

Many of my clients confided that being around me was the first time they could talk openly and honestly about their sexual desires, and how liberating it was for them; they did not feel judged and the newfound ability to explore possibilities was akin to a sexual awakening for them. This was an aspect that I got legitimate enjoyment from because it was nice seeing a person completely relax and open up, feeling free to be themselves for what might very well be the first time in their entire lives.

My client was still wearing his towel and watching the television when he placed his hand on my thigh. At this point, it had been about ten or fifteen solid minutes of watching this blonde lady getting pounded into oblivion, and I was bored. Trying to follow his cues, I glanced over at him coquettishly and flashed a smile, trying to communicate that his touch was acceptable, but his gaze was still fixated on the screen. Finally, he broke the silence.

"It is real?" he asked, his voice sounding almost philosophical through his accent.

I was taken aback; this was not a question I expected.

"Is what real?"

"Their penises. Are American men really that big or is it only in these shows?" as he spoke, he gestured toward the male porn star dominating the screen.

The scene was a close-up shot of a massive dick going in and out of a woman's vagina. Now the client was looking at me, practically boring a hole into my soul with his eyes, needing an answer.

Before I could speak, he slid the towel off from around his waist. Beneath his pudgy belly, I could not see his penis. I did a double take but still saw nothing; while the testicles were visible, the rest of his genitalia were not.

I had witnessed enough overweight men smoosh down the fat around their penises to even be able to see it, so I figured my client just needed to move some chub out of the way. Seeing me looking, he leaned back a little on the bed and spread his legs wide apart, so his crotch was fully exposed for my examination. I looked closely at the spot where you would expect to see a penis and saw nothing.

He could see my mounting confusion and looked amused. With near clinical-like expertise, I took to examining every inch of his pubic region with my eyes, taking everything in. It was weird; I could see his balls clearly enough, which were normally sized, but no ding-dong was anywhere in sight. Finally, feeling like I had exhausted my ability to understand what was happening, I spoke up.

"Can I touch you?" I asked politely.

I always asked first before putting my hands on anyone, in an attempt to set the proper example for what consent looked like, hoping my clients would follow suit.

After he nodded in approval, I leaned over and poked the pudgy area beneath his protruding belly with a single finger. He was leaning back, resting all his weight onto his elbows and grinning. Whatever was going on, he was enjoying it. Maybe he could tell I wasn't going to judge him harshly for his uniqueness, and instead of being self-conscious, he was having fun with how utterly bewildered I was.

He let me poke around for about five minutes before taking over and laying the mystery to rest.

"Look. Watch," he said as he climbed off the bed and stood in front of me, completely nude.

Reaching down, he pushed the pubic chub inward, as I initially expected, and did his best to show me what he was working with.

And that was when I saw it.

Right in front of my eyes was the smallest penis I had ever seen in my entire life, babies included. I would not have recognized it as a penis unless he had pointed it out to me, which he had helpfully done.

I was speechless. I didn't know it was humanly possible for a dick to be so small; I had seen many instances of male genitalia that I considered tiny, but none of them even came close to this. It was an aberration, a freak mutation.

After remaining silent for what felt like an eternity, all I could manage was to mouth the word *wow*.

I didn't know it at the time, but having what was called a micro-penis was a real medical condition. I am no doctor, and I'm not claiming to diagnose this guy retrospectively, but good gravy was it small. Like, shockingly small. If what I saw that day wasn't classified as a micro-penis based on medical guidelines, then I don't know what would be.

I have small hands, I always have, and this guy's love noodle was similar in diameter to the smallest final digit of my pinky finger on my non-dominant hand. It looked like a very tiny, shriveled hole was occupying the space where his penis should have been.

To be sure, it was a cruel twist of nature that would be comical if it wasn't so sad; a real person was sitting in front of me, having lived each day of his adult life with that thing sitting between his legs. I felt terrible for him but knew his small penis couldn't be nearly as debilitating as I thought it was: wrapped snuggly around his chubby little finger was a solid gold wedding band, meaning this guy was married.

Being that he was married, like most of my clients were, I had questions. Questions like: *did you wait until marriage to have sex, and if yes, what in the actual fuck is wrong with you? Was she mad when she found out?*

Does she like it?

Does she have a lover?

Are you good at head?

Taking it all in, I could see the questioning expression remained visible on his face. He really, truly wanted to know if male porn stars were some ridiculous, impossible standard that was purely a concoction of

109

Western fantasy. I stared at him for a moment, wondering if this guy was for real, and it dawned on me that perhaps he truly had no idea just how far from the status quo he really was.

Maybe he hadn't seen other men naked before, or maybe he thought it was normal for Asian men to have a smaller dick. That is the prevailing stereotype, right? That Asian guys are small? I had heard this so many times before as a joke, so there was a less-than-zero chance that this man had heard the same comments before in passing conversation.

Putting it all together, I could see how he could have gone his entire life thinking he was normal, especially if he was the shy type and hadn't been around other naked people before. I reasoned with myself that not every person feels comfortable being nude in a locker room, and that some people get changed in the stalls.

No matter what he thought, though, I had a sneaking suspicion that no one, not even his wife, had ever told him he was different.

So, there I sat on the hotel bed, with a ruddy-faced Asian man staring intently into my eyes and waiting for an answer to what was likely the question heavy on his mind for his entire life.

Fuck.

I was faced with a dilemma and unsure how to proceed. This guy was in his mid-forties, married, and seemed harmless enough. I saw no advantage to being the one to enlighten him and subsequently smash his ego into bits. Besides, if I hurt his feelings, was he going to give me a tip? Not likely. So, weighing my options, I decided the best course of action was to lie.

"Those guys? Psh. Yeah, *no one* is that big. Those are special actors. I've seen tons of guys' junk, and no one looks anything even *remotely* like that."

I watched his face closely and smiled as he ate up every word of my falsehood. Would the world suffer if this man thought everyone was walking around with a tiny penis? Probably not. I didn't see the harm in being dishonest.

I felt a tangible weight come off my shoulders because I was not the best when it came to lying. In fact, I was terrible at it; I was the type of person who would get lost in endless stammering and turn red when trying to execute even the most minor attempt at guile.

The only way I managed to be even slightly deceptive at work was by remaining mostly genuine. When asked about myself, I would leave out just enough information about myself or my interests, so I wasn't technically lying, but I wasn't giving up personal information, either. My easiest workaround was redirecting the conversation back to the client because they were *so exciting to me.*

The awkwardness I felt festering deep inside me was practically painful; the guy standing in front of me was hilariously small. I wanted to laugh, take a picture, and then look at the picture later with other people so we could laugh again. Was it wrong to feel that way? Maybe. I never claimed I wasn't an asshole.

As I struggled to suppress my giggles, part of me was grappling with the guilt I felt for lying through my teeth. Surely there was zero point in telling him the truth, but it still felt wrong. Why hurt his feelings? I had nothing to gain from having no discretion in this circumstance. Besides, he had lived his whole life this way, and let's be honest, when it comes to most things, ignorance is bliss. I didn't want to be the one to upset this guy about a facet of his life he had no control over.

After I was sure he believed my lie, I embraced the moment and decided to have fun with it. After all, when would I ever get to see a penis that small again in my life? I had to know if it functioned normally, and how he used it. Looking at it, the physical aspect of its use was unclear to me.

"So… What do you like to do with it?" I said softly, teasing him with each word.

I smiled my devilish grin and stroked his inner thigh lightly with my fingertips. I loved how comfortable he was in his own skin and felt reassured that I had made the right choice by not revealing the truth. My kindness was rewarded, too, because he proceeded to show me something I would never forget.

To put it in perspective for you, so you are really capable of appreciating what I am about to describe, I want you to imagine holding a penis in your hand. Picture yourself holding it, and the stroking up-and-down motion you'd normally employ to move up and down the shaft. Now, think carefully about how you would accomplish that same task for a penis that was a fraction of the size. You can't just grab it like you would a banana, it is too small. How then, would you go about doing the same motion if the thing you were grabbing was a third the size of a small baby carrot? My client, bless his heart, was about to show me.

He pushed his flub down with one hand, exposing his groin area, and used his thumb and pointer finger on his other hand to grab hold of his penis. How he was grasping it was very similar to how one would pick up a Cheerio or a small pebble; he used a pincer-like grasp and was holding it in between the tips of his two fingers, with his remaining digits flaring out to the side.

As stated before, there was no usable length to stroke up and down; there simply wasn't enough shaft to accommodate that sort of movement. It was a puzzling sight indeed, and I watched with growing curiosity, wondering what he would do next.

Leave it to men though to find a way. He started twitching the back of his hand up and down, resulting in a very quick, small movement with his thumb and pointer finger. He used the resulting 'vibration' to masturbate. I had never seen anything like it before and couldn't help but watch; small and fast, it was reminiscent of a hummingbird and I had to do my best to keep from giggling.

Sitting on the bed, encouraging him to wiggle his tiny willy with every bit of earnestness he could muster, was the highlight of my shift. Hell, it was the highlight of my week. It was so different from what I was expecting, and I was completely mesmerized.

At that point, I had become thoroughly invested and needed to know what it looked like when he sprayed his spunk. Would there be less? Would there be more pressure pushing it out of the hole? The tube was so small, so I wondered if there would be less man-goo when he finished. I told myself that I wouldn't leave until I knew the answer to these questions; I simply couldn't count on getting another opportunity to see this again and knew that it could very well be a once-in-a-lifetime opportunity.

Egging him on, I watched as he worked himself over with one hand while straining to hold back his fat with the other. His balls were flopping around, moist and sticky, smacking into the side of his hand as he went full throttle. His whole body was turning beet red and sweaty, and the heavy scent of his exertion began to fill the small space of the room.

He was struggling, and while I was invested in seeing him finish, it wasn't nearly enough to help him out. For one, it looked like hard work, and I was not interested in killing my arm. He also hadn't tipped me extra, so the only thing keeping me so committed was an undeniable morbid curiosity. I waited, never taking my eyes off his crotch, with high hopes and an unwavering focus. Eventually, I got my wish.

With a gasp, his back arched, and a sudden torrent of white-ish goo spewed forth. Despite his size, he produced what appeared to be a normal amount of ejaculate. Now satisfied, his weenie sunk inside itself like the head of a frightened turtle covered in clam chowder. A small puddle of his spunk pooled over where his penis was just moments before and began oozing downward into the crevice of flesh. I suppressed a gag as the heavy scent of sweat and cum settled on my tongue. Hopping off the bed, I slipped into the bathroom and hastily pulled my clothes over my lingerie before heading out the door.

CHAPTER TEN

Don't Tell

While searching for a way to regain a sense of control over my life, I re-read a book called *The Gift of Fear*. It was an interesting, in depth piece that explored the power of intuition. I had read it for fun as a teenager and decided to re-read it in response to my shifting worldview.

For me, it was the best self-help book money could buy; most of my work relied heavily on snap judgments, and trusting my gut. I remember digesting the book thoroughly, highlighting and re-reading sections as I went. Applying some of the concepts to my job on a daily basis helped me stay more alert and feel safer.

Client Simon

One night, I arrived at a booking in a very remote area. It was an expansive property that housed a double-wide trailer, and not much else. There were no neighbors or services for at least a couple of miles, and the lack of streetlights left the area dark and quiet.

I parked my car and looked around, remarking to myself how empty and desolate the place was. The only light was from the porch, and I could see moths and small gnats flying around it. Looking out my car window, the sky was full of constellations I had never seen, and I took a moment to appreciate the lack of light pollution.

Other than how isolated it was, nothing seemed out of the ordinary; it was a mostly well-kept-looking manufactured home out in a field. Driving through rural areas, this was a pretty common sight, so I thought nothing of it.

I sat in my car, enjoying how peaceful the area was, when the door opened and a very young man waved at me. He couldn't have been a day over twenty-five and was of average height and build. He smiled and beckoned me to join him.

Once inside, I did the usual thing and changed into my dance attire in a cozy bathroom. Per his instructions, he had me meet him at the very back of the trailer in a small room. I padded lightly in my fishnets down the hallway, the only one that there was, and made my way to the far bedroom.

It is worth mentioning that the trailer had only one exit that I could tell: the front door that I came through, which was situated at the opposite end of where I was headed. He was young and charming, so while I took in these small details like I did at my other shows, I felt completely at ease.

The back room was quite small and based on the laundry and lived-in look of the bedding, I guessed it functioned as his bedroom. The cramped space left just enough room for a lap dance show on the bed. While I gyrated and slid my breasts across his bare chest, I observed a multitude of photos and posters covering the walls.

Scores of scantily clad women in suggestive poses littered the walls and left little to the imagination. There was even a cheesy eighties' style paper calendar tacked onto the wall with nude women for each month. I knew that men enjoyed pornography, but this seemed oddly excessive.

I was lost in thought, mindlessly performing having given easily more than a thousand lap dances in my life, when I noticed he wasn't getting hard. As a veteran entertainer, I understood that some men needed a little extra, but they were usually over fifty.

I playfully asked how I could be sexy for him and get him excited. He had his hands on my breasts, toying with them idly, and told me he liked what I was doing. Not wanting to pry, I shrugged and continued dancing until he broke the silence.

"Can I tell you something?" he whispered, both his tone and expression serious.

I stopped dancing and gave him my full attention.

"Yeah, you can tell me anything. What's up?"

"I'm gay," he said, looking away, "I like men."

He then looked at me nervously, carefully gauging my reaction.

To be fair, this was not what I was expecting; gay men did not pay hundreds of dollars to spend time with a naked woman. Considering how unusual it was, I would have been less surprised if he had told me there was a hamster up his ass.

Caught off guard, I started dancing again and decided to ask some follow-up questions since it seemed like he wanted to talk about it. The posters of nude women all over the walls were suddenly less comical and more depressing. Why was I even here?

"Well, that's okay," I answered kindly, "but how do you know for sure?"

"I have always known. I have tried to... like women... I just can't." With these words, he let go of my breasts and looked away from me, a pained expression clear on his face.

To be honest, I felt bad for the guy. He was clearly battling some kind of inner demons related to his sexuality, and in my opinion, no one should feel ashamed about being gay.

I was very used to seeing men fuck other men and women going down on each other, so while I felt for him, I couldn't truly empathize. I existed in a world of open sexuality, where kinks and fetishes were encouraged and embraced with open arms. While small fries to me, his sexuality was a serious source of internal conflict.

After a few moments, he smiled and chuckled darkly to himself.

"It's so funny. You know, I've never told anyone that before. I've never told anyone that I was gay," as he spoke, his lips quivered, and the tone of voice had changed ever so slightly.

Something was off, but I couldn't put my finger on it. Suddenly overwhelmed with uneasiness, I decided to call it quits and told him my time was up. He didn't object and told me he would step out so I could get dressed.

Alarm bells were going off like crazy in my head, and I didn't like it. Somehow, something barely perceptible had kicked my brain into high gear. The subtle change in his voice had unsettled me in a way I couldn't quite put my finger on, and there was now a voice in my head urging me to get the fuck out of there.

My hands were shaking slightly as I got dressed, and was quietly thankful that he didn't argue with me about staying. I had only been there for about thirty minutes, so I was definitely leaving earlier than expected.

When I walked out of the bedroom, from the end of the hallway I could see him standing in front of a radio. It was at this moment that he turned the volume of the music, which I hadn't noticed before, way up. Deafeningly loud.

Seeing him there, his back facing me with the music blaring, I became one hundred percent sure that this man intended to murder me. I didn't think and instead ran as fast as I could to the door and straight to my car.

On my way out, he was startled, and tried to stop me, but was too slow. He watched me from the doorway as I sped away, his fleeting image in the rearview filling me with terror.

Maybe I was overreacting, but maybe I wasn't.

To this day, I will never know if I was truly escaping danger, or if I was overthinking things. Even though I was very scared, I never reported my suspicions to the police. For one, no crime was committed. The other reason was the same reason I couldn't report the rape: fear that I would be arrested and not taken seriously.

CHAPTER ELEVEN
All Natural

Worker Darla

I had already done my hair, makeup, and prepped my body for a night of scantily clad adventures schmoozing my various clients when my phone buzzed. After plugging the address into my GPS, I gulped down an energy drink and headed out the door. The moon was full and a subtle zing in the night air perked my senses into high gear. Based on my years of experience, I knew this was the beginning of a long night.

While driving, I thought about the other woman I was reserved with for the upcoming two-girl show. I had several run-ins with her before, and like most of the other women I worked with, she had her quirks; she was tall, blonde, smoked weed, and most notable of all, she didn't like to shave *anything*.

At the last few bookings, she showed up with hairy legs, hairy armpits, and a full-on seventies' style bush. Don't get me wrong, I am all for feminism and challenging the status quo, but this was not the business for making a statement. Our job was to sell sexual fantasy, and following society's beauty standards was essential.

I would spend time perusing the internet and popular women's magazines for what looks were 'in'. I wanted to be the penultimate representation of a male fantasy in order to earn tips, and looking that way didn't happen by accident. I did my hair and makeup in line with the popular trends of the time and took care when choosing clothing. I wasn't exceptionally skilled with makeup or curating outfits, but I had a naturally beautiful face and figure that more than made up for my lack of talent. In addition to hair and makeup, during the entirety of my career, and even to this day, it was in vogue for women to be free of most body hair.

This meant keeping up with hair removal in order to portray the ideal image. I knew that some of the women at the agency used laser hair removal or electrolysis to permanently remove unwanted body hair, but I only shaved or waxed. Being that I didn't see the job as anything beyond transient, I opted for more temporary means to keep my hair in check. I spent extra time in the shower but didn't have to fork over thousands for silky smooth skin.

Given the taboo nature of being a hairy woman, it struck me as very odd that this particular woman was so intent on looking like a sasquatch while working in an industry that revolved entirely around superficiality. Most men, at work or otherwise, were turned off by a woman with excessive body hair and weren't shy about it. I never understood her abject anger and pissy fits when the clients teased her about it, because it was obvious her decision was going against the norm.

After doing a few shows with her and watching her get absolutely roasted by the clients, I harbored a sneaking suspicion that there was more than meets the eye when it came to her grooming habits. Considering how the men at parties hassled her, I suspected she was compensated handsomely by discrete persons with a kink for hairy ladies.

If that was the case, she had little competition; it took a week or more to grow hair out to the length she had, so the company's options were limited. Keeping your hair that long was not something that could be faked or substituted, either, so if a worker intended to target that specific niche, she had to be committed to the lifestyle twenty-four-seven.

I could have asked and gotten some clarity, but I made a point to avoid letting my personal life bleed into my professional life. As far as I could tell, I had nothing in common with the other women at the agency; they would chatter and gossip about abusive boyfriends or their ever-growing broods of children with absent fathers. In contrast, I spent my time reading books, painting, and contemplating the futility of the universe. I was a pensive, socially awkward mess, and didn't exactly fit in.

This personality mismatch became evident within the first couple of months employed at the agency. Even within the small world of outcasts and misfits I was now a part of, I still did not fit in. I noted that for many of the girls at the agency, the job was their entire life and personality; they seemingly reorganized their entire lives around pleasing clients, an idea that seemed alien to me. If there was a mold for 'stripper' or 'sex worker', I did not fit neatly inside of it and instead bent it crookedly around myself in order to suit my needs.

Because I only ever saw this woman when we were booked together at a group party, working with her mostly didn't bother me. Sure, the body hair was weird, but I actually considered getting paired with her as a lucky break because it meant I would likely be walking away with the majority of the tips. With her around, I had no trouble becoming the party favorite, as most men were less than zealous about having a huge bush of curly pubic hair thrust into their faces.

The other way that I secured the majority of tips when paired with her had nothing to do with looks, and everything to do with personality. Diversity and uniqueness are wonderful, beautiful things, but they don't belong in a sales environment. Personally, I found that the clients enjoyed a friendly, positive, non-judgmental woman who possessed a good balance of both sexiness and silliness, yet capable of exercising a firm hand when needed. My naturally awkward demeanor lent itself well to silliness, and the languid part was all practiced. This cocktail of traits, common to the majority of us, made us more approachable and set clients at ease.

This other woman challenged the status quo and adopted what I would call the classically bitchy, catty, 'Karen' attitude. I loathed her and couldn't stand being within five feet of her bullshit. She was entitled, rude, demanding, and prone to dramatic outbursts; temper tantrums and whining fits were the norm when she didn't get her way, and since she was very hairy and unkind, this happened fairly often. Because she came across as such an awful human, I made no effort to defend her behavior to clients. I knew that we were expected to act as a united front, but it was hard when she was behaving like a petulant child. I had to look out for myself, and being associated with her would not garner repeat clients.

When I arrived that night at the address for the party, I was impressed. The home we were called out to appeared modern and expensive, and there were even a couple of fancy cars parked in the driveway. The neighborhood, tucked away and mostly private, hinted at upscale living; the streetlamps reflected perfectly in the nearby man-made lake, and strategically cultivated landscaping enhanced this effect. There was no trash in sight, and even the air smelled clean and fresh. With the sky being mostly clear that night, I understood the appeal of living in this community; it was a gorgeous, tranquil, idyllic neighborhood. It was the kind of place you saw in movies where the happy family raised their kids without a care in the world.

I was enjoying the stunning view when the other girl arrived. She stumbled out of her car, looking as she always did: like she just rolled out of bed and hadn't bothered to prepare in the slightest. Her clothes had the visual quality of having been worn multiple days in a row, and her sloppy makeup made her look worse, not better.

I didn't approve of her unkempt and lazy appearance, because it reflected poorly on the agency. Any negatives posed a threat to securing repeat customers; I couldn't make a great first impression on first-time callers if the person standing beside me stank of skunk weed and looked like she lived in a cardboard box on the side of the road.

If we walked into a job looking like a complete mess, it wasn't as easy to negotiate tips; imagine a streetwalking, nasty hooker with only two teeth telling you her blowjobs usually cost seven hundred dollars a pop, would you believe her? Probably not, and I seriously doubt you would pay for it even if you did. When my partner showed up for a booking looking like hot garbage, it shattered the illusion of pricey exclusivity the agency tried so hard to create, and bargaining power plummeted.

Frowning, I watched with narrowed eyes as she hit a joint, holding in the smoke and erupting in a fit of sputtering coughs. Her eyes were bloodshot, her hair an uncombed mess. I felt hot anger boiling inside me, the promise of a lucrative evening slipping between my fingertips like grains of sand.

It was then, the very moment I saw her flicking a cigarette butt carelessly into the dry grass, that I decided to keep a positive attitude just to spite her. She would be the bad apple, and by being nice and friendly, I would look all the more appetizing to whoever wanted a bite of my forbidden fruit. The approach was underhanded, and wholly against my normal operating principles, but I didn't care. This was how I made my living, and I had to do what I had to do, even if it meant being a conniving bitch.

When she was done smoking, we said our hellos and walked side by side to the front entrance. From a foot away, the not-so-faint smell of marijuana bombarded my senses. I rolled my eyes, unable to recall a time when she didn't reek of recent drug use.

In the past, my numerous run-ins with coworkers using at work had left a sour taste in my mouth. Not only was it gross to witness a person shooting up or snorting lines off a dirty bathroom counter, but it was also incredibly dangerous; being high or drunk meant you couldn't keep an eye on what was happening around you, and you were more likely to get raped or attacked, or even murdered.

My stance was that if they wanted to be irresponsible, fine, that was their business, and I respected their autonomy. However, they needed to do it on their own time and not put me at risk. Staying safe was always the main priority at any booking I ever went to, and most girls understood this. For two girl shows, it was an unspoken rule that one girl was supposed to look out for the other at all times. We all knew the job was dangerous, so we had to stick up for one another. But if one of them was high, it created a safety liability, and the dynamic was jeopardized.

I often wondered, on nights like this, what I would do if things suddenly took a turn for the worse and I had to escape. Would I try to save the other girl from danger? Attempting a speedy exit with someone who couldn't walk straight, or even comprehend what was going on, was a bad idea. As awful as it sounds, I would have no choice but to leave her behind and call the authorities, hoping things worked out okay for her until they arrived.

Another factor was the looming danger of the authorities themselves; if the other girl had hard drugs on her, she created more risk for both of us. I didn't want to catch a felony possession charge because the other girl, unbeknownst to me and trying to save her own ass, slipped a baggy of illicit substances into my purse when the cops showed up. We all worked together amenably, but when it came down to it, I knew any one of them would throw me under the bus to save themselves. I wasn't a drug user, so I couldn't empathize with the insatiable cravings that caused them to bring highly illegal, dangerous substances with them everywhere they went.

After a few moments of silence while we waited for the client to answer the door, the sound of footsteps could finally be heard from within. Two younger men answered the door and immediately invited us in, quickly shooing us inside and away from the watchful gaze of nosy neighbors.

The interior mirrored the exterior, and I was surrounded by luxury furnishings, tasteful décor, and cutting-edge electronics. There were high ceilings, and even higher price points for design choices of the home; everything looked like the priciest, most exclusive option available. Aside from the recent evidence of drinking beer and eating snacks on the coffee table, the home was immaculate.

Pleased, I turned my attention to sizing up the clients. It took me all of two seconds to determine that unless they were prodigal financial gurus or had struck it rich via the lottery, there was no way this house belonged to them. It was an expensive, massive home with a waterfront view in a posh, pricey area, and neither of them looked a day over twenty.

Their fresh faces didn't betray a hint of weariness, and their hands, after touching them intentionally to confirm, were very soft and free of callouses. Additionally, they gave off an air of immaturity while displaying little respect for their surroundings; they both had glasses of dark colored liquor in their hands, which were spilled onto the floor carelessly whenever they erupted into fits of drunken laughter. Indeed, both were adorned in similarly styled collared polo shirts, khaki shorts, and boat shoes. Sizing them up, I determined the most plausible explanation was that they were spoiled-rotten rich kids and were likely housesitting while their parents were off on a business trip.

It could have been because I grew up poor, or it could have been that snobby, pretentious assholes annoyed everyone, but I didn't like them. Even if they had money to spend, it was a meaningless commodity

123

to them, and it made me feel cheap. I didn't like the idea of being a convenient plaything for a person with no real understanding of the value of money. Perhaps it was foolish of me to be disinterested in the wallets of young, naive men, but I wanted nothing to do with them.

As far as work went, I preferred older men to younger twenty-something-year-olds any day of the week. I didn't care about nice abs or common interests; in my experience, the more mature men were more likely to treat me with dignity and respect and came with less drama overall. It was unlikely that an older man would get pouty when I refused to give him my personal phone number, and I rarely had issues with older men not tipping. Older men knew that my attention came at a premium and were under no illusions about who I was or why I was there.

In contrast, the younger guys often thought that I would be physically attracted to them, and for that reason give them special treatment. More than once, a man with rock hard abs and a pretty face had zero money to tip me, and proceeded to get angry when I didn't want to just *hang out* with him while he did bong hits since I was *already here* and he was *such a cool guy*.

They would also get grumpy when I refused to accept *as much pizza and beer as I want* as payment or agree to meet them outside of work to go on dates with them. For some reason, it was a repeating trend that a man with no money would ask me out on a date, telling me he didn't mind if I was his sugar mama and paid for everything, and that in exchange he would have sex with me. It took every ounce of professionalism I possessed to not scream at the dirty, twenty-something stoned blue collar workers trying to pull this shit. Nothing was more vexing than getting pulled out of bed at three a.m. on a Thursday night to deal with a broke jerk with the personality of a tree stump.

Still, despite my disdain for the men who ordered me, I couldn't just turn around and walk out; no matter how much I personally disliked the client, I wanted to look out for the reputation of the company. If the people who ordered us had a bad time, they could spread the word, and I risked losing potential business long-term. It didn't help that the person I was booked with was a train wreck, so I couldn't risk dipping out.

Plus, even though I loathed the coddled brats that called, not every escort had the same hangups that I did. I was certain there were plenty of other women at the agency more than willing to empty their bank accounts.

After a brief pause, I settled on remaining cool as cucumber, and positive to boot. I shrugged off my growing disdain and projected a façade of friendly flirtatiousness. I smiled, had the two men sign the credit card slip for the booking fee, and stepped away to check in with my boss.

Once we emerged from the bathroom in our lingerie, we joined the clients in the living room to go over the usual spiel. We told them that they paid to have us there for up to an hour, and that the booking fee included a striptease to nude dance show, and that anything else would cost extra. I went over the available upgrade options, including the most popular choice of an all-nude lap dance show with unlimited dances and non-sexual touching allowed for three hundred dollars an hour. Eyeing the conspicuously huge bush of blonde pubes jutting out the sides of my co-workers tiny thong, the clients exchanged glances and declined to tip, stating they were okay with the basic show included with the booking fee.

I smiled, not really caring one way or the other, but the other dancer was peeved. She started complaining immediately, saying things like *we came all the out here, and you don't want to tip?* and *you got two beautiful women in front of you, and you don't got one dollar in your pocket?* Her voice was grating and nasally, and I hated listening to it. I had no desire to join in on her plight, but I did want her to shut up, so I slyly jumped in and explained to the clients that they could pay as they went with twenty-dollar a piece lap dances.

This must have been what they wanted to hear, because they agreed and sat down, beckoning us over to them. I was picked first by the guy who paid the booking fee and snickered internally; it was no surprise that I was the favorite, but I relished how it bothered the other worker.

We put on music and got started, and overall, the guys were actually surprisingly pleasant for a couple of drunk preps. The man who picked me was intentional about not touching me without permission and made friendly idle chatter with me as he bought dance after dance. After a few songs, I agreed to let him touch me during my dances as long as he

125

didn't try to suck on my nipples or stick anything into my vagina. I was content that the seemingly spoiled rich kid was not treating me like a piece of disposable garbage, so I played nice. We were having a merry old time, making the best of things in our own little world, but the other guy was not so lucky.

My co-worker was non-stop complaining about not getting any up-front tips and was unabashedly confrontational. Instead of dancing, she was standing in front of the other client with her hands on her hips, demanding money from him. He was drunk, seated comfortably in front of her, and completely indifferent. He was relaxed, downing alcohol like water, and honestly seemed mildly amused by her ridiculous behavior.

The more he ignored her, the louder and more direct she became. Her attitude was completely sour, and she would not stop insisting that she *needed a tip*, and how *we weren't getting any tips*, and how she *wouldn't dance without a tip*. As she raged, he grew progressively more drunk, and unable to hide his amusement.

Wanting to stir the pot, I started butting in with passive aggressive comments about how we could *just have a good time anyway* and *maybe you should earn your tip from him by doing something sexy*. I knew I couldn't say what I really wanted to say, which was to shut the fuck up, so I did my best to remain professional while fanning the flames.

My words, of course, were not helpful, and the other woman grew increasingly agitated. Delighted with my minor victory, I grinned devilishly, letting my enthusiasm spill over onto entertaining my client. With my back to him, I bent at the waist, using my hands to slowly, sensually play with my butt cheeks to entice him. I was rhythmically bouncing each cheek up and down, smacking them lightly as I went, being as much of a huge, playful tease as I could get away with. I enjoyed the feeling of being desired, and since I was stuck waiting due to a strict company policy forbidding us from leaving separately, I intended to tease the client for my own amusement.

Spreading my legs apart, I bent over further in front of him, turning my head to maintain eye contact as I languidly caressed my body in a series of prolonged, exaggerated movements. His eyes widened and his lips parted ever so slightly; I had seen this hazy look many times before, and knew he was hooked.

He watched me, his gazed fixed upon me like a helpless puppy, as I ensnared his mind with my body. I knew that I wouldn't do anything with him, but he didn't, and the idea tickled me pink. I was something he wanted but couldn't buy with daddy's money, and the mere thought filled me with glee.

While my relentless onslaught of sexuality beguiled my client, the other girl was having a meltdown. She would not shut up, and the client wasn't even paying attention anymore. I couldn't help but giggle as she stamped her feet to emphasize each angry word while he played games on his cell phone, oblivious.

My client, on the other hand, was becoming more mesmerized which each dip of my hips, and I could see the desire smoldering in his eyes. Seeing this, I redoubled my efforts and climbed onto his lap, rubbing my bare breasts against his face, and teasing the tip of my nipples onto his lips. I could feel his erection through his shorts and giggled playfully while I grasped it. I managed my best surprised face while lightly stroking the outline of his unimpressive genitalia.

It was while I was rubbing my breasts against his crotch that he pulled out his phone and motioned for my attention. I batted my eyelashes coquettishly, wetting my lips as I made eye contact.

"I'll give you five hundred dollars to come upstairs with me right now and sleep with me," he said, his eyes never leaving my tits.

Lust and determination glimmered in his eyes, and I knew instantly that he was serious, but five hundred dollars was a laughable amount. I smiled devilishly, letting my fingertips trail along his straining erection, keeping my eyes firmly locked on his.

I hated that this rich, spoiled brat thought he could dangle a trifling, meaningless sum in my face and purchase carnal knowledge of me so easily. Pausing for only the briefest of moments, I winked at him before I tongued my nipple mischievously. Staring into his eyes, I mouthed the word *no* and continued on with my dancing.

He was flustered, and obviously not used to being told no. I was no stranger to people who had grown up with a silver spoon in their mouth, so I wasn't surprised; they always got their way, and hearing *no* was as alien as a three-headed dog. At first, he struggled to comprehend what just transpired and looked puzzled over the rejection. He regarded with me a curious eye as I continued to dance, a muddled expression growing with each passing moment.

After a few moments, it appeared that a lightbulb went off in his head, and he relaxed into his seat, a smug grin plastered across his face.

"Isn't this what you do?" he said coyly, looking both triumphant and pleased with himself, "don't you want my money? I'll give you a thousand dollars. Right now. Cash."

With these words, he pulled out his wallet and opened it, revealing a wad of cash neatly tucked away within the sidefold. He then took the money out, counting it in front of me as if to prove he wasn't bluffing. Once counted, he held it up and fanned it at me with a devilish grin on his face.

I could see that he had interpreted my rejection as nothing more than a ruse to finagle more money from him and giggled. I blew him a kiss, facing him as I ran my hands along the length of my curves.

Cheeks flushed anew, it appeared that he was getting turned on by the supposed power his wallet provided him. I took my time with his offer, even letting my fingertips brush up against the money timidly, before I slowly and very deliberately shook my head *no* and continued with my erotic display.

He flinched, not expecting another rejection, and appeared more confused than ever. I winked at him and spread my legs wide as I bent over in front of him. I fingered myself for a moment before turning around and licking my fingers while he watched. I could tell he was completely enchanted with me, as I could see a growing wet spot of pre-cum sprouting on his shorts.

In a final attempt to win me over, he pulled out his phone and directed my attention to the screen. It was his bank account, and he was boldly showing me the balance. Surprisingly, it wasn't much more than five thousand dollars, which I thought was very odd for a rich, spoiled brat. I wondered idly if this was just one of his accounts but said nothing.

"This is my bank account. Do you see this? I'll pay you five thousand dollars to fuck me right now," his voice was thick with desire as he spoke, with just the slightest edge of desperation.

He wanted me, and he wanted me bad.

He was pointing to the balance, insisting that he was good for the money.

In truth, five thousand dollars for what likely would amount to two minutes of sloppy flopping around didn't seem like a raw deal, but I was committed to my game. Sure, the money would have been great, but I wasn't greedy, and my bills were already paid that month.

Not being an overly material person, I didn't *need* the money, so I didn't feel bad turning it down. Besides, more satisfying than any payday was teaching a rich little prick that money couldn't buy everything.

Eyes wide, he wet his lips as he waited for me to accept his offer. I could see he was eager to scoop me up and drag me into the upstairs bedroom to have his way with me. He took me in like a wolf circling an injured lamb, licking his chops in anticipation. It amused me that he thought I was helpless to resist his offer.

I continued to dance, grabbing my butt cheeks and caressing my inner thighs enticingly. I was moving slower, letting soft moans escape my lips, and trying to be as sensual as possible. I let him stew in anticipation for a few moments while I pretended to think it over. He was suffering internally, and his misery sustained me.

After a few minutes of silent teasing, I dropped to my knees and crawled to him, comfortably positioning myself between his thighs, inches from his crotch. I toyed with his belt buckle, loosening it slightly, before telling him in the most indifferent tone I could manage: *nah, I'm good. I'll pass.*

Flabbergasted, the client started stammering, the gears of his brain struggling to compute what had just happened. I was an escort, after all, and he had personally ordered me from a list of available women on the agency website to provide him with erotic entertainment. Our job revolved around accepting money in exchange for satisfying the lewd desires of men, and turning down a large sum of money was not in the job description. We were, as far as the clients were concerned, attractive women who were within reach for the right price, completely attainable and willing.

And yet, I had turned him down flat.

Watching his mind unravel was even more delicious than I'd imagined, and I savored every minute of it. I suppose being rejected by what was presumably a dirty hooker after offering her a decent sum was baffling. Pride wounded, the spoiled kid in front of me was not taking it well. He pleaded with me, demanding an explanation, but I wouldn't budge. I decided to let the unknown fester inside him, letting his insecurities fill in the gaps I wouldn't.

After I was finished wreaking havoc on his ego, I called over to the other woman and let her know our time was up. She was still standing arms crossed in front of the other client, loudly complaining about not receiving any tips. Drunker than ever, the client was now openly laughing as she pestered him.

In what was possibly a final act of desperation, my client stopped me at the door and promised that he would show me such a good time in bed, that I should be paying him. I giggled, rolling my eyes, but listening as patiently as I could.

He regaled me with stories about his masculine prowess and how good he was at giving oral sex. He promised me he would eat me out as long as I wanted and give me the best fuck of my life. He was now offering me the five thousand from his bank account with an additional one thousand he had stowed away in his wallet. Beads of perspiration speckled his forehead, and his smug demeanor had shifted to one of pleading.

Whether it was at work, or in my regular dating life, I learned that men who bragged about how well they pleased women were the absolute worst in bed. I found that the guys who knew what they were doing didn't feel compelled to brag or convince anyone of anything.

It also seemed like there was a direct relationship between how well-endowed a man was, and how lazy he was in the sack. The bigger the dong, the less effort they put forth, and nothing was fun or exciting about mindless pounding.

Once a client removed his towel and surprised me with the largest penis I had ever seen in my life; it was roughly the size of my forearm, and incredibly beefy. The man that it was attached to was a short, lanky Caucasian man that looked like the type of guy who got beat up for his lunch money. He stood in front of me, gesturing to his willy, and told me that he was ready to show me the time of my life. He then explained that he ordered me at eleven o'clock at night fully convinced that I would have sex with him *for the experience.*

To be honest, even if he had offered me money, I would have said no. He was enormous, and I wasn't willing to risk hemorrhaging to death. It was incredibly thick, reminiscent of a soda can, and besides that, it was far too long to fit comfortably inside me.

That night I left after informing him his best bet was gay men and collected exactly zero dollars of the booking fee. He had wrongly assumed that his penis was payment enough and was subsequently blacklisted by the agency.

But back to the rich brat.

In the doorway, my co-worker overheard the offer of six thousand dollars, and her eyes nearly bugged out of her head. She started throwing herself at him, stroking his chest and offering herself in my place. She prattled off reasons why she would be the better choice, breathing heavily in his ear and kissing his neck.

She was purring at him like a kitten, but after her antics for the past hour, he wasn't interested; he politely brushed her aside by physically removing her from his person and taking a step away from her. Flabbergasted, she stormed off towards the street in a huff, ranting loudly about how *the men who live in that house are gay faggot losers.*

For clarity, in any other scenario I would have been livid if another dancer brazenly attempted to steal a client. This man was offering a large sum of money, and she tried to take it for herself. This kind of behavior was a considerable faux pas, usually exhibited by newbies who didn't know better. Amongst the more seasoned entertainers, it was an unspoken rule that we didn't mess with another girl's money or try to distract a client when he was paying attention to someone else. It was underhanded, dishonest, and depending on who it was done to, it was the kind of behavior that caused a physical altercation.

Since my payment that night was the client's emotional damage, I let the poor conduct slide and instead focused on the desperate man still begging for me. He hadn't given up his efforts to convince me what an amazing lover he was and took to brandishing the cash openly.

I frowned internally, well aware of the power of seeing cash in hand garnered; he was trying every trick in the book to convince me and reminded me of a slimy car salesman.

I decided to deal the final blow to his ego. I took a step back and eyed him up and down, making it obvious I was appraising him physically. I pretended to be lost in thought, making questioning expressions while looking at him. I even put my hand to my face, rubbing my chin in the stereotypical thinking gesture. Finally, satisfied with how much I had toyed with him, I said *meh, no thanks* before leaving him mentally broken at the doorstep.

CHAPTER TWELVE
Oysters

When I first got into the business, I strictly did not offer what we called 'full service' or 'extras', that is sex acts in exchange for money, for any price. I would go to bookings as a call girl, and entertain clients in a multitude of ways, but never actually have sex or perform sex acts with anyone.

I would go on dates, accompany people to night clubs while pretending to be their girlfriend, perform at bachelor parties, or do private nude lap dance shows. I would charge extra for clients to be able to touch me during the nude dances, but there was a clear boundary in place wherein they could not put fingers inside me or lick my nipples.

It was normal for clients to try and push the rules, and I often had to correct them or warn them that if they didn't stop, I would leave and there would be no refunds.

These rules protected me mentally from feeling like I was doing anything wrong, or even questionable. I didn't *think* what I was doing was prostitution or sex work; no explicit sexual acts were being done, and no exchange of money for anything beyond lewd behavior.

Insulated by this grey moral cloud, I was able to keep my sense of dignity and pride. Customers would make demands, and I felt okay denying them. I was not at risk of contracting any diseases, nor was I potentially jeopardizing my freedom by breaking any laws. I was toeing the fine line of legality and making a decent profit in the process.

After becoming an escort, I started to enjoy a more lavish lifestyle, and for the first time in my life, not worry about bills. If I saw something I wanted, I bought it, and there were no financial consequences. I ate what I wanted, worked as much or as little as I wanted, and overall grew comfortable.

Growing up poor, financial freedom was new to me, and incredibly exhilarating. I felt confident, sexy, and fiercely independent. It was a lovely, magical time that I thought would never end.

Until it did.

The company had some clients that were eager to book new girls to see how far they could go with them, so when I started out, most of my calls were from these people.

Testing my limits was almost a game to them, and they called again and again, eager to see if I could be bought. I would dance and entice them, and sometimes let them jerk off while I watched, but I wouldn't give them what they truly desired.

I was a terrible tease, and an expensive one at that. Most clients wanted a call girl they could reliably get sex from, and that wasn't me. After a while, my newness wore off, and so did my calls. My once reliable stream of income had transformed into a painfully slow trickle.

I still got sporadic bookings for bachelor parties, which were not inherently sexual shows, but I started to grow concerned about my finances. I went from spending all night out doing shows to waiting up all night hoping my phone would go off. I had bills looming on the horizon, and each passing day without a call only heightened my despair.

The sudden influx of cash had caused me to foolishly live beyond my means and sign into a contract for a luxury living space I could no longer afford. I had also upgraded my car and spent money on work costumes and makeup without a second thought. At no point did I consider that I would need that money later to pay rent. Because I had grown accustomed to coming up with everything I needed for required expenses the day before it was due, I hadn't been saving anything.

Even though the signs were on the wall, I didn't comprehend how damning my situation was and failed to make appropriate adjustments to my lifestyle before it was too late. By the time things really started to spiral out of control, I was behind on everything and teetering on the edge of homelessness.

I remember around this time that I did a two girl show with a lovely Korean woman who was gabbing away to me about her recent liposuction. She had a very, very nice car and a way with the clients I simply couldn't match; they adored her and followed her around like puppy dogs.

I studied her carefully, watching her witty banter and enchanting demeanor capture the attention of the clients. She was like a summer breeze, warm and relaxed, and the customers loved it. Her every action seemed to draw them in closer, and try as I might, I couldn't put my finger on what she was doing differently. After the show, she pulled me aside, confused that I had only made three hundred dollars.

"E., what are you doing here?" she implored kindly.

Even when she spoke to me, I felt entranced. She was absolutely hypnotic, and I longed to be her.

Flabbergasted at first, and didn't know how to respond. I stared at her and made confused sounds that weren't exactly words.

"Don't you want to make money? Look at this."

At this, she pulled out a stack of recent credit card slips from her purse and showed them to me.

My eyes grew wide as I leafed through them in disbelief. Her slips were all for outrageous amounts of money and made my tips look pathetic in comparison.

"Listen E., you need to know your worth. I charge these men all kinds of money. They pay. Trust me," she said sweetly, then winked.

These words were spoken with both confidence and a motherly concern; she was trying to make me realize that I had been doing things all wrong, and for a long time.

This moment, as brief and innocuous as it was, was a pivotal turning point in my career. I suddenly knew that there was a way to make much, much more than I ever thought possible. I remembered how the agency told me just a few weeks prior how the top performer had made over a million in credit card tips *alone* last year. They asked me why I wasn't doing as well considering how beautiful I was and told me to think about what I wanted out of the agency.

It was when I was sitting alone in my apartment, broke and anxious, that my mindset started to shift. I was becoming more desperate, and afraid of what would happen to me if I ended up on the streets. I was alone in life and had no one to rely on. There was no way I could afford to pay rent, and an eviction would make it impossible to get a unit anywhere else.

With the due date for my bills drawing closer each day, I was becoming frantic. I called my employer multiple times a night and asked them to recommend me for clients if they called. They agreed, but reminded me that sometimes there were dry spells, just like any other business.

I remember that night and the excruciating psychological pain of slowly coming to terms with how my life was falling apart. Snuggled in blankets on the couch, I was watching the first half of my favorite film, *Les Misérables*.

Onscreen, a young woman struggled to support her estranged child after her lover abandoned her in old-timey France. Apparently being a single mother was a huge deal back then, so she had to hide her past and pay an innkeeper man and his wife to care for the child.

In the film, she is banished from her stable job and forced onto the streets. A sad reverie follows, where she sells everything she owns, her hair, her jewelry, and even her teeth to get money to send to her daughter. By the end of the scene, she accepts that she must sell her body and become a prostitute since she has no other options. It was a somber tale, made gritty by the fabulous cinematography, and on that particular night, I burst into tears.

Safe in my home, I felt the helplessness, the misery; her plight resonated deeply within my soul, and in that moment, I realized I had reached the proverbial bottom. I had been struggling with the idea that I would have to do more in order to remedy my situation, and the tragedy on screen brought this reality to the forefront of my consciousness.

This was the night I accepted my fate. To avoid destitution, I had to let go of my personal truths and cast aside the last remnants of my dignity and self-respect.

Mentally raw, I crawled into the shower and cried. As the warm droplets fell in tiny rivers over my flesh, I felt terribly alone. I was angry at myself for being so dumb and foolishly getting caught up in a lifestyle I couldn't sustain, and angry at the consequences waiting for me.

People make jokes about hard to swallow pills, or having to knock on wood, but I didn't truly grasp the meaning of those phrases until I was living it. I had lost, so to speak, and accepting failure was no easy task.

I used to think I would never do *x* or say *y* thing given a hypothetical scenario, but I was wrong. It turned out that when it came down to the nitty gritty, the person who I thought I was, and the things I thought I stood for, crumbled away. Faced with hardship, my steadfast morals suddenly became waxy and flexible.

That night, after I got out of the shower, I took a good look at the girl in the mirror. She was petite, frail, and tired. I frowned, suddenly feeling uglier than I ever had in my entire life. I did my hair and makeup, picking darker colors for my eyes and lipstick than I usually would. I felt repulsive, and for the first time since becoming an escort, I felt shame.

I didn't dare cry again, because I didn't want to ruin my makeup. I needed to look beautiful so I could sell myself. No one would want a girl who was crying.

Client Heath

When the phone rang later that evening, I read through the booking details with a strange, lofty indifference; I was about to step into uncharted territory, and my former confidence had faded. So many thoughts were racing through my mind, but first and foremost, I was afraid of getting arrested for solicitation.

It was easy to imagine getting busted by a cop, and the idea scared me. I paced in my house, half afraid to send the confirmation message that I had received the booking.

As I pictured myself in jail, I also saw another possibility: ending up starving on the streets, alone with nothing to my name. I went back and forth as I mechanically gathered my things and kept coming back to losing it all after already sacrificing so much.

I had already let men touch my naked body, and was used to degrading myself for their amusement, so backing out now would make all of that meaningless.

When I finally grabbed my keys and walked out the door, I knew the night was going to change me. There would be the time in my life before this booking, and all the time after it. Nervous, I bit my nails as I walked, afraid of being seen. Even though I had left my home for innumerable bookings before, I now felt exposed, like someone was watching my every move. Guilty, I looked over my shoulder and was greeted by nothing but my own shadow.

During the drive, I rehearsed dialogue in my head to calm my jitters. My goal was to come up with a plan on how to offer myself for sale and not get arrested in the process. I had no practice identifying law enforcement because before now, it didn't matter.

I gulped, drowning in a sea of unfamiliar territory. Sure, many clients had flat out tried to buy me in the past, but the offers weren't consistent, and I had no practice initiating that sort of conversation.

Price was an issue as well; I knew that some of the other women in the company made a ton of money, but I had no clue how much they charged. It was common knowledge that each woman had unique rates for services, so I had no real reference point to work with.

How could I put a price on sex? Or a blowjob? The only real clue I had was that it needed to be substantially more than what I already charged for a nude lap dance show.

I was catastrophizing every scenario my mind could possibly come up with, and by the time I arrived at the booking, I was a bundle of nerves. Shaking slightly, I had to steady myself before I got out of my car. I glanced at myself in the rear-view mirror, checking that my makeup was perfect, and took several deep, calming breaths.

I was here, I was ready, and I was going to follow through with it, no turning back. Glancing in the mirror again, I touched up my eyes, adding another layer of dark, sultry broodiness. With a final parting smirk, I got out of my car, mentally prepared to do whatever it took to survive.

When my client answered the door, I was surprised that there was not one, but two men in the doorway to greet me. Usually, the booking information included how many people were present, and two men booking one girl was a little unusual. Confused, I double-checked my phone and confirmed that it was, indeed, only one man who had ordered me.

I shrugged, and went inside anyway, as it had been my first show in weeks. The apartment seemed nice enough, and their haircuts and overall demeanor screamed military. Judging by their baby faces, they couldn't be a day over twenty.

My muscles relaxed as the tension left my body; these were not *just* military men, these were young, stupid military men who were ripe for the plucking. I loved clients like these because guys in the service had plenty of credit cards and not nearly enough free time to use them.

A sense of calm washed over me, and my jitters faded completely away. I was dealing with a type of client I had loads of experience with and started my standard routine with them without hesitation. It was remarkable how easily I switched gears into work mode, leaving behind the timid, terrified girl and embracing the seductive vixen.

After hearing my spiel, they readily agreed to a nude lap dance show, and paid extra for the ability to touch. They took turns picking songs while I danced, and I went back and forth between them while they groped my naked body.

It was easy, after collecting a decent tip just for a dance show, I felt so relieved that I was giddy. Still, while my stress melted away, I couldn't deny one inescapable truth: this wasn't enough money, and I would need to do more in order to get more.

After I spent about thirty minutes teasing them, the man who paid for everything asked me during a dance if I would go to the bedroom with him.

My dancing slowed to a halt as my mind switched off autopilot. It was the question I had been dreading all night, and it needed an answer. My heart pounded out of my chest and my knees felt like jello; this is where I would usually explain that I didn't do that kind of thing, except this time, I did.

Unused to responding in the affirmative to this kind of question, I didn't have a repertoire of casual, rehearsed responses ready. My fingers lingered on his chest, playfully trailing up his neck as I stalled. With careful calculation, I formulated a nonchalant answer and let it slide through my lips like butter.

Keeping up a façade while navigating the unknown was no easy task, and I felt my pulse quicken as anxiety wracked my brain anew. I was smiling at the man, stroking his chest when I remembered that we were not alone.

In all my catastrophizing, the prospect of having a spectator along for the ride had never once occurred to me. I felt weirdly judged. Perhaps I was imagining it, but I could feel a pair of eyes piercing into my back. The lack of privacy made me incredibly uncomfortable and self-conscious, so I encouraged my client to lead me into the bedroom and away from the prying gaze of his nosy friend.

Once the bedroom door shut, the butterflies set in. On the couch, we hadn't discussed details, and I felt queasy at the thought; having never actually negotiated the sale of my body, I had no clue how to broach the subject. Did I come right out and say it? Did I lead him into the idea and let him ask on his own? Unsure, I stalled by luring him into bed and upping the spice with more sensual dancing.

Not being nearly as shy, my military man cut to the chase and bombarded me with questions I hadn't considered. Would I go down on him? Could he go down on me? Did I do anal sex? Do I kiss my clients? Do I really have to pay more for you to pretend to like it, or is that only in the movies?

I was so naive, completely unprepared for the depth involved when selling sex. Every ask seemed sensible, and I listened quietly as the client unknowingly helped me uncover all my boundaries.

Unprepared, I didn't have a clear answer to his questions at first. Some of the probing was an easy pass, but other requests required more thought. For the most part, I wasn't entirely certain of where I would draw the line. Needing more time to digest the implications, I told the client I only offered regular old peen on vag action, with no kissing involved.

To my surprise, there was no bargaining or argument. He paid me an agreed amount, and we awkwardly did the thing. We fumbled a little at first, and I wondered if this was his first time as well. We were strangers, and unlike a one-night stand, there were no alcohol or lust goggles acting as a social lubricant.

What happened though, after all the nervousness and fear disappeared into throes of physicality, was something I had never anticipated.

I liked it.

In fact, I *loved* it.

Instead of feeling ashamed, depressed, and utterly emotionally destroyed afterward, my cup overflowed with an overpowering sense of exhilaration.

I had always been a sexual person and loved the feeling of being desired by men. In my personal life, I took various lovers and enjoyed them until I was bored. Sex was a hobby for me and provided entertainment and joy in an otherwise bleak existence.

This new thing, being so desirable that men were literally willing to pay me to sleep with them, was intoxicating. I was so wanted, and there was clear, tangible evidence I could measure.

There was finally a source, albeit an unhealthy one, for the validation I had craved for so long. The sadness that had gripped my soul washed away as the aftershocks of my decision echoed in my mind. Not only had I gotten what I needed for my expenses, but I also received currency to fill the void and felt absolutely drunk from the sensation.

Suddenly, the world was at my feet; getting another call now meant getting paid and having a great time in the process. My mundane routine had been flipped upside down, and the world seemed colorful and interesting again. I found myself aching to get another call, to feel that lovely high of intense desire, and to see how much I was worth.

During the drive home, I knew there had to be ground rules in place or I would get out of control. I wanted a good time, not a disease or a black eye. As streetlights passed by, I reminded myself that money and admiration are fleeting, but everyone knows that herpes is forever.

That night, I did as much reading and studying as I could on ways to identify STDs and how to practice safe sex as what was considered a 'high risk' person. Graphic photos of venereal diseases lingered on my computer screen, and I decided that I would be extremely selective about who I slept with, no matter what the price. My previous elation was now swirled together in a tornado of undeniably pertinent information. Shutting my eyes, I methodically processed what I had learned.

In order to avoid disease, I had to be prepared to say 'no' even when faced with copious amounts of money. If someone offered me extra money to forego a condom, for example, it was a huge red flag because they weren't concerned about contracting diseases from me. In the past, I had already encountered clients that offered absurd amounts of money to fuck me raw, and even then, I was puzzled. The behavior seemed careless, if not extremely reckless; I was an escort, and the presumption was that I had sex with lots of strangers regularly, making me a high-risk partner.

Such a request also meant that the client likely slept with other sex workers without a condom, and other people for that matter, if he could get away with it. I thought of my co-worker Peaches, and shuddered, not wanting to be exposed to whatever she had festering in her cooch.

To avoid potential issues with law enforcement, the nude lap dance show would be my chance to size up a client. I could ask carefully crafted, seemingly innocuous questions to make broad stroke judgments, and proceed from there. If they seemed gross or sleazy, I would decline to offer any entertainment beyond the dance routine.

This was, after all, what I had been doing before, anyway, and I hadn't encountered any medical problems. It was a safe middle-ground option if I had any reservations.

Another choice I settled on was a thorough examination of their genitals for any obvious signs of infection and refund them if I saw anything out of the ordinary. I knew that some things even a condom couldn't stop (i.e., herpes due to viral shedding), so I was always rolling the dice no matter how careful I was.

This constant, nagging anxiety about contracting a disease heavily flavored my decision to be as exclusive as possible and to charge a significant amount as well. My logic was that a client who could afford my prices would have no financial barriers to medical care, so it was marginally safer.

I also drew a hard line regarding illicit drug use, which I read was a very high-risk behavior. Sharing needles was an amazing vector for blood-borne pathogens, and anyone willing to put a needle in their arm to get high wasn't exactly practicing sound judgment.

As a final measure to protect myself, I didn't offer anal sex or offer services to men who had sex with other men. I read that anal sex caused more tearing and thus made it easier for a virus to enter the body. Men who had sex with other men and sought company from sex workers seemed like a dangerous combination, so the choice to exclude them altogether was easy.

It wasn't difficult, either, to ask during my dance show about the sexual and drug habits of my clients, because they were already primed for lewd conversation. I would dance, seducing them with my body while dissecting them with my mind.

So, saying I was paranoid about disease would be an understatement. Looking back now, with the knowledge that I never contracted any diseases during my entire career as an escort, I am thankful for being overly cautious. I turned down clients all the time, even if they looked healthy, just on a hunch. I let the smallest hint of a problem be a deal breaker, and luckily it never steered me wrong. But while I was navigating the turbulent waters of selling my body, it wasn't just diseases I was concerned about.

As I mentioned before, I loved sex, and I was promiscuous outside of work. I wanted to make sure I wouldn't destroy the intrinsic value sex held for me by charging money for it, so my favorite sex acts were not for sale. For me personally, this meant that blowjobs were off the table. I had a kinky fascination with going down on men, and didn't want to spoil it with something as common as money.

For my own sanity, kissing was also on the no-no list. The mere idea of planting my lips on a man with stale alcohol breath made me want

143

to puke. Gagging was hot, but not when it was followed by chunks of half-digested food and bile.

By the end of the night, I confidently established that I would only offer hand jobs and regular penis-in-vagina sex for my clients.

With the important stuff handled, my thoughts turned back to exuberance. I couldn't wait to see some of my more attractive regular clients and have sexy fun with them for the first time. Was it weird? Maybe. Perhaps even shameful, depending on who you asked, but I didn't care. I was blessed with a flexible moral center that permitted me to engage in activities most people would never dream of.

As an added bonus, my depression was gone; relief and giddy elation ebbed their way into every molecule of my being. Late bills or poor client retention were a thing of the past, and that assurance translated into pure sexual energy.

Desire and positivity were radiating off of me like a horny, sex starved sun, and I couldn't wait to go to my next show. Since I had already made enough to cover my rent by sleeping with the military guy, the pressure was off, and I could have fun.

I found myself winking at strange men in the grocery store and batting my eyes at the men across from me pumping gas. I enticed men in public for the hell of it and enjoyed watching them fumble around after me. I was shameless, and I was having the time of my life.

Suddenly, I felt like the world was my oyster, and I could fuck that oyster. From that day forward, I shed my misgivings, put social expectations far behind me, and proudly embraced being selectively slutty for the right price.

CHAPTER THIRTEEN

But Why?

Client Josh

It was very early in the morning, and I was exhausted. I was at home cozy in bed, looking forward to finally resting after a steady stream of calls had kept me busy since nine o'clock at night. I was fairly tired, and content with my earnings thus far, so I was more than ready to call it quits and shut off my phone. My body ached and the words of my book blurred together as I tried to read; I was spent, and thankful my shift was finally over. I curled up in my blankets, pulling myself into a makeshift burrito, and sank into my pillow; the only thing on my mind was drifting off into dreamland. As my eyes closed and I felt myself melting into the warm embrace of soft sheets, my phone went off.

Fuck.

I looked over and groaned; it was almost five a.m. and getting a show at this hour was the absolute worst. Most clients were already asleep by now, long since having satisfied themselves one way or another, and had gone off to bed. The only customers left awake at five in the morning were usually drug users who had been awake for twenty-four hours or more, or men so drunk they could hardly stand. Neither of which was profitable, and both of which were an absolute pain in the ass.

I covered my face with the blankets, cursing myself for being scheduled so late into the night in the first place. We rarely ever got calls after four in the morning, and the only reason I kept myself on into the wee hours of the night was to stay in the good graces of the agency. It was only once in a blue moon that I had to deal with the consequences of my schmoozing, but it still left me sour.

I sat in bed scowling for a few minutes, holding my eyes firmly shut before grumpily tossing my blankets aside onto the floor. There was simply no getting around it: even though I had already gotten washed up, undressed, and settled into bed, I had to go back to work. I reluctantly sent a confirmation text to my boss, letting them know I received the booking details and was now on my way. This was the norm for our company, and if I didn't text back promptly, I would receive phone calls until I responded.

Grumbling as I got ready, I tried to imagine what kind of man had called for an escort at five in the morning, and the only thing I could come up with was a drug addict. It was a Tuesday, so the odds of it being a drunk guy were exceedingly low. Generally, I only ran into those types of men on the weekends, when working the next day was off the table.

After a very busy evening seeing multiple clients, I didn't know if I possessed the patience necessary to tolerate a junkie's shenanigans. I wasn't going to sit there politely as he picked at his face, or tried to tell me how the government was out to get him. Frowning, I stuffed my lingerie into my dance bag and began brainstorming all the bitchy things I would say if mister-five-a.m. expected me to put up with his shit.

I decided right then and there that I wasn't going to bother feigning sexual interest, and instead resigned myself to full bitch mode. A meth head probably wouldn't care if I was mean to him anyhow, so it didn't matter if I had an attitude. Chronic drug users seldom had spare funds to throw at a person like me, so I had no expectations of making any money. Most of the time when people with a habit called for an escort, they demanded full service for the base booking fee and grew hostile when they were told *no*.

The idea that wherever I was going was likely a total waste of time kept nagging me, adding to the bad mood my sleep deprivation had started. Even though I was certain it was a waste of time and effort, I knew that I had no choice but to go. Like it or not, it was my job.

Unlike a lot of the women that came and went rather quickly at the agency, I treated being an escort like a real job. This work ethic made me very reliable and kept me one of my employer's top choices when offering a girl to an inquiring customer. The women who constantly refused bookings or accepted them but then didn't show up on time (or at all) were not recommended, and sometimes my boss even talked the client out of picking them altogether.

The boss didn't like sending unreliable workers unless the client was specifically requesting them, because they put the company at risk of losing money in the short and long term. My agency was not the only one in the area and losing a long-time regular customer because of a flakey new person was not something my boss was keen on doing.

As I grabbed my keys and headed out the door of my small apartment, I got a follow-up text from my boss containing only one word: *sorry*. I gritted my teeth and stuffed my phone into my bag with a huff. Stomping down the stairs to the sidewalk, I mentally went over different scenarios where I told her off or even quit while telling her she could take the job and shove it up her ass.

She knew it was late, and since she was the one who personally arranged all my calls, it was understood between us that I had already been out all night and shouldn't be expected to go on one last booking. Another reason the booking irked me was that it was well known among all the people in charge that I had regular obligations during the day, so going to work at five a.m. was cutting into my normal life.

Once in the car, I took several deep breaths and calmed myself. Instead of sending back a snarky, passive-aggressive remark, I responded that I was on the way and that it was no problem at all. I wanted to be on my boss's good side, and this was unfortunately the price I had to pay.

Checking the mirror, I realized that I looked cute, but very tired. The black eyeliner framing my eyes was smudgy after a busy night and made me look borderline gothic. It wasn't bad per se, and even found that some men were really into that sort of thing, but most weren't. Using my fingers, I did my best to wipe away some of the black resting beneath my eyes but failed miserably.

The far-off, empty stare that emanated from my eyes only exacerbated the broody, gothic effect, and I sighed deeply. I wouldn't be able to pull off a chipper, fake personality due to my exhaustion even if I wanted to. The client was going to get what he was going to get, and that was all. Because I already had all the money I needed from being out all night, I didn't particularly care.

In my mind, this man was lucky I was coming at all. I was only showing up to make my boss happy, and I didn't plan on putting in the necessary effort needed to make a good impression. The last thing I wanted was a repeat client that regularly called me into work at the butt crack of dawn.

I grumbled while struggling to keep myself awake for the entire drive into the quaint residential area flooded with too-close-together middle-class homes. I lucked out that the drive was only twenty minutes away, because I was barely capable of staying alert enough to drive. I knew that I could stop for coffee or an energy drink along the way, but then I would be committing myself to staying awake after the one-hour booking. What I wanted to do was sleep, and the artificial alertness caffeine offered would last far beyond the single hour I would spend with the client.

It was an unfortunate conundrum, where I had to decide between being able to safely drive or the ability to fall asleep when I got home. If I stayed awake, I would inevitably crash during the day and be entirely useless when it came to my obligations. I often encountered this problem working overnight as a person trying to balance a normal life during the day. Since I couldn't fully commit to either lifestyle, I was left constantly chasing sleep and squeezing it in wherever possible. There were times that I was so exhausted that I would pull off at a rest stop between bookings and take a power nap in my car. It wasn't safe, but it kept me from falling asleep behind the wheel.

The other gripe I had about the booking had nothing to do with the time of day, but with the way the client was paying the reservation fee. He used a credit card, which was the popular choice for clients for tipping higher amounts, but it came with downsides.

Unlike cash, credit card payments had to be managed through the agency, which meant waiting on processing times and related fees. Any tips charged and my share of the booking fee, which was about thirty dollars, would not be paid out to me the same day it was charged. With cash, I immediately had my share the second it was placed in my hands, but with credit cards, sometimes the wait could be days.

Despite its downsides, avoiding credit cards in lieu of cash was impossible; it really did seem easier for a man to sign a slip of paper for several thousand dollars compared to a stack of cash. Something about seeing it in person made customers more hesitant to part with it, so they were stingier when it came to cash tips. I always thought of it as a strange psychological trick that somehow made it harder to part with a physical, tangible representation of a large sum of money versus a digital one. For this reason, my largest tips were always on credit cards.

The company was well aware of this phenomenon, too, because they imposed a sizeable processing fee on any credit card tips received. For the booking fee, it was a flat ten-dollar rate, so girls would end up walking away with about twenty dollars instead of thirty. As far as the tips went, the agency took between ten to fifteen percent of the total. It was equivalent to highway robbery, but I had no choice in the matter; as a singular person, I was incapable of using a client's credit card to transfer money directly into my account, so the middleman was entirely necessary. I paid a hefty price for the luxury of offering credit card payments as an option to my clients.

Considering all the annoying details about credit cards, I grit my teeth angrily as I drove. I knew that the five a.m. booking meant that I was not only making less of a base amount just for showing up, but that I would also lose a decent chunk of any tips I was lucky enough to make. I would also have to wait several days to receive any payment for my services, so I couldn't even use the booking fee to buy gas on the way back. I was pissed and looking forward to being a total cunt just because I could.

When I finally arrived at the client's home, I waited by the front door, trying to be as inconspicuous as possible. His home was situated at the end of a dead-end street on a cul-de-sac. There were a ton of cars parked along the road and all around the circular portion of the dead-end road, so I had trouble finding a spot to park. The area was unusually crowded, and I was worried that someone would see me walking from my car and then standing outside the client's front door. Privacy and discretion were major selling points for the agency, so part of my job was being as invisible as possible.

I was standing there, looking over my shoulder and hoping none of the neighbors would see me while I waited for the client to let me in. I was explicitly instructed by my boss not to knock on the door, which experience told me was a sure sign that he had roommates. If a client had roommates, he probably had poor cash flow, and I glowered again.

Not long after texting my boss that I was at the door, I heard the sound of footsteps from deep within the house. I waited, quietly, anticipating the dark flitter of light on the peephole that would indicate my client was observing me. I saw the dark flash, and the door slowly creaked open, my client making as little noise as possible.

I saw two dark brown eyes peering at me, and a crooked toothy smile. The door opened all the way, and my client joined me on the front step. Illuminated by the soft glow of streetlamps, I could see that my client looked to be somewhere between thirty-five and forty-five years old and was dressed as if the punk band *The Misfits* was his entire personality.

Dear God.

It was painful to look at. He had a devil lock, jet black hair, horribly applied thick, dark eyeliner framing his eyes, and silver piercings all over his face. He was tall, had a prominent beer belly, and was wearing a *Ramones* band t-shirt. He was wearing fishnet stocking gloves, skinny jeans, a chain wallet connected to his belt loop, and black chucks with black laces. Even his fingernails were painted black; he was a walking advertisement for *Hot Topic*, but in the worst of ways. Staring at him, I wondered if he had bought his entire wardrobe there.

It was my manner to avoid being overly judgmental, because I functionally was a social pariah due to my job, but it was hard for me to remain impartial. My client was middle-aged and unabashedly perpetuating a teenage stereotype. Honestly, it made me feel a tad uncomfortable.

150

He was so exceedingly cringe that I didn't want to be seen with him; I was embarrassed just standing next to him and afraid that the neighbors would see me with him and assume I was his lover.

After making an excuse to hurry us inside, my expectations for maxing out his credit card dwindled every minute; as he led me to the back bedroom, he quietly whispered that this was actually his sister's house, and the family (including some kids) were all slumbering away in the other rooms. His requests to not knock and be as silent as possible made sense, and I groaned internally.

He wasn't *just* painfully awkward, he was the weird, creepy uncle who lived in the spare room. I was instructed to tiptoe around to avoid waking anyone up, and that if I did happen to bump into someone, I was supposed to tell them that I was his girlfriend.

Barf.

I couldn't wrap my head around his concerns about me making him look bad; how could buying an escort make him look any worse than he managed to do on his own? I frowned, hoping that I wouldn't have to tell anyone I was romantically interested in him and get roped into an excruciating family breakfast on my way out of the door. I was patient, but not that patient, and knew that the curious peppering of questions from a concerned family member would likely cause me to break.

Normally, I didn't mind lying for clients to save face, with discretion an expected part of being a paid companion, but this guy was so unbelievably embarrassing that I felt physical discomfort from simply looking at him. I strived for professionalism but told myself that if one of his family members woke up and saw me, I would tell the truth. I was a bad liar on a good day and knew that I lacked the guile to pull it off, anyway. I reasoned that if things turned to shit, at least I would have a legitimate excuse to leave early.

When we got to his living quarters, I could tell that the room was as much a reflection of his tastes as his clothing was. CDs were scattered everywhere, trash and laundry littered most available surfaces, and the walls were yellowed from years of smoking cigarettes indoors. It was disgusting and smelled like a mixture of dirty socks and stale nicotine. I had to brush loose ash and clutter aside with my arm just to make enough room on his desk to process his credit card.

When clients paid with a credit card, I had to get a physical imprint of their card for the bank on a carbon transfer sheet. The process involved using a specially designed, antiquated contraption with a sliding plastic bar. I would place the credit card underneath the transfer paper and slide the plastic bar back and forth, repeating the process until I had a clear imprint of the client's credit card. The transfer paper also functioned as a receipt and created three copies of the imprint: one for me, a merchant copy that required a signature, and an extra for the client's records.

Clients would frequently pay the booking fee in cash and put any high-dollar tips on a credit card. This meant keeping a large stack of blank slips in my dance bag at all times. It only took me once to learn my lesson about always having slips handy, and the mistake cost me hundreds of dollars. Keeping a pen in my bag was crucial as well; if the client didn't sign the slip for a processed transaction, he could easily dispute it at the bank, and I would lose my earnings. I pushed my luck with this only once and learned the hard way that if a client could dispute a charge and get away with it, they would.

I usually only ran into these kinds of problems at work after I cleaned out or organized my dance bag. I would get distracted and forget to put an item back inside, and this absentmindedness would cause hiccups. If I forgot the credit card imprinting device, but otherwise had the slips, I had to get creative or forfeit the tip altogether. Using a coin with the carbon paper wasn't an option, because rubbing the metal on the paper made the slip too dark to be legible at the bank. It took a delicate hand to get it just right, and after some practice, I figured out the best way to get a copy of a client's card was by gently rubbing the tube section of a pen across the transfer paper itself. The result was easy to read and never resulted in a rejection from the bank or a verbal lashing from my boss.

The next step after procuring a physical signed copy of the credit tip was to call the company and immediately attempt to process the transaction. This was crucial, because it wasn't uncommon for cards to get declined, especially for larger amounts. Sometimes credit cards would get rejected not because of a lack of funds, but because the client had maxed out their daily limit. If this happened, we would walk them through calling the bank to have more funds released. It was a fairly common problem to run into, so all the women I worked with were well-practiced at coaching clients through the process. ATM withdrawals had similar restrictions as well, with clients only being able to pull out four hundred dollars a day before having to contact their bank.

It was very important to make sure the credit card transaction fully cleared before beginning a dance show or providing any extras; I had clients offer me absurdly high amounts of money for services, probably thinking that the company wouldn't process the card right away, and then look mortified when I told them their card was declined.

Their expressions seldom gave me the impression of true surprise, and it really annoyed me when clients tried to pull a fast one. If a higher tip amount was rejected, we couldn't rerun the card for a lesser amount without a new signature, which meant no tip at all. The clients were no fools, and the frequency with which they tried to get something for nothing was staggering. After having countless clients try to trick me with a tip they knew would decline, I learned to never trust anything they told me.

Some clients had no money to negotiate with and instead employed other tactics in an attempt to get what they wanted. I heard every promise imaginable from broke men, detailing why I would be paid after I had completed whatever service they were after. Things like *I'll pay you extra if you do a really good job* or *I want to see if you are for real* and, my personal favorite, *you need to trust me*. These empty promises were so common that I wondered if some man out there was spreading false knowledge about their efficacy. No matter what these men said initially to try and weasel their way out of paying, the primary goal was convincing me that I was somehow obligated to prove myself to them to get paid.

Another tactic broke men used to try and get free services was making promises to pay me at a future date. This was arguably a weaker strategy than the former, but that didn't stop men from trying it. I would get a sob story about how they thought the booking fee included everything, and how they had no cash to spend until their next payday. I

153

was told that if I did whatever they wanted and gave them my personal phone number, they would keep in touch and make sure I was paid the following week.

All of these promises were, of course, completely and totally bogus. My response, no matter how lengthy or convincing the client tried to be, was always the same: all tips were due upfront, no exceptions. I was no fool, and I knew that nothing was forcing a man to keep his promises. I couldn't exactly call the police and demand legal intervention to make him pay if he cheated me, either, since the transaction was legally grey at best. If the prospect of spending a month's rent on an hour with a beautiful woman was already dicey, it was exponentially more so after the sobering effect of post-nut clarity set in.

I found it particularly amusing when men like this would throw adult temper tantrums after their attempted manipulations failed. When sweet-talking me didn't work, some of them would try to bully me into sexual favors or even threaten physical force if I didn't comply with their demands. As I would pack up my things and leave, as a last-ditch effort, these men would often tell me how I was losing a customer forever, not understanding that their 'business' was a joke to people like me.

On the other end of the deceptive spectrum, I had clients go through the motions and agree to exorbitant tips, only to have every single credit card in their wallet declined one after another. I would sit patiently at the foot of the bed as they argued with the bank over the phone about getting their credit limits increased. In these scenarios, the bank always said no, and after a few failed attempts, they would give up and flop down on the bed in exasperation. Strangely, when money wasn't an option, some of these men expected me to entertain them for free, as a consolation prize for at least *trying* to tip me. They were nice guys, and how dare I refuse them when they tried so hard on my behalf.

But back to my wannabe punk-rocker client. He agreed to sign the pre-authorized merchant copy for the booking fee, as they all do, so I got to work trying to squeeze a little extra money out of him. I took an inventory of the room, trying to determine what angle I could best utilize to get a fat tip.

154

I could hear a punk-rock mixtape playing quietly in the background and noticed evidence on the walls of what his life had been like thus far. There were photos of him and a woman, both dressed in a similar fashion, at multiple music venues and concerts. They looked committed to their lifestyle, seeming very punk rock, and also very much in love. They were holding each other close in the photos, smiling huge, cheesy grins, and looking fantastically happy together.

The photos appeared to span years because you could see them aging, ever-so-slowly, and then suddenly the woman vanished. In the more recent photos, only my client could be seen, and instead of a woman, there were deep, creasing wrinkles accompanying the man in the photos. Where had the woman gone? Did she die? Was there a nasty divorce? Nothing in the small bedroom hinted at what became of her, but I did notice something else. I paused, taking a closer, more focused look at all the photos, and then frowned.

I looked very much like the woman in the photos, even more so with the dark, smudgy makeup smeared around my eyes. I took another look at the pictures and silently cursed my boss; this guy probably specifically requested someone who looked like his ex, and I was the best match. She had probably known this but didn't tell me, letting me walk into this creep's house without warning. I clenched my teeth, mentally making myself promise to share my displeasure with her bullshit later.

Looking around the room again, I sighed, wishing more than ever that the night was over. The room was dingy and smelly, and I was too tired to care. I pushed aside some dirty laundry and sat in the swivel chair at the desk, letting my legs flop out in front of me. I lit up a smoke and stared at the pathetic specimen in front of me. He was smoking himself, watching me curiously from his bed. Exhausted, I decided that the best I could do was respond if he started calling me by her name. I felt bad for him but still planned on leaving the second he started crying or telling me he still loved me.

Unfortunately, dealing with newly single or divorced men was par for the course, so I was used to scenes like this. I was already at the booking, and that meant at least trying to make some money. Half enthused, I began my pitch, selling the allure of an all-nude, steamy lap dance show with touching.

Touching, a key selling point in all my negotiations, consisted of giving the client permission to touch my naked body, with the exception of my genitals. This non-sexual touching amounted to lots of groping my tits and squeezing my ass. Before I was an escort, touching like that was purely sexual in nature and was associated with doing the deed. Now, after almost of year, it was meaningless to me and held no element of sexuality whatsoever. It was all in a day's work and was about as exciting as filling out an incident report or alphabetizing paperwork.

With the touching, like any of the services I offered, I expected clients to push these boundaries. Of course, they all did. No matter how clear I was about where touching was permitted, stray hands or fingers somehow always wound up in places they ought not to be. If I was feeling particularly grouchy, I would slap them in the face for the slightest transgression. If I was in a good mood, I would let things slide a little and playfully remind them to follow the rules.

That night, I told my client that I would give him a brief strip tease with minimal touching but made it clear that I would leave directly afterward. I don't know if it was the dead look in my eyes or my uncanny resemblance to his past love, but he accepted my terms with meek resignation.

Once we had the tip business squared away, the client stretched out on his stained bedding and started speaking in my direction while he smoked another cigarette. I knew he was talking to me, but I wasn't listening or putting in the effort to act interested. He only tipped me one hundred dollars, which wasn't nearly enough for me to pretend to care. I was exhausted and saw no value in making this man a part of my regular roster, so it was in my best interest to be a cunt.

He rambled on, pausing his monologue only when taking a drag on his cigarette, while I zoned out. I didn't possess the patience or mental focus necessary to nod along at all the right times, and the client didn't seem to care; I got the impression he was talking as much to himself as he was to me. The small tidbits that managed to float into my awareness were about his ex-lover, and I began to grow slightly nervous that the grown man in front of me was chattering himself into a self-imposed mental breakdown. I watched the orange ember of my cigarette glow as his ceaseless rambling filled the background, and wondered how much sobbing and pleading I could sit through if he started bawling about his ex-lover. I grinned to myself, watching the tip smolder as the end turned grey and ashy, anticipating cutting the booking blessedly short and seeing myself out. A man on his knees and covered in snot was in no shape to chase me out the door, and likely too embarrassed to admit to anyone what had happened.

When I was more rested, I occasionally gave these types some grace. It was so banal, these broken men with their broken relationships, and I had seen more than I could count. They would cry, explaining their point of view about an unresolved argument, and I would just sit there and listen. I would nod along, say *uh-huh* at all the right moments, and watch as the clock dragged.

If I was feeling particularly heinous, I would sometimes say things like *maybe if you bought her flowers instead of spending this money on me, she would have taken you back* or *that's what you get for cheating on her*. The men would implode into uncontrollable, bitter sobs and wailing, and I would get dressed and leave without issuing a refund. It was awful, but so were they.

I was deep in thought, with images of my soft, plush bed ebbing into the forefront of my consciousness, when an unexpected comment from my client snapped me back to reality.

"You want to see something cool?" he said casually, almost like an afterthought.

In an instant, I was laser-focused on the scene before me. Years of experience taught me that I *always* wanted to 'see something', and that those 'somethings' had never disappointed me before. Without missing a beat, I responded in the affirmative and began waiting with high hopes. My client was already a bit on the weirder side, and in two seconds my mind was already racing with the possibilities of what he wanted me to see.

I watched intently as he started taking off his clothes, hoping that the surprise wasn't as boring as a human tail or an extra nipple. First, his shirt came off, and I could see that his nipples were pierced just like his

157

face. It was fascinating to learn that you could have more than one piercing on a nipple at a time, even going in different directions. I could also see that even his belly button was decorated with multiple piercings as well, which as far as I knew, was an unusual choice for a man.

Considering the entire picture before me, it was pretty obvious that this guy had a serious thing for metal. I found him extremely unattractive and thought that his body jewelry only amplified this effect. Despite my aversion to him physically, I had to admit his dedication to becoming so extensively pierced was intriguing. As he removed more of his clothing, I saw that he had piercings all over his body in strange, unexpected places. It was hard to look away as he got more undressed, akin to witnessing a car crash, or a horrific accident.

It was while staring at his nipples and noticing how thin and delicate the layer of skin around his piercings was that he began unbuttoning his pants. Before I could object, he slid them off in one fluid movement, boxers and all, and then gestured towards his crotch with a proud flourish.

He was nude, and I was not ready.

His dick looked like a pin cushion bursting at the seams with an enormous amount of metal. I had never seen so many piercings concentrated on one body part in my entire life, and of all places it was his *penis*. Metal rings and bars ran down the shaft, while studs decorated the skin of his scrotum. The bulk of the piercings were located on the head of his penis, where metal rings and rods poked in and out of the meat in ways I never thought possible. It looked uncomfortable, and I wondered how it felt to have metal touching his urethra. He had a particularly large ring that was centered on the head of his penis, and he pointed to it with a smile.

"This one is new. What do you think?" he said, beaming with pride.

The skin around the newer piercing looked pink and in the early stages of healing. I stared, lost in thought, trying to gather the ability to speak. I could see stray glimpses of flesh visible through all the metal, but mostly it looked like a perforated flesh tube bursting with silver bars and rings of all sizes. I slowly covered my mouth with my hand and stared in abject horror at the monstrosity before me.

Even in the wildest sci-fi or porn flicks, I had never seen anything quite like it.

It was baffling how a professional shop was okay with doing this to him; it seemed borderline unethical and likely restricted the practical functionality of his genitalia. The weight alone of all the adornments probably prevented him from getting proper erections, that is if there was enough intact skin left over to even allow for it. I imagined that even the most seasoned piercing professionals did a double take when confronted with his dick, and I wondered how many turned him away.

So, there I was, unapologetically gawking at his dangly bits, and the client loved every second of it. He was obviously very proud of what he had accomplished, which made a lot of sense because body modifications that extreme didn't happen overnight. I couldn't begin to speculate on how long it took him to transform his appendage and was curious if each new piercing was fully healed before he got the next one.

I had so many questions swirling around in my brain about his life choices up until this point, and my mind shifted to the natural follow-up question that such a sight inspired: what would happen if they were removed?

Did urine trickle out in little streams from every orifice along the shaft like a deranged watering can? What about when he ejaculated? Did all those little holes ooze white goo and crust up shortly afterward? Did he remove everything in the shower, put a shower head to it, and let water run through it like a sprinkler?

I also mused about the smell; I remembered from having my piercings done that there was an unpleasant odor from dead cells accumulating within the puncture hole itself, which required regular cleaning. I thought about the people I knew with gauged ears, and how they joked about how awful the smell was and then shuddered. Did his dick smell like old, moldy cheese?

I was becoming more and more uncomfortable, but it was still too early to leave without a legitimate excuse. Since I didn't know what to say, I said nothing, and the two of us sat in silence for what felt like an eternity. Finally, I managed to collect myself enough to mutter something along the lines of *how long did that take?*.

This must have been the response he was hoping for, because he began to prattle away happily about his unusual life choices while I listened politely. It wasn't the real answer I was looking for, so wasn't particularly interested, but I let him fill the silence so I wouldn't feel obligated to do it myself. I was grateful that he was so content just lying on his bed and telling me his story, and decided to let him eat up as much time as possible talking.

Apparently, it had taken years to get to the point he was at now, and he had a special guy who handled all his piercing needs. This tracked; this guy probably spent a small fortune maintaining his lifestyle, and a dedicated piercer probably appreciated the regular business.

As he spoke, disappointment and confusion were plain on his face. He admitted astonishment that I wasn't crazy horny after seeing his penis. He had fully expected me to jump his bones after the pants came off, and when I didn't, it surprised him. When he not-so-subtly hinted at how good all the protrusions would feel rubbing against my insides, I did my best to avoid vomiting.

I didn't know what kind of life he had been living up until this point, but I personally knew of a grand total of zero people who fostered die-hard kinks for overly pierced genitals. Remembering all the pictures of his ex-lover covering the walls, I suspected that perhaps his former girlfriend had something to do with this and probably got wet seeing all the metal. It looked like it had been a long-term relationship as well, so his expectations weren't entirely based on fantasy. Considering his behavior from that perspective made it easier to tolerate him but did nothing to change the fact that he was super gross.

Using every ounce of my professional ability, I convinced him that I, unfortunately, couldn't indulge tonight because of the fresh piercing. Having sex before it was completely healed was out of the question, so there simply was nothing I could do. I remembered the importance of cleanliness from getting my ears pierced, so it wasn't so much of a lie as it was a convenient truth.

I doubled down with my lie and layered on fake disappointment thick as mud. In my best coquettish tone, I played into his fantasy by pretending to be wholly spellbound by his self-imposed genital mutilation. In truth, I *was* fascinated, just not in the way he wanted. I toyed with him, imploring him sweetly with a myriad of questions about his penis until my ten-minute warning timer blessedly chimed, signaling that it was time to wrap things up.

Once he knew my time was almost up, he indicated his desire to get off before I left. This was common, so I didn't protest. There was no way I would touch him or let him come anywhere near me, so I told him I didn't have any issues with watching him jerk off if he paid me extra. He seemed crestfallen, but I reminded him we didn't want to risk anything since the newest piercing was still healing. Reluctantly, he agreed to my terms, and I blithely charged a few hundred more dollars to his credit card.

Secretly, I was ecstatic; I had wanted so badly to ask about what happened when he ejaculated but couldn't think of a way to do it without sounding rude. Now, I watched with keen anticipation, thrilled that I was being paid to satisfy my morbid curiosity.

Watching him masturbate in itself was very strange because physically there were so many piercings between his hand and the shaft. It was the same up-down stroking motion that all men employed, but it wasn't entirely clear to what extent he could feel his hand on his flesh with all the metal in the way. Watching closely, I wondered if the pleasurable sensation he got was from feeling the movement of the piercings themselves within his flesh. I shuddered at the thought, pressing my lips into a hard line to keep from making a face. Whatever was happening, the client must have enjoyed it, because he spent years plugging himself up with metal.

Eventually, after what felt like the longest ten minutes of my life, the moment of truth arrived, and he finally ejaculated. I wasn't sure what to expect, but a big part of me had been secretly hopeful to see his cum slowly ooze out of every orifice like a grotesque, X-rated Play-Doh extruder. Instead, in the most normal, unspectacular way possible, his man-goo weakly spurted out the tip of his metallic meat rod and dribbled lamely down his hand.

E. S. Silversmith

Driving home that morning, the sun was on the horizon and blinding me. It was close to seven a.m., and the highway was filled with traffic. Usually, the roads were deserted and barren, and I was not used to stop-and-go commuter traffic. I reflected during my slow grind home about what I had seen and realized that I walked away that morning with a new personal boundary: maybe I was a prude, but there was no way I would ever let a metal-studded meat stick like that within an inch of my vagina. I tried to be as open-minded as possible, as sexual deviance was my forte, but what I had seen was too extreme even for my taste.

I was hopeful that morning when I settled into bed that I would never see him again. He didn't pay well, and he had called me at the butt-crack of dawn, both things that were on my no-no list. But, as it goes, every few months he would call the agency, request me specifically, and summon me back to his house just before dawn. I began to suspect that whenever he got a new piercing, he would book me, if only for the reason of showing it off to someone.

We would then go through the same song-and-dance where I would sadly explain that I couldn't have sex with him because of it and would sit bored out of my skull while he jerked off in front of me. One of my only regrets about being an escort is that before I retired, I never got to see what it looked like for him to ejaculate without the piercings.

CHAPTER FOURTEEN

Plastic Wrap

Contrary to popular belief, it was not just single men requesting our services. Every so often, we encountered women. This was usually in the form of a woman being present during a group party, or because a couple called requesting an escort together for a spicy night in. I wasn't against female clients, but I wasn't exactly crazy about them either; women posed unique challenges when it came to charming them and generally were not good tippers.

Whenever I arrived at a group party and saw that a woman was included in the group, I groaned internally. I was definitely all about equality in any other circumstance, but at work I hated dealing with them. I knew it wasn't intentional, but they often had an annoying habit of getting in the way of making money.

Sometimes they would try to assume the role of liaison between me and the male clients, which was entirely unnecessary, and other times they would drunkenly get naked and start giving shitty lap dances to the partygoers for free. A drunk chick at a party who is doing everything she can to keep shifting attention back to herself was not good for business, even if she was puking in the sink and making a spectacle of herself.

Free is free, and people liked getting something for nothing. Women like that had a real chance of having sex with a man at the party, and it's like they could smell it in the air. A man busy convincing the drunk chick to go upstairs with him is the same man not succumbing to my feminine wiles. If I was lucky, she would end up on her back off in a bedroom somewhere and out of my hair.

Another issue was when the woman present would scoff at my up-front tip price for a dance show, making it harder for me to seal the deal. The last thing I needed was someone injecting a sense of financial responsibility into a situation where I primarily profited off of poor judgment.

I always chalked up this bizarre behavior to insecurity and did my best to not let it get under my skin. A common way I would see this manifest is by the woman present at the party throwing herself at her man of interest in order to distract him from the entertainers.

I also observed that they would start arguments with male guests, who I presumed there was a romantic connection with, because I would hear heated arguments from the other room. It was a mess, and a real downer for everyone else if a dumb, drunk bitch was screaming and crying her eyes out in the bathroom.

Rarely a woman would approach me privately and ask me nicely to avoid entertaining a particular man because she was interested in him, and I would happily oblige.

There were other times though when having a woman present was anything *but* irritating, and whose presence was actually beneficial for my cash tips. Every now and then, a woman would be part of the group because she actually wanted a lap dance or sexually charged interaction with an exotic dancer. This was fun for me because I loved giving women lap dances and didn't have to worry about their insecurity causing me problems while I did my thing.

It meant I could squeeze their boobs, kiss their necks, and be very suggestive with them, which was great for driving a crowd wild. When the group of men at a party saw two chicks making out, they went crazy. Watching two women together in any sexual context was always a huge hit, and the men would pay top dollar to keep us going at it.

If the woman in question was particularly free-spirited, I would drag her out to the middle of the room, lay her down on her back, and make a huge production of giving her a sexy floor dance. I would grind on her, rub my tits all over her, spank her bottom, and anything else I could get away with.

I would encourage her to slap my ass or suck my nipples, and everyone loved it; the woman was getting exactly what she wanted without causing me problems, and it drove the men bananas. I would also have the woman give me a dance, which made the men especially rowdy because they got to see someone they actually knew behaving in a sexual way. This was always tons of fun, and while I charged them for the privilege of doing it, the levity it added was priceless. As an added bonus, it gave me a golden opportunity to rest and do nothing but sit.

Couples were a different story entirely, and far less common than the stray female party participant. These people did not waste time; when a couple called, they wanted to fuck, plain and simple. The story I usually heard was that they had been looking for a long time but were unable to find a woman to share that met both of their stringent physical requirements, i.e. not ugly or fat.

In my personal life, I had sex with couples periodically for fun and knew from experience that the best approach was always to pay more attention to the wife/girlfriend instead of the guy. No matter how strong they purported their relationship to be, I always ran the risk of the other woman getting jealous or upset, and this was also true for bookings with couples as well.

The idea of seeing your partner with another person is a very fun one indeed, but not everyone could actually handle the reality of their partner boinking another person two inches away. I was always concerned about pissing the other woman off, having her freak out, and then dealing with the backlash of a suddenly unsafe situation. Case in point, a woman once went as far as throwing a shoe at me when her boyfriend sprung an erection after seeing me naked.

It is worth noting, however, that not every couple is prone to a huge breakdown when including another woman. There are some people who are truly comfortable and secure in their relationships, and those were my favorites.

Couple Miller

One afternoon I got a text indicating I had a booking, and then a follow-up text specifically indicating that it was a couple that requested me. The booking fee was higher for meeting a couple, but a good chunk of the booking fee went directly to the company. This was always a difficult situation for me because the high price often led couples to believe it covered an all-inclusive experience.

Since I wasn't desperate and only slept with clients if I wanted to, my hard line with couples was directly proportionate to how attractive the wife was. If the wife was a beautiful lady, I would consider entertaining her for free.

When I arrived at my booking, I was surprised at how young the couple was; they looked to be mid-twenties and were both very attractive. Usually, couples who called were in their forties, so this was a pleasant surprise.

After collecting the booking fee, they explained to me that the husband was in the military and that he was about to go on a long deployment. Apparently, they had decided as a couple that the wife was permitted to have a female lover in his absence, and today was her trial run to see if her inclination towards women was anything more than a passing fancy.

I was a bit of an asshole, so I told them I understand their situation, but I needed to see her naked first. She got undressed and was stunning. She had cute, perky tits, mid-back length hair, and was just the right amount of slender. Her skin was pale, and her eyes were a lovely shade of green, which was a combo I was particularly fond of when it came to aesthetics.

She was very good looking, and before I gave them an answer, the husband told me he had a gift for me. He disappeared for a moment, then produced an envelope and handed it to me. Peeking inside, I could see it was full of cash, and I didn't ask any questions about what they thought it was for. I had already decided I was going to have sex with them simply because I wanted to after seeing the wife's beautiful body, so if they were choosing to give me money, I wouldn't say no.

The encounter ended up being fun for everyone involved, and it was nice to see how much the couple obviously loved each other. I didn't run into any snags, and it was refreshing to have some no-strings-attached fun.

Worker Tara

There were other times, though, that weren't bad but weren't exactly good, either. When I was booked with another woman to entertain a couple in the middle of the night, I had mixed feelings about it. I knew the woman I was working with very well and had recently enjoyed an off-the-clock sexual encounter with her and her spouse, so that was a plus. But requesting two women for a couple was highly irregular, and I suspected I was about to be subjected to things I wouldn't want to see or do.

When we arrived, we understood immediately that it wouldn't be smooth sailing. The couple was visiting from Europe and spoke poor English. We managed to ascertain that the husband wanted to watch another woman perform oral sex on his wife.

The wife, oddly aroused, was moaning and writhing around on the bed dressed in nothing but her underwear. I could see her occasionally touching herself while she looked at me or Tara, rolling her eyes in the back of her head as she let out pleasured gasps.

I suspected drug use right away and didn't want anything to do with it; I was okay with sleeping with clients periodically if I truly wanted to, but I drew a hard line if illicit drug use was involved. Based on what I had read, it added another layer of unnecessary risk to an already risky situation, and I wasn't interested in getting an exotic STD from a drugged-up foreigner.

Tara, on the other hand, was less picky. She had no qualms about accepting cash from the husband and eating out the woman while she squirmed around in ecstasy. The husband, naked and hairy, was watching from a hotel chair beside the bed and furiously masturbating.

I was left as the odd one out and watched the scene unfold with little interest. Yes, the intoxicated woman was into getting her pussy eaten, big surprise there. Yes, the husband was stroking a rock-hard erection while he watched some girl-on-girl action, neat.

Seeing sexual acts and being involved in sexual situations in general was such a common occurrence for me that I didn't pay much attention. There was nothing fun or exciting about what they were doing; honestly, it was pretty vanilla and nothing I hadn't witnessed a hundred times over.

Bored and unable to leave, I stood there playing games on my phone and scrolling through social media waiting for them to finish. When they were finally done, I couldn't help but wonder about my co-worker's choice.

To be honest, Tara's willingness to engage in high-risk behavior was a relatively new development, especially for such a small sum of money. If the couple had been offering a large amount, it would have at least been reasonable, but this wasn't the case at all; they barely had any money for a tip on top of the booking fee, and if someone had offered me that kind of money I would have laughed in their face.

What I didn't know at the time was that my co-worker was harboring a pretty nasty drug problem and was spending a sizable sum maintaining her habit. Looking back, it made a lot of sense. There were so many times that I was left waiting for over an hour for her to arrive at a booking, and she also had an uncanny tendency to come down with and recover from the flu on a bizarrely regular basis.

It wasn't until far later when I saw a small wound developing in the antecubital space of her left arm that the puzzle pieces finally fell in place. All the mysterious illnesses and running late all the time suddenly made sense.

I felt terrible for her but knew there was nothing I could really do to help her. I had known her for years, and I saw her descend into a very sad, dark way of life right before my eyes. When we met, I knew she had a history of using, but to my knowledge, she had been sober for years. I don't know why she started using again, and I never asked, but from what I could tell, it destroyed her life.

Being addicted to drugs and forced to make compromises was a serious fear of mine. Being an escort, you constantly had people pushing drugs and large sums of money on you in exchange for fairly heinous requests. Without a drug habit, I maintained my ability to choose and declined offers that would jeopardize me physically or mentally. But if I was addicted to drugs and needed to use in order to keep myself from getting sick, suddenly that option would fizzle.

My co-worker was in that boat, and towards the end of the time I knew her, she needed to shoot up or she would become very sick and be unable to do anything for days while she went through withdrawals. She couldn't work while she was dope sick, either, because she would have frequent diarrhea, a fever, and sweat profusely. She had no choice but to get high just to be able to go to work. As she spiraled deeper into the throes of addiction, she began to look more haggard and undesirable, resulting in less bargaining power when negotiating tips for non-sexual acts.

It was a vicious cycle that left her with few options; she couldn't get a regular job that would pay enough to support her habit or offer a flexible enough schedule that allowed her to use and acquire drugs as needed.

I used to wonder about the women I saw walking the streets selling their bodies, or the way sex workers are portrayed on television, but watching my co-worker's gradual descent filled in all the grey areas. She didn't start out that way, it was a slow, gradual process that left her backed into a corner and struggling to survive. I don't know what ended up happening to her, but the last thing I heard was that she sold her house, blew through all the money, and was now homeless and living in hotels when she could afford it.

CHAPTER FIFTEEN

Minivan Mistress

Because a certain amount of self-confidence and entitlement was necessary to perform the job, the agency had a tendency to attract an enormous amount of self-important, stuck-up cunts. Many times, I would be paired up with another woman for a two-girl show, and she would parade around like she owned the place and behave rudely to everyone, myself included.

For these women, it seemed that being attractive and having a vagina somehow made them the best thing since sliced bread, and getting paid for companionship only boosted their toxic egos. I can't say that I was a perfect angel myself, because I was certainly quite the asshole, but I was never operating under the delusion that I was the center of the universe and that my shit didn't stink.

Some of my co-workers were notoriously more difficult to get along with than others. I don't know if it was me specifically, or if these particular women took out their frustrations on the world around them. I considered a certain amount of competitive and underhanded behavior normal, but these women took it to the next level.

Worker Sally

This awful dynamic shined its brightest when it came to Sally. Now, Sally is what is colloquially known as 'a raging cunt'. She would make snide, passive-aggressive comments to me in front of the clients whenever she had the chance. I found her behavior childish, and embarrassing; she somehow missed the memo that men could deal with a bitchy woman at home for free.

I remember the first time I met her, we were in the hallway of a hotel, and I was trying to helpfully give her the rundown for a booking she was about to walk into. The client had wanted more time, but I wasn't willing, so instead I hung out until my boss got another woman out there.

When she arrived, I was perplexed; she was very short, petite, and obviously missing one of her front teeth. Her makeup looked like it was from yesterday and she seemed to be shifting back and forth in place like a real-life video game character.

Judging by her erratic nature, I immediately suspected she was high on methamphetamine. She seriously reminded me of a skittish raccoon that had just clawed its way out of a rolling dumpster fire; angry, unpredictable, and probably riddled with disease.

To make matters worse, she wasn't alone, either. Standing beside her was what I presumed to be her boyfriend, and wow was he a sight. He was dressed like an extra from a rap music video, but if rap music videos were made in white trash America with a camera phone and no budget. While I'm sure he meant to be intimidating, it was comical having a man who looked like a caricature of a Hollywood gangster give me dirty looks while flashing his grill.

Strangely, the shifty-eyed woman fidgeting in front of me looked like she had a personal vendetta against me, and I had no idea why. This was the first time I had ever seen her at work or otherwise, and the only reason I was even speaking to her was to warn her about the asshole waiting in the other room.

I was as patient as I could be, trying to explain some of the details about the client to help her out, but she cut me off rudely and told me she had it under control.

Now, to be fair, I get not wanting help from what was essentially a rival, but there was absolutely no reason to be a bitch about it. I had been an escort for years at that point and knew from experience that girls at my company normally adopted an us-versus-them mentality when it came to the clients.

So, when this new girl had to be physically restrained by her boyfriend to keep from assaulting me, I was taken aback. Instead of arguing with her, I said fuck it and walked away, leaving the poor client to deal with whatever bullshit she was about to drag kicking and screaming into his night.

The next run-in happened when I was added as a second for a two girl show with one of her regulars. Apparently, he had a friend fly in from out of town and wanted an extra girl present to entertain them both. When I got the booking details that afternoon and saw her name, I groaned; I already did not get along with her, and the boss told me up front the situation with the client being one of her regulars. This meant that she would be fiercely protecting her right to him in order to preserve her stable income.

Knowing what kind of woman she was, I was not at all interested in stealing a client who fancied her. I found her so utterly unattractive that the idea of her bumping uglies with a lecherous creep was positively nauseating. As I got dressed for the show, I decided my best bet was to go minimal to avoid any unnecessary conflict; looking my best for an extra two hundred bucks in my pocket was not worth the trouble that it came with.

When I arrived at the seaside resort, the smell of salty air hit me in the face as the wind whipped my hair from side to side. The beautiful weather swept away my bad mood and invigorated my spirit; my anxiety stemming from my co-worker faded away as the sound of seagulls and waves filled my ears. I breathed in deeply and felt my whole body relax, the humid air moist on my skin.

My serenity was interrupted when a junky minivan clambered its way into the parking lot, loud music blaring as its driver crookedly pulled into a space. I frowned, knowing who it was before they even stepped out: my lovely co-worker.

She climbed out, slamming the door loudly behind her. Even though it was barely noon, she was dressed like a cheap hooker walking the streets at two a.m. Recognizing me, she walked stiffly towards me while flicking a cigarette, her skintight, bright pink spandex mini dress hugging her tiny frame in the worst of ways.

It was no secret that she had a few kids and was left with loose skin folds over her tummy, and the dress only accentuated this fact. It clung tightly to her body in a way that the fishnets she had layered underneath could not fix. Her hair looked like she hadn't even bothered to run a comb through it, and her black heels were scuffed and damaged; perhaps in the wee hours of the night when men were deep in their cups, this look worked, but during the day she looked like a ripe pimple on a butt cheek.

"You ready, E.?" she muttered impatiently, rolling her eyes and flicking her cigarette in my direction.

My brow furrowed and I gritted my teeth; I had actually been waiting about fifteen minutes for her to arrive, and her tone made me want to shove her in the bushes. Instead, I took a deep breath, refusing to let her antics get under my skin.

Since she had been there before, I let her lead the way and pretended to listen politely while she prattled on about how this was *her* client, and how I was only present to keep the other man company. I rolled my eyes, saying nothing as she shot me dirty looks in the elevator, wishing that my boss had chosen anyone else for the show.

In front of the client's door, she gave me one last hateful glance before knocking and switching on her fake, plastic-looking smile.

Barf.

Her pretend smile looked worse than her usual bitchy expression, and I frowned again; I didn't understand how someone so unappealing could be an escort, and I hated being associated with her. As we stood waiting for the client to answer the door, she became oddly fidgety. She picked at her arm, and darted her eyes around, apparently searching for something. But the hallways were empty, and the upscale condominium building was not the kind of place to have boogeymen hiding behind corners. I sighed again, realizing that she was probably just high, like the first day we met.

When the client answered the door and smiled affably, I was relieved to no longer be alone with her. He was an older man, probably sixty, and had a shock of grey hair coupled with too-tanned skin. He was barefoot and wearing a vibrant pair of swim shorts, and around his neck was a fluffy white towel. Ice clinked in his glass as he took a sip of dark colored liquid, and he grinned.

"You girls want to get in the hot tub?" he teased, waggling his eyebrows.

My coworker dramatically fell into him, embracing him tightly as she squeezed her tits into his chest. She then planted a soggy kiss on his neck and asked for a drink. He smiled again, happy to oblige, and led us both inside. I groaned internally, unimpressed by her over-the-top possessive display.

The kitchen was set up for guests, and various bottles of booze and mixers were displayed on the counter along with an ice bucket. I politely declined the offer, not especially interested in imbibing before eleven a.m., while my coworker poured herself a full glass.

The older man was clearly smitten with her and regarded her with a toothy, lusty grin that made me sick to my stomach. It was disgusting watching him visually devour her, and I knew that spending two hours with them while he pawed all over her would feel like an eternity.

Looking around, I noticed that the booking fee was neatly laid out in cash on the counter. I grabbed it, stuffing it discreetly into my purse, not trusting the other woman to drop off my share for me. I didn't want to risk being on the hook for my cost of the show, and I had serious doubts about her ability to hold onto cash long enough without spending it on drugs. I texted my boss that I had the money, and sighed once more, suddenly feeling very bored.

The condo was fairly plain, with a couch and small television, a few paintings on the wall, and a large glass window overlooking the ocean. I walked over to the window and took a moment to enjoy the vastness of the sea; from the thirteenth floor, it seemed to go on forever, and was quite the view.

Other than the single bedroom and a bathroom, the condo also had a special balcony room with a hot tub. You could sit inside, warm and toasty, while the cool ocean breeze kissed your cheeks. I wasn't a fan of heights, and not particularly inclined towards the ocean, but I had to admit it was pretty nice. I slid off my shoes, letting my bare feet rest on the cool tile beneath them, and smiled. Even if the company was bad, the accommodations were top notch.

After a moment, it dawned on me that the plus-one was missing; I had been told there would be an extra man, and I had yet to see him. After nosing around, I spied him relaxing in the hot tub room, his arms stretched wide as he soaked in the warm waters. Not wanting to deal with the nauseating sight of the old man and my coworker swapping saliva, I excused myself to the bathroom and got changed into my work uniform.

It was hot that day, and after pulling on my thigh highs, I opted to take them off instead, exposing my bare legs. After looking at myself in the mirror, I decided to forego clothing altogether and go full nude at the start, figuring that I would end up naked in the hot tub anyway.

Besides, I didn't predict selling a nude lap dance show in my near future; judging by the way the client was squeezing my co-worker's ass and sticking his tongue down her throat, it was clear that dancing was not what these men were after.

Exiting the bathroom, I groaned when I heard obnoxious laughter coming from the hot tub. A brightly colored pair of swim trunks lay on the tile floor, not far from a bright pink pile of clothing that I recognized as Sally's. They were naked, their bodies stewing together like nasty soup in the steaming water, and now I had to get in with them.

Fuck.

"Hey, look who decided to join the party!" the client said loudly, now regarding my naked form with the same lusty, inebriated gaze.

His eyes, glassy and bloodshot, surveyed my nude form and he licked his lips. Disgusted, I managed to smile meekly in response as the three made room for me in the tub, splashing as they went.

They were drunk, they were wet, and I did not want to join them. I kept repeating to myself that this was my job, and that this was what I was paid to do. Suppressing my instincts, I dipped in a toe and reluctantly sunk into the warm water. My nipples grew hard in response to the sudden temperature change, and the client hooted, *now that's what I'm talking about!* My co-worker glared at me for the briefest of moments before reverting back to her fake smile, and I sighed again.

It was never any fun being the only sober person in a room full of drunks, and this was no exception. The friend from out of town scooted over next to me and placed his hand on my thigh. I could tell from his tan lines that he normally wore a wedding ring and had slipped it off before we arrived. I could smell alcohol and cigarettes heavy on his breath as he flirted with me, squeezing my thigh as he spoke.

His fingers were less than a hands breadth away from my bare vagina, and it made me extremely uncomfortable; I didn't know what my co-worker was used to selling, but I seriously doubted I offered the same services. I had already seen her open mouth kissing the other guy, which was something that I never did. My main concern was that the client had given his friend expectations on what he could do with me, probably with a monetary value attached, based on his dealings with my coworker.

Mulling this over, I calmly accepted that I would make nothing but my share of the booking fee for my two hours of time. No matter how you sliced it, I simply could not compete with bottom-dollar blowjobs or whatever the fuck else she was selling to stay afloat with her looks.

Accepting defeat, I tuned out the friend, being sure to nod at all the right places during his riveting tale about a recent fishing trip. I was lost in thought, thinking about my grocery list for the week, when I felt a hand grip my shoulder tightly and shake me.

"Hey E.! I got a couple hundred bucks over here, how about you show me a good time in the other room?"

I blinked, startled back to the present, and reflexively turned in the direction of the person grabbing me. It was my worst dream realized: the hand on my shoulder belonged to the regular client, and my coworker was staring me down, fire in her eyes and venom in her teeth. She looked like she wanted to eat me alive, but knew she couldn't say anything, or tell the client he couldn't have me.

We were supposed to be a fantasy, and a fantasy woman does not get jealous. She lets her man do whatever he pleases, even fuck other women, and doesn't bat an eye. She is cool, she is sexy, and she thinks it's hot when you lust after other women. We were escorts, and this was our way.

I froze, unsure how to answer. The client's eyes, glassy from too much to drink, were fixed squarely on my tits. His lips were curled up into a creepy smile that I recognized from years on the job, and I knew without a doubt that he fully intended to fuck me.

To be clear, I would have said no even without the ultra-low price. He was gross and creepy, and I had standards. Besides, my nude dance shows alone cost more than that, and it was all I could do to keep from giggling.

"No thanks," I said sweetly, "but Sally over there looks like she would *love* to spend some time with you."

My coworker, confused, eyed me suspiciously. Yes, I was redirecting the client's drunken attention back to her, but it seemed like she hadn't forgiven me for inadvertently seducing him in the first place.

"No, I don't want Sally, I want you. Two hundred, right now. What do you say?" he said sloppily, sliding up next to me in the hot tub. The water sloshed as he moved, accidentally filling his friend's glass of booze with chlorinated liquid.

"Um... no, I can't, actually," I said, scooting away slightly, "I do things differently than Sally, and I just can't, but thank you for the offer."

The client took a long swig of his drink and set the glass down on the tile counter beside the hot tub. Far from discouraging him, my rejection only emboldened him. He reached an arm around my waist, squeezing me tightly, and then leaned his head close to mine and sniffed my hair.

"Okay, okay, I'll play nice," he breathed huskily in my ear, "how much?"

I could taste the stink of his breath floating into my mouth and felt like everyone was watching, waiting for my response. My coworker was seething quietly, smoking a cigarette, and looking like she wanted to flay me alive. Based on the abject rage apparent on her face, the two hundred dollars he was offering was a big deal to her.

I decided to play hard to get, and resort to the old trick of pricing him out of my services. In my experience, letting the client be the one who chooses to say *no* keeps them from treating you badly when you still have time left on the clock.

"Oh… gee," I said innocently, "I don't think you could afford me, hon."

He leaned in closer, his skin now pressing against my naked flesh. I felt a shiver go through my whole body as I suppressed the overwhelming urge to escape. I hated the way his shriveled, pruney hands felt on my body, and there was no way I was letting his century-old sausage anywhere near my lady parts.

"How much?" he whispered loudly in my ear, too drunk to properly conceal what he was saying.

"Oh, I usually charge fifteen hundred dollars, and that's just the base fee," I said matter of factly in my sweetest voice, hoping the large number would scare him off.

While I did totally make up the number, it wasn't entirely a lie. The truth was, when it came to prices, I charged whatever I wanted to, and it varied wildly from client to client. Sometimes my prices were sky-high, and other times they were modest and affordable; it all depended on my mood that day, and how personally attracted I was to the client. Most of the time, though, I had zero attraction to the client. So, when a smoking hot fitness nerd wanted to roll around in the sheets for an hour, I secretly provided a discount.

At my words, the drunken client made a surprised face, my coworker audibly scoffed, and then he slid away back towards Sally. While he groped her tits, she had a smug, triumphant look on her face, and I let her think that she won. The old man started licking down the side of her neck, letting his saliva drip onto her collarbone as he breathed heavily. It was gross, and I turned away, not wanting to burn my corneas.

I was so thankful that day that I didn't have a drug problem; the idea of putting up with that kind of behavior for any price was nauseating, and the mere idea of allowing it for a measly two hundred dollars made it even worse. Now that I was out of reach financially, the friend lost interest in trying to get into my pants and instead engaged in normal, pleasant conversation about what he did for a living.

Worker Tiffany

One lazy summer afternoon, I got a call from my boss, telling me I was booked for a two girl show. Apparently, it was two younger guys at a notoriously seedy apartment complex, but the upside was that they were paying with a credit card.

While the zip code was disheartening, the allure of a possible credit card tip put a smile on my face. If they had money for a two girl show on credit, they likely had plenty more to spare. I grinned as I packed my dance bag, images of ruining a naïve young man's credit score dancing blithely in my head.

At the time, my deadbeat, dirtbag stoner boyfriend still lived with me, so I shook him to wake him up. If I didn't let him drive me to the booking and wait around in the parking lot, he would punish me later with a pissy attitude. He didn't work, being that I made enough on my own to keep us afloat, and was instead intent on forcing his way into my job and making himself a part of it.

Even though we were using my car, he told me that since he drove me to the shows and was my personal bodyguard, half the money was his. He made a point to remind me constantly how I could never do the job without him, and how replaceable I was. If he got upset, he would angrily tell me how he could just find another girl to do my job, and that I was worthless.

In the beginning, I kind of believed him, but I was no fool; I handled all the expenses myself and never gave him any actual money. Nor did I consider his 'services' helpful or necessary; once when he was particularly mad and telling me how easy it would be to replace me, I told him to go ahead, and to get the fuck out of my car. Leaving him at a gas station on the other side of town mellowed him out for a few days, but it didn't take long for him to return to smoking weed all day and blaming me for all his worldly problems.

So that afternoon, I woke him up, and he stumbled sleepily out of bed and groped around for his bong. I had to be at a show within an hour, was already dressed, and he was slowing me down. He wanted to take his time to eat and get high before we left, and had cleverly held onto the car keys so I couldn't leave without him.

I was starting to fume, worried about being late, when he came out of the back room with bloodshot eyes and reeking of marijuana. I clenched my jaw, finding his drug use a waste of time and money. I did not use any drugs myself and considered any habit like that a weakness. The only reason I tolerated his drug use was because it made him easier to deal with, and I hadn't quite worked up the nerve yet to kick him to the curb. My life was incredibly lonely, and as much as I hated to admit it, he kept me company when I wasn't at school.

Once we were in the car, he lit up a cigarette and drove us sleepily to our destination. He stopped at a gas station to buy himself an energy drink despite us already pushing the line timewise.

Ever since I was a child, and even now as an adult years later, being late to anything gave me serious anxiety. Additionally, punctuality for my bookings meant that the customers were nicer to me. If I was late, many customers used it as an excuse to be mean, or as a bargaining chip to get services at a reduced price. Either way, it was a colossal pain, so I avoided it like my life depended on it.

When we eventually arrived, I scrambled to identify the correct apartment building as he chain-smoked in the car; all the buildings were identical, and the numbering system seemed almost random. After a few passes cruising through the complex, I finally spotted the unit I was looking for.

I could see that the other escort, a woman I had never met before, leaning against her car waiting for me. She looked annoyed that I was late, and rightfully so; I was over twenty minutes late.

As I prepared to get out of the car, she sauntered over to the driver-side window and leaned in towards my boyfriend. She smiled innocently, but after working with women like her for so long, I could tell she was up to some shit. Her eyes, angry and vindictive, gave her away.

"Hi E., and you are...?" she said, leaning closer to my boyfriend.

As she spoke, she swirled a lollipop on her tongue, popping it in and out as she batted her eyelashes. She also wore a low-cut top and was pushing the cleavage from her big, fake tits right in my boyfriend's face. I could smell her perfume and was not amused.

Being the stellar man that he was, my boyfriend accepted the attention and chatted back and forth with her while I watched silently from the passenger seat.

Now, I wasn't particularly attached to my boyfriend, but what she was doing was completely out of line. I could have said something, and gotten mad at them both, but decided against it; my boyfriend was a piece of shit, and this was just another nail in the coffin that hardened my resolve to eventually leave him.

Once they had finished fawning over each other, I got out of the car and walked to the apartment door. I said nothing and watched as she flipped her hair and shot me a smug look as she passed by.

There was no doubt about it, she was a cunt with a capital 'C'.

When we got to the door, she pursed her lips at me and daintily knocked, apparently disgusted by the layer of dirt and grime on the door. Her self-important, stuck-up attitude made me roll my eyes and brought my already low patience down to zero.

She was thin, athletic, had a nice face and beautiful hair, and also had a huge pair of double D's. Our clients loved huge tits, and it probably contributed to her overinflated ego.

I heard the sound of footsteps from inside, and soon the door swung open, revealing two early twenties guys who stunk of alcohol. They were moderately attractive, but a total mess; their grubby appearances matched the tone of the neighborhood, and the furnishings present reflected a lack of financial freedom. I guessed that the couch had been salvaged from the side of a road somewhere, and that the eclectic assortment of other furnishings was not an art statement. These guys were barely scraping by, and it showed.

I stepped carefully through the apartment to the living room on the filthy carpet, trying not to cough; the walls were yellowed, and the air musty from years of smoking indoors. The stink had settled on every surface, and the multiple overflowing ashtrays throughout the apartment made me wonder how often they cleaned, if at all. True to the spirit of a

181

real bachelor pad, there were bits of ash and dirty dishes scattered on every surface.

My coworker's pink lips were furled back in a sneer as she tip-toed through the dirty apartment. Perhaps it was because I already hated her, but I found her behavior ridiculous; in all my years, I had yet to see a single client who wanted to deal with a sassy drama queen.

Part of what clients paid for was the agreeable disposition they couldn't get from the normal women in their lives. The agency constantly drilled this into us, and even still, she continued her snobbiness in front of the two men seated comfortably on the couch.

Rolling my eyes, I joined her, standing beside her as the two men cheekily regarded us with intoxicated smiles. After they signed the credit card slip, I started my spiel, but my coworker cut me off mid-sentence and took over.

Flabbergasted and not wanting to make a scene, I remained silent; this was a new employee, and I wasn't positive she knew what she doing. Arguing while clients looked on was not good for business, either, and I didn't want to deal with my boss if the customers complained. Instead of confronting her, I swallowed my pride and let her speak.

To her credit, she mostly knew what to say, and even requested what I considered a reasonable price for a full nude lap dance show. After I got another signed slip for the tip, they picked music while we got changed. Once the bathroom door shut, she demanded that I hand over the credit card slips so she could make sure that they got dropped off with the boss. I stared back at her blankly and responded in my calmest voice *no*.

She looked shocked for a moment at my refusal, but then scoffed and flipped her hair, ignoring me completely as she turned her back to me while getting dressed.

What a bitch.

The sound of alternative rock hits at full blast filled the tiny apartment, and I grabbed my bag and headed out of the bathroom. We had already negotiated tips, so I didn't see a reason to wait for her to finish, and any moment I could manage away from her was a victory.

The men were laughing and drinking beer on the couch when I found them, and I got started with my routine. I did a couple of lap dances, slowly removing my lingerie as I went, giving the young men the appropriate amount of tease for what they paid for. I was mid-song, grinding away on one of their laps, when my coworker came out of the bathroom.

She was dressed in expensive-looking lingerie and high heels, both of which seemed out of place in the shitty apartment. Her big, fake boobies were beautifully framed with a lacey pink bra, and her smooth tanned skin glistened, reflecting beautifully with each step.

I had to admit, she looked nice, but it was a bit overdone for the level of clientele we were entertaining. I had only tossed on some random dancewear from the bottom of my bag and didn't even bother touching up my makeup. These men were home in the afternoon on a weekday, and based on how they were dressed, they didn't require much impressing. Besides that, we had already been paid and they were positively sloshed. I doubted they would even remember calling us the next day.

She waltzed over to the living room and started dancing on the other man. She shimmied and moved her body to the music, her body heat wafting the smell of her perfume into the air. It was floral and heavy, and a welcome change from the scent of old cigarettes. I could also see that she had applied body glitter to her ample bosom, torso, and thighs as a finishing touch.

As I watched the light reflect off the glitter, highlighting her more erogenous zones, I understood her choice; even though it seemed a bit much at a glance, the effect was actually quite aesthetically pleasing once she got moving. I began wondering if perhaps I was outclassed and didn't realize it and suddenly felt self-conscious.

I shut down slightly, focusing on the music and my client and stealing glances at the other woman whenever I could. As I was rubbing my bare breasts in my client's face, she stood up in front of her client and seductively broadcasted that she was about to remove her top. The man watching her was blind with drunken lust, eyeing her like a hungry puppy. She batted her eyelashes at him, and unclasped the back of her bra, letting her big, fake titties flop free.

As I watched her boobies bounce in time with the music, I couldn't help but feel like something was off. I observed her closely now, determined to figure out what felt 'off'. Sitting in the client's lap, I peered over, still not able to put my finger on what seemed out of place.

When she turned and I saw her full-frontal nudity for the first time, it hit me: her nipples.

She obviously had her tits done, but the surgeon had made a horrible, tragic mistake. Her nipples were asymmetric, and with the size of her areolas, it gave her chest the appearance of a cock-eyed, questioning owl.

Caught off guard, I snorted, then erupted into a full on fit of laughter. I couldn't help myself; seeing her nipples point in different directions was just too good. Here was this prissy, stuck-up cunt that had been treating me like trash, and underneath all her glitz and glamour was a hilariously bad boob job. She saw my expression and shot me a dirty look, and my moment of insecurity faded; this woman was probably such a bitch because she was self-conscious about her physical shortcomings in a profession where looks meant everything.

As the hour came to a close and I wrapped things up, I left the booking feeling less bothered by the rude behavior of my coworker; she could be a jerk, flirt with my boyfriend, and have nice legs, but at least I had normal nipples.

As I chuckled, I wondered what her private shows were like. It was a well-known tactic for clients to insult the escort/dancer, in a bid to lower her self-confidence and curb negotiations in their favor.

These men would say mean, hurtful things that exaggerated physical shortcomings, and even act entirely disinterested, claiming that we weren't *good enough*. This was always immediately followed by the client *feeling sorry* for having dragged us out to his house coupled with an egregiously lowball offer for high ticket services.

It was transparent and it had happened so frequently that we all recognized it for what it was and laughed it off. But for someone like my coworker, who was still green and possessed an obvious, glaring physical imperfection, I couldn't even begin to imagine the awful things they said to her. I wondered if when she was having a bad day, she let the craftier clients get to her and allowed herself to be taken advantage of.

It was all very sad to me, and by the time I got back to the car, I had shifted from hating her to feeling sorry for her. It wasn't as if she planned for the surgeon to so thoroughly botch her boob job, and she was left dealing with it until the mistake was fixed.

Once I got in the seat and closed the door, I saw my boyfriend looking around for my coworker. He was doing a poor job of hiding it, and I rolled my eyes; he was on his way out the door with me anyway, so his dirtbag boyfriend act wasn't getting under my skin.

CHAPTER SIXTEEN

Meat Flap

C ompany policy was to have a woman at a client's home within an hour after calling unless the address was particularly remote and far away. This meant that if one of the workers decided not to show up at the last minute, our boss would scramble to still get the client an acceptable substitute within the time frame.

The newer workers were more prone to this kind of behavior and often called in crippled by the 'stomach flu'. I did my best not to judge and rolled my eyes when I saw track marks on these women at work, and kept to myself. We all had our own demons, and drugs seemed to be a common issue for my co-workers. For the most part, their behavior didn't bother me, except for when it cut into my free time; as a seasoned and reliable employee, I was generally sent out whenever they didn't do their job.

Client Mark

One night, I got a text around dinner time telling me I had been booked for a one-hour show and that the other woman bailed at the last second, so I had to stop whatever I was doing and get my ass to work immediately.

That particular night, I had been studying for hours while watching movies to keep it interesting and wasn't anticipating going to work. I had taken the night off and hadn't planned to be entertaining any men that night, so I needed to shave, my hair was a mess, and I wasn't wearing makeup. It was a hassle, but my boss had promised a larger cut of the booking fee and swore it would be my only call of the night. I agreed, reluctant to leave the cozy solitude of my home, knowing that staying in her good graces was far more valuable than any extra cash she could offer.

After reviewing the address and seeing it was less than thirty minutes away, I decided to take my time and make myself extra sexy and presentable. I was already going to be late, so spending a couple extra minutes refining my look might be the difference between a grumpy customer and an eager lap dog. I skipped to the bathroom, grabbed my razor and turned on the shower, trying to shift my mindset from stay-at-home frump to fantasy dream girl.

For reasons I don't fully understand, neither at the time or now over a decade later, that night I was feeling exceptionally sexy and had a whole-body sensation of walking on cloud nine. I was almost giddy as I shaved my legs, my mind a racing haze of hopeful positivity. Instead of grumbling and brooding about how much I hated my job, I smiled as I did my hair and makeup, enjoying the process while practicing sultry smiles in the mirror.

Finished, I gave myself a quick up-and-down and felt like an irresistible tigress; my hair fell perfectly, free of frizz while framing my face, and my body was a pillar of femininity. I was brimming with an insatiable zest for life and felt waves of sexual energy radiating off of me like a perverse, horny sun. Whether or not I was actually irresistible was irrelevant; I was unshakably confident and viewed the glass as half full in every thought and action.

Leading up to that night, I had been getting one good booking after another. It had been well over a week of friendly patrons that fed both my ego and my wallet, filling me up with top-dollar tips and flattering words for easy work. The stars were aligned, and I felt invincible.

Not wanting to break my streak, I picked out an extra skimpy, black lacey number for my dance routine, complete with matching thigh highs. The cascading waves of my hair and smokey, seductive makeup paired perfectly with the slinky, sexy ensemble I selected. I even decided to break my own rule and donned my favorite slutting dress, an item usually reserved for picking up men for my personal amusement during my off time. As a finishing touch, I completed the look with my lucky heels, so named because I wore them when I was really hoping to get lucky.

Normally, I always chose flats. As a matter of personal safety, I avoided wearing heeled shoes to work because they inhibited my ability to escape quickly and effectively should unforeseen shenanigans ensue. Additionally, heels were a poor choice for foot protection against broken glass or debris, which I encountered regularly when navigating seedy motel parking lots and crossing city streets.

Still, despite my better judgment, I chose to wear them anyway and admired myself in the mirror. I felt like a tiger, but if a tiger was an early twenties woman dressed like a cheap skank and on a mission to empty men's wallets. I could feel lightning coursing through my veins as I knew for certain that it was going to be a night to remember. Something spoke to me, stirring from the depths deep within my soul, and I was convinced that I was about to have a darling evening with a passionate, handsome man. I would love every moment of my job while he swept me off my feet and made sweet, sweet love to me.

I tittered to myself, lost in my internal fantasy world of sensual romance and the promise of falling in love. I had just finished watching the movie *Pretty Woman* moments before my boss called me, and no one could tell me it wasn't my destiny to meet my rich, intelligent, charismatic Mr. Right at work.

I sang along to sappy love songs the whole ride to the client's home, raising my voice to cracking, awful falsettos with each passing chorus. I flashed playful winks at myself as I drove, my attention split between the road and my elaborate daydreams. He would be tall, blonde, have a friendly smile that warmed up the whole room, and striking green eyes. I blinked, imagining my Mr. Right, surprised when my GPS chimed that I had arrived at my destination. So lost in thought, I only partially remembered the drive, and giggled with excitement.

I fished through my purse, hastily reapplying my lipstick to a perfect shade of crimson and darkening my already smoldering eyes. I fretted over my hair, parting it on either side before deciding on the left, and spritzed myself with fruity perfume. I couldn't keep myself from smiling, and the muscles of my face were starting to feel tired. I gave myself one last excited grin in the mirror before I squealed lightly and stepped out of my car.

Right away, something was wrong. The house was in a lower middle-class neighborhood, and the grass looked like it hadn't been cut in months. Instead of tasteful contemporary art pieces, the yard was decorated with rusting lawn chairs and broken cars. Confused, I double-checked the address on my phone, puzzled as to why my prince charming was here instead of at his lofty, high-end condo on the other side of town.

Even the car in the driveway was an older model, and the dull, sun-bleached paint of the house looked like it hadn't been touched up since before I was born. Dumbfounded, my mind began racing, struggling to make sense of what I was seeing. Was this his friend's house? Was he undercover for a covert operation that required him to 'lay low' and avoid raising suspicion? Or maybe he was housesitting for his ailing grandmother, tending to her every need and treating her with love and care as she slowly said her final goodbyes to a cruel, dark world. I shut my eyes and smiled.

Yes, his grandmother, how could I be so dumb?

I immediately grabbed hold with one hundred percent certainty of what I considered the only rational explanation for what was in front of me. It wasn't a mental stretch to do this either, because *obviously* my dream man doesn't live in this dumpy hovel, and *obviously* he drove a nice car.

Gosh, he is such a kind soul to care for his dying grandmother. I love him. I thought to myself as I gathered my things and took my keys out of the ignition.

I smiled to myself, blushing as my errant thoughts renewed my confidence. I actively dismissed any idea that questioned my beliefs, refusing to betray my hapless optimism.

Adjusting my bra so my tits were loud and proud on display through the deep V of my blue dress, I strutted to the front door and rang the bell. I did my best salacious pose on the grimy doorstep, wanting to be sure I made a good first impression to start the evening off on the right foot.

My Romeo answered the door, and the shroud that had bewitched my heart and snared my soul melted away in an instant and left me stunned as reality smacked me in the face.

My client was a big guy. No, not big, *huge*. He was obese. The kind of obese where the folds had folds, and the chins had chins. This was the type of man I would see in public and wonder, with complete seriousness, how he could manage to walk, wipe his ass, or simply clean himself in the shower. Maybe it was cruel to harbor those kinds of thoughts and judgments, but for someone of his size, I couldn't help but wonder.

Because of his weight and thick, blocky glasses, his age was not entirely discernable. It seemed that he was vaguely more than thirty but less than sixty, his wrinkles, if any, were filled out with a generous layer of adipose tissue. I frowned, surveying the large U-shaped bald spot nestled on the top of his head, and grimaced when I saw a halfhearted attempt to conceal this baldness by combing a few stringy, greasy strands over it. His face was riddled with cystic acne and scraggly facial hair that trailed past his ruddy cheeks and down the entire length of all of his chins. Judging by the bits of food and unidentifiable gunk nestled within the hair on his face, it appeared that he hadn't shaved or washed his face in anticipation of my arrival.

His clothes, which looked in dire need of a wash, barely fit him. His giant, hairy flap of an underbelly was visibly hanging beneath his t-shirt and folding over the front of his pants like a grotesque flesh-colored apron. A pair of suspenders, which I suspected were the only thing holding up his pants, were holding on for dear life under the massive strain.

And the smell.

My stomach turned. My curiosity pertaining to how people so large bathed properly was, in part, partially answered because there was *no way* he smelled that badly if he took showers on a regular basis. He was exuding a scent akin to souring milk and rank urine that lingered heavily in the air. My stomach lurched, twisting into knots as his stench filled my nostrils, and I almost yakked right onto his feet.

My client, seemingly used to such reactions, ignored my revulsion, and his lips twisted into a crooked smile, revealing a mouth full of yellowing teeth. His meaty sausage fingers casually gestured me forward. The hairs on the back of my neck raised as a chill ran down my spine; I was about to spend an hour with this man, this giant, awful, stinky man, and there was nothing I could do about it.

Aghast, I watched as the enormous specimen awkwardly shifted his body to maneuver into the dark entryway. Loud thuds filled my ears with each heavy step as he waddled slowly onward, not bothering to turn around to ensure I was following.

Regret permeated every pore of my being; perhaps if I wasn't so dressed up and out of place I could have pretended to be at the wrong house and had an easy out. I could have possibly pulled off being a new neighbor needing a cup of sugar or even claimed that I had broken down in front of his house and needed to use the phone.

But, due to my provocative attire, there was no mistaking it. I was too out of place for the area and looked exactly like what I was: a call girl. Regular people didn't wander around residential areas on a Wednesday night knocking on doors with their tits out on full display.

I sighed, grimly aware that it was too late for me to ditch without getting in trouble, so I rallied myself mentally for whatever horrors awaited me. I crossed the threshold, my legs heavy as lead, and reluctantly followed him inside. My optimism faded and was replaced with a cloying depression that suffocated me as the door shut behind me.

Fuck.

I had let that stupid movie captivate me, ensnaring my better judgment with its irreverent fairy tale fantasy of true love and overcoming the odds.

The walkway was dim and felt faintly claustrophobic as I stepped deeper inside. Slowly, my eyes adjusted, and the contents of the home came into focus. Have you ever heard of the term for people who never throw things away, called hoarding? This man's home was the poster child for this mental illness. There was aging junk stacked literally everywhere: books, newspapers, paper plates, bags of trash, dishes, loose cat litter, you name it. I could see what looked like a plate of half-eaten dinner, fork and all, turning black with mold on top of a pile of yellowing towels.

For me, a person who needed to feel clean at all times and practically panicked when someone so much as sneezed on them, I was in hell. The client, also apparently used to such reactions from strangers when they saw his home, chuckled darkly in response to my disturbed reaction.

A hard lump filled my throat as it dawned on me that this twisted son of a bitch knew exactly what a gross fat fuck he was and enjoyed that I had no choice but to tolerate him since he ordered me from the agency. I was trapped, his prisoner for the next sixty minutes, and he was getting sick satisfaction from it.

I kicked myself for wearing my favorite dress and lucky heels, knowing they would be tossed straight into the garbage after tonight. Defeated, I silently continued following him, dodging stray bits of trash as I went.

As I did my best to breathe as little as possible to avoid gagging, I carefully made my way through a small snaking path that led through the towering piles of decaying trash on either side. It began at the main walkway by the front door, passed by the kitchen, and then took you through the hallway and to the master bedroom. The living room and bathroom were both connected to the hallway and had their own little paths cleared out to make them accessible. Despite his size, his body made no contact with the rotting garbage surrounding us, the path vertically expanded to accommodate his rotund form.

Eventually, after proceeding at a snail's pace, we made it to his living room. There, amidst the debris, was a television and couch that sat flush against a large window overlooking the front yard. Like the rest of the home, the couch was also covered in what appeared to be years of decaying junk, rendering it useless except for the large, body-shaped recession molded into the trash.

I gagged, having never seen something so disgusting in my life. I began to wonder if the home was a biohazard to myself and his neighbors, teeming with pestilence and potential threats to human life. Ignoring me, my client collapsed into the couch, perfectly fusing into the available space while trash hugged him on either side.

He farted, letting out a pleased grunt, and I frowned. He was staring at me now, beady-eyed and expecting me to do something, so I said the only thing I could think of.

"I need to collect the booking fee and check in with my boss. Do you have somewhere I can change into something more comfortable?" I uttered my rehearsed line robotically, trying to show as little emotion as possible.

Yes, he was a nasty fuck, but if I was outwardly rude about it, he might take offense and not offer me a tip.

Without a word, he nodded his head towards the hallway. I had seen the bathroom door on my way over and shuddered at the thought of what it looked like inside. After collecting the booking fee and stuffing it into my purse, I made my way out of the living room, dreading each step as I went.

My share of the booking fee was only thirty dollars, and if I didn't make any tips, I would have exposed myself to all this filth for nothing. My client, hulking and grotesque, was not worth any amount of tips he could possibly offer, and a cloud of misery settled over me. I would likely make no real money and gain only an insatiable urge to take a shower for having been there. I shut my eyes, wanting to cry but unable to ruin my makeup, and desperately wishing I could be anywhere else.

Once I got to the bathroom, I hesitated; I didn't want to touch the knob, and honestly barely wanted to open the door. If there had been enough space, I would have changed in the hallway, but it was too cluttered with years' worth of junk. I gulped, staring at the dirty, stained wooden door in front of me, unable to will my hand forward.

I didn't want to know what was on the other side and felt my pulse begin to quicken. After seeing the state the rest of the house was in, I was concerned about exposure to diseases from his bathroom. This man didn't clean his house, or even his body for that matter, so I had real doubts that he washed his hands after taking a dump. And based on his smell, I wasn't positive he even *wiped* himself after taking a dump, either.

I stood there, petrified of the potential germs I might encounter by simply touching the doorknob. My mind raced, frantically trying to remember anything I could about how long bacteria and viruses could survive on various surfaces.

My brain, hellbent on preventing me from entering the bathroom, assaulted me with an onslaught of images showcasing people stricken with exotic diseases. Each time I started to move my hand toward the metallic surface, memories of my disgusting client and his pungent odor left me paralyzed.

Frozen by fear, I cannot say if I stood there for five minutes, or fifteen. My life, and all the choices I had made leading up to that point, flashed before my eyes, and for the first time in a long time, I questioned what I was doing with my life.

Knowing I could only get away with deliberating in the hallway for so long before the client complained, I swallowed my fear and reached for the knob. My hand shook slightly as the sensation of cold, moist metal collided with the warmth of my palm. I could feel the molecules of my skin fusing with the filthy, germ-riddled surface and wanted to scream. I gagged, my mouth filling with copious amounts of saliva, my stomach threatening to spill its contents on the already soiled carpet.

Holding my breath, I firmly gripped the doorknob, twisting it slowly and sealing my fate. With a final nudge, the door creaked open, and I shut my eyes, expecting to be hit immediately with a wall of unbearable, crippling stink.

Instead, the gentle scent of air freshener intermingling with fresh laundry tickled my nose. I opened my eyes, surprised that the bathroom, while awful, was not nearly as bad as I thought it would be. Sure, the toilet bowl looked like it had never been cleaned *ever*, and was covered in a layer of thick, black sludge, but it wasn't the worst I had seen at work.

I thoughtfully noted that all the surfaces had soap scum, and that the wallpaper was peeling in all the corners revealing black mold behind it, but it still could have been worse. The piles of bunched up bath towels and dirty underwear were certainly off-putting, and the collection of frayed toothbrushes on the sink was surprising, but nothing close to the pile of rotting excrement that I had pictured. Taking another look at the toothbrushes, I felt surprised; with how bad his teeth looked, I wouldn't have guessed he brushed at all. All the signs in the bathroom pointed to regular use, so I shrugged and began getting changed.

Was I overly judgmental? Yes, definitely, and I suddenly began to feel very bad for expecting the worst. There was evidence that he was at least trying in some capacity to better his personal hygiene, which was more effort than I gave him credit for. Yet, with all the good graces I could muster, I simply could not look beyond the glaring fact that he was a humongous, smelly bastard. Even the linoleum was nasty, peeling up in some places and stained dark brown from years of neglect.

No longer shocked, I giggled in the mirror as bemusement took over. Deciding to live in such filth suddenly seemed hilarious, and I reflected on the absurdity of it all while getting changed. Knowing that the chances were slim I'd ever see such a deplorable space again, I decided that a photo was needed for prosperity.

Tittering deviously, I snapped a photo of the dastardly toilet with just the tips of my thigh-high covered toes poking into the frame. Feeling especially mischievous, I posted it to social media with the description *if you can afford me, you can afford to pay someone to clean your house* and began laughing hysterically.

Looking back, this was in incredibly poor taste, and I never should have done it. I did end up removing it a couple of days later after being chided by one of my very few close friends, realizing that perhaps the photo gave away more information about my personal life than I ever intended to share.

When I had finished taking photos and getting dressed, I collected my thoughts and decided I was ready to get things over with. I was no longer a germophobic, barely functional shell of myself, and was more optimistic about dealing with the fat fuck waiting in the next room. I left the bathroom, carefully using a napkin from my bag to avoid touching the doorknob a second time, and made my way to the living room with the confidence of a prowling lioness.

He was sitting there, not having moved a single inch, waiting patiently for me on the couch with his suspender straps pulled down on either side. I observed that his belly flap was resting snugly between his fat thighs and covering his crotch, and the gears in my mind began to turn.

His meat flap obscured access to his genitalia, and I wondered if he could reach it at all. No stranger to fat clients, I knew all too well the challenges of contending with excess flub; a client struggling to push down enough fat to cause their penis to pop out was a normal part of my life. Without blunt physical force keeping the fat at bay, their cocks were swallowed completely into an abyss of their own poor dietary habits. How they managed to pee without getting piss all over themselves was a mystery to me, but judging by the pee smell emanating from my client, I reasoned that perhaps some of them couldn't help it.

His heavy, strained, open-mouthed breathing sent a shiver of disgust down my spine; his yellowed, crooked teeth were twisted into another demented grin, and I knew I needed to get out of the booking fast. The problem was, I couldn't just leave because he was gross without catching hell from the agency.

Weighing my options, I determined the easiest way to pull off a speedy escape without losing any brownie points was to price the client out of my services. All that was actually included with the booking fee was a strip tease to nude dance show, and the rest was up to negotiation. If he couldn't pay, he couldn't pay, and I wouldn't be in the wrong for cutting things short. I frowned as a microcosm of spittle dribbled down his fat, lower lip, and felt a pang of queasiness demanding urgent execution of my plan. The idea was to make my services so absurdly expensive that he would have no choice but to settle for the basic show, and hedging on the state of his home and yard, that wouldn't be a challenge.

I grinned, patting myself mentally on the back for being so clever, and let out a sigh of relief knowing the nightmare would soon be over. There was no penalty for leaving a booking early if all they could afford was the basic show, so I was essentially ten minutes of bullshitting away from being completely off the hook.

Standing up straight and tall, I looked at my client coquettishly and planned my attack; I thought of a number that I knew was ridiculous, and doubled it. I began prattling away about the general rules of the agency like always, then casually dropped the bomb of my sky-high prices. I
196

looked down at my nails, pretending to absentmindedly examine them while I spoke matter-of-factly about how not everyone can afford me, and that without the tip all you get is the basic show.

Before I could finish, he held up a credit card between two fingers.

Son of a bitch.

Frozen in place, my brain struggled to register what it was seeing; he had called my bluff, and I had just locked myself into an entire hour of nude lap dances. I did my best to maintain my composure as I silently took the credit card from his hand and examined it closely.

Surely, it was a fake, because the room I was standing in was probably days away from being legally condemned. I held the card inches from my face, pouring over every detail, praying it was counterfeit.

Nope.

A hot, tight lump grew in my throat as my fingertips grew white, firmly pressed into the hard plastic. I took a breath, calming myself, convinced I had missed a detail. Surely it was expired, because a person so vile and repugnant couldn't afford me. My eyes nervously flitted to the four little numbers that could grant me my freedom.

Nope.

My hands trembled slightly as panic set in. It was clean, it was shiny, and it had his mother fucking name stamped across it in neat, orderly letters. The card was real, and I had ruined my one chance at escaping that hell hole by not asking for more.

I blinked, biting my lip and unable to speak. There was nothing I could do now, and going back on the bargain was out of the question. Since the agency took a whopping ten percent of all credit card tips, if I changed my mind and they found out about it, I would be in deep shit.

Begrudgingly, I started going through the necessary motions needed to process the transaction and take his money. I tried to stall as much as possible, dragging out the process for as long as I could while he silently waited on the couch, regarding me lustily with his beady little eyes. I hemmed and hawed, pretending to have technical difficulties, and even 'accidentally' dropped the card several times, interrupting the process altogether. My final attempts to burn the clock, while pathetic, were all I had left.

I gulped when I got the confirmation text, the audible ding of my phone a peal of sorrow. With the transaction finalized, I was out of excuses. I looked at the disgusting wretch of a man resting on the couch, his forehead dripping with sweat from the summer heat, and steeled my nerves.

With no other choice, I did the only thing I could do: shift my focus from the insufferable reality waiting for me to calculated pragmatism. My head tilted to the side while I pensively eyed the challenge the enormous flesh apron created.

How the hell do I give a lap dance with that thing in the way?

Being a natural problem solver, my mind set to work addressing the conundrum set before me. The easiest answer would've been for him to lie down on his back, but I doubted his ability to breathe properly in that position due to his weight. Due to the piles of trash on either side, I couldn't ask him to recline back to thirty to forty-five degrees, either. Asking him to hold it out of the way wasn't practical, either, considering how sweaty he got from just walking over to the couch. I had serious doubts that he was physically strong enough to lift it away for moments, let alone for thirty minutes while I danced. I had serious doubts that I would fair any better, and even if I did, I couldn't exactly give him a lap dance at the same time.

Studying him, I had a nagging anxiety building within me about what sort of *things* were lurking beneath the flap since lifting it was such an issue; I imagined bits of food, a yellowing, cheesy substance, and a smell so intense that I would pass out.

He was already quite smelly, and I speculated that lifting the flap would only make things ten times worse. Would he make me keep going if I was actively gagging and vomiting? I wasn't sure, but I didn't want to find out. Encountering unusual kinks was an almost daily occurrence, and nothing surprised me anymore. Knowing my luck, this could be the one guy on the planet who got off by making women spew chunks. His previous behavior already told me that he was a sadistic fuck, so picturing him feverishly masturbating while I splattered my lingerie with streams of puke wasn't much of a stretch.

Sighing deeply, I opted to do my routine on his lap as best I could, which boiled down to dancing on his knee while his nasty belly rubbed and pushed against my bum. While I danced, his body moved right along with mine and started to heat up. The foul stench of his body intensified the hotter he got, and I had to bite my lip to keep from screaming.

As I gyrated on his knee, thoughts of what horrors lurked beneath the flap haunted me; I would get little whiffs whenever he repositioned in even the smallest of ways, and each time it made my stomach spasm in protest. I sat there, dancing robotically, waiting for the sweet chime of my alarm to set me free.

During the portion of my routine where I was bent over and rubbing my ass cheeks provocatively, he motioned for me to stop. Confused, I stood up and faced him, out of patience for any last minute bullshit.

He leaned back, pressing himself deeper into the trash, and using all the strength of his dominant arm, he pulled up the belly flap so his crotch was visible. The skin underneath was shiny and pink, with bits of white in the cracks. It smelled absolutely foul, like a mix of souring milk, sweat, and urine. The smell filled the room and smacked me in the face, almost flooring me. Even though I was mentally screaming, I didn't want to give that asshole the satisfaction of seeing me fall to pieces in front of him.

Taking a closer look at his groin region, I realized that he was not wearing underwear or bottoms of any kind underneath. My eyes scanned his pubic region, and slowly trailed their way to the center of his crotch, my curiosity too strong to avoid taking a peek.

Like most profoundly heavier guys I had seen, he needed to push back the pubic fat around his penis in order to make it more accessible. This was to be expected for someone his size, but this was the worst I had ever seen. There was no evidence of his penis at all, and it seemed that his body had swallowed it whole. Based on the growth pattern of his pubes, I had a strong inkling of where his penis *should* be but only saw a concentrated fluff of hair in that spot.

While I stood there dumbfounded, my client reached over with his other hand and started pushing down hard into his blubber. Based on the hand placement, I knew he was trying to force back his girth in order to bring his penis to the surface.

It was clear that physically, this was a challenge for him. Holding up the belly apron while simultaneously pushing down into his fat was a struggle for him, and he began grunting and turning bright red from exertion. Sweat appeared on his furrowed brow as he grunted and puffed, struggling against the weight of his own massive form.

I watched, utterly mesmerized, unable to look away from the bizarre spectacle. As he fought to reposition his body fat, one thought popped into my mind and would not leave.

How does this guy masturbate?

Physically, it didn't seem possible, and images of wooden planks rigged with ropes danced in my mind, and I giggled. He was barely able to get his penis to poke out from his belly fat, and without a third hand, it didn't seem possible to make it work. I was doubtful, but years in the sex industry had taught me one thing: men always found a way.

So, I watched, of course not offering any help, as he strained against the self-imposed limitations of his own body. Eventually, he managed to maneuver himself in such a way that I could make out a penis poking through. He was now turning quite red and growing sweatier by the second, the battle of attrition against himself unfolding before me. Now that I could get a good look at his privates, I had the impression that he likely hadn't properly cleaned his genitals in ages. Which, to be fair, made sense given how much work it was for him to even expose that part of his body to the ambient air.

He was looking intently at me now, growing more exhausted with each passing second, jerking his head towards his crotch. His nonverbal communication, frantic as he continued his onslaught against gravity, told me everything I needed to know. I was no fool, but blessedly, he didn't know that.

I stood there, staring blankly back at him, unmoving. What was he going to do, chase me? Force me to touch him? He could barely touch himself, and in his state, the idea of forcing me to do anything was laughable. I could walk at a normal pace and leave him in the dust if things went awry, so I fearlessly decided to play dumb. Instead of obliging his unspoken request, I just stood there quietly, watching his mounting frustration as his cheeks grew scarlet red from exertion.

I never understood guys like this; be it at work or in my personal life, it was almost like they thought that since I was there and they were aroused, I was obligated to pleasure them. Yes, contextually it probably made sense for the client to feel that way, but I was still a person and maintained the right to choose regardless. Besides, we had not negotiated anything beyond a nude lap dance show, so making assumptions was his fault alone.

The more I ignored him, the more frustrated he grew with my outright lack of obedience. He was huffing and puffing like a chimney, but it didn't faze me in the slightest. I could care less about implied social conventions, and certainly not ones that pressured me into performing sex acts.

Turning from impatient to angry, he started barking orders at me to touch his penis, demanding to know what I was waiting for. He was a hot, sweaty mess, and reminded me of an overcooked baked potato. Almost shaking, he was barely maintaining his unnatural positioning, so I decided to take full advantage of his lack of mobility. I ignored everything he asked and stared vacantly off into space.

I picked up my phone and began to fiddle with it absently; there was no way I would willingly touch his cheesy red rocket, and his angry complaints meant less than nothing to me. As far as I was concerned, I was already paid, and engaging with him further wasn't required. He continued to yell at me, pausing to catch his breath as he strained between words, as I waited patiently for my alarm to release me; I was under zero obligation to touch his repulsive meat stick, and didn't plan on it.

Perhaps sensing this, he suddenly let go of his flab just long enough to fish out his credit card. Furious, he chucked it across the room at me. I watched in slow motion as the card hurdled across the room and collided with my cheek before falling to the floor. I made a show of tilting my head towards the card, and then back at the client, before very deliberately shaking my head *no*.

201

My rejection paired with his mounting exhaustion was seemingly the final straw. He screeched obscenities at me while I blankly stared back at him, unfazed.

What a guy.

As my client went to pieces and roared that I accept his money, the sweet, sweet sound of my alarm began chiming. A smile spread across my lips, and I mouthed the word *goodbye* before quickly making my exit. I could hear him, enraged and furious, still yelling at me to come back as the front door slammed shut behind me.

CHAPTER SEVENTEEN
Puddles

It would be unfair to say that my job was all work and no play. While there certainly were no shortage of assholes that pushed my patience to the brink, there were also some real gems. But I am not referring to a steamy rendezvous or an overly generous tip. I am talking about something far rarer, and much more valuable: a unique kind of man that not only paid me, but allowed me to scratch an elusive itch that otherwise left me in wanting.

Client Terrance

It had been a dry couple of weeks, and I wasn't anticipating getting any calls. This was the unpredictably predictable part of being an escort that I had grown used to and now found mind-numbingly boring. Things would randomly slow down, and before I knew it, I wasn't even shaving my legs.

After being home every night for weeks, I was hairy, unkempt, and sort of smelly. I had grown comfortable with doing nothing and secretly wished it could go on this way forever. I found that I didn't mind lazing around all day getting lost in books and exploring various creative endeavors. If I didn't have to waste time putting on makeup or styling my hair, I had more opportunities to delve deeper into neglected hobbies.

I welcomed the sudden ability to practice my talents; work itself had become an endless stream of monotonous routine sprinkled with the same dull requests over and over again. I was bored, and even before the dry spell, I had been dragging my feet in response to getting a call.

Being an avid reader had not prepared me for the banality of existence. I wanted the excitement and adventure inherent in all the stories I read, but was stuck in the inescapable rut that was my real life.

It had been years since I took the job at the agency, and the dazzle had long since faded into the grimy reality of getting naked for strangers. Life was a never-ending stream of stale cigarettes and bad manners, and I craved substance. I had become a shadow of my former self and was uninspired, unmotivated, and subsisting primarily off of coffee and a bad attitude. I was desperate for something new to kickstart my soul and inject some living back into my life.

When I got the text from my boss that night, I was confused. It had been so long without work that I thought I hallucinated when I heard the ding from the other room. Glancing at the phone, I realized the booking was real and that I was completely unprepared; I needed a shower, to shave, to do my hair, my makeup, the whole shebang.

GPS calculated that this guy was at least thirty minutes' drive away, which cut my prep time extremely short. I scrambled, frantically trying to undo weeks of neglected personal hygiene, shaving with one foot propped in the bathroom sink and hoping eyeliner alone would suffice.

When I grabbed my bag and bolted out of the house, I looked OK but wasn't up to my usual snuff. Feeling my best made me more confident, and that confidence was the difference between a good tip and a great tip.

I needed to top up my accounts since I hadn't been to work in weeks, and I was mildly concerned my one shot at redemption was about to be a colossal flop. As I sped down the road, I fretted over my makeup; at stoplights, I managed to apply lipstick, brush on a few coats of mascara, and even smoke out my eyeliner.

The lack of relaxed preparation had left a funk hanging over me like a dark cloud. Switching gears so quickly from lounging to rushing left me discombobulated, and I thoroughly disliked the sensation; a calm headspace was essential to project my fake personality at work, and I worried I couldn't pull it off. Men who called me were not interested in an uber-nerdy, socially awkward weirdo. At work, executing my fake persona was everything.

During the drive to the client's home, I paused at the outskirts of the neighborhood to take a look around. The area appeared pleasant enough and gave strong upper-middle-class vibes.

I was still working on getting my act together when another car pulled up beside me full of rowdy twenty-somethings. It was late at night, and I guessed the designated driver was shuttling his inebriated buddies. The men leaned out the windows and made crude, sexual comments, jeering at me as they tried to convince me to follow them home.

I hated drunk men, and having to deal with them when I wasn't at work filled me with contempt.

I felt my blood pressure rising as my face grew hot. My knuckles gripped the steering wheel, and my eye began to twitch as my threadbare patience grew precariously close to snapping. They obnoxiously carried on, loudly trying to get my attention as I seethed.

Normally, I would have coyly dismissed them, but being that I wasn't mentally prepared for shenanigans, I cussed them out and drove off in a huff. Speeding away, I breathed heavily and turned my music to full blast. I was a mess, and even if I looked my best, I was in no shape to go to a booking.

By the time I pulled into the client's driveway, I was a tangled ball of nerves. I was lost in a downward spiral that centered entirely around my disdain for men coupled with a burning hatred for my job; I hated men, therefore I hated my job.

When I knocked on my client's door, I had the charming disposition of a pouty teenage girl. I stood there, arms crossed and hip jutted to the side, glowering at the flowers on the porch. The soft sound of footsteps padding their way toward the front entrance alerted me to my client, but I didn't care. I continued examining the flowers, muttering to myself.

The footsteps paused just behind the door, and a flash of darkness over the peephole signaled that he was scoping me out. Unable to control myself, I rolled my eyes and stared directly back at him.

As I defiantly locked eyes with the peephole, the lock slid out of place and the door opened. My client invited me inside, putting his finger to his mouth while saying *shhhh*.

Great. So my client was some dickhead with a sleeping baby in the backroom, or his wife passed out drunk on the couch. I didn't have the mental willpower to fake pleasantries, so I scowled and entered his home without a word.

Once inside, I crossly surveyed my client with all the allure of a prickly cactus. He was about six feet tall, thinly built with a little bit of a pot belly, with dark hair and a clean-shaven face. He smelled faintly of soap and cologne, a likely indicator that he had just gotten out of the shower. For a total stranger, he was remarkably affable, and I suspected right away that this was someone's husband.

The rows of tastefully arranged pictures of his wife and kids dotting the walls of his house confirmed my assumptions; he was indeed a kept man, and a well mannered one at that. His wife was positively radiant, arguably more beautiful than myself, and he looked genuinely happy with her in the photos.

There were no fake-looking smiles or any evidence otherwise of an unhappy marriage; their faces had the cheesy, full-faced, shit-eating grins that only true joy created. Even the kids looked happy, which was saying something.

I also noticed small things around the house that told me that the couple was thoroughly in love with each other. His and hers sports equipment, matching canvases from boozy paint nights, and other products that displayed abundant quality time as a couple. I stared at the various photos and knickknacks and frowned. This was a happy marriage. Why was I here?

It was very common for a married guy to call me once the wife and kids were safely out of town, but it was normally a different dynamic. I didn't have any moral hang-ups associated with entertaining a married man, and in all honestly, most of my clients *were* married men. Unlike my other clients, this house advertised every sign of a healthy relationship, and I felt a twinge of guilt for sullying an otherwise perfect union.

I sighed deeply, put my hangups aside, and collected the booking fee. He gestured towards the bathroom and told me to meet him in his back bedroom when I was finished getting changed. I eyed him curiously, as his manner suggested an air of familiarity with this routine.

It was odd, but at its core this straightforward, cut-to-the-chase attitude was why I generally preferred married clients. Yes, it was terrible that a man was unfaithful, and yes I did feel awful when the marriage seemed like a happy one, but I always remained firmly in the camp that it was better for a man to call someone like me than have a full-fledged affair.

With me, there was no risk of an unexpected pregnancy or an emotional attachment that could break apart a functional family unit. No divorce, no custody disputes, no nothing. Discretion and anonymity were among the many perks our agency offered, and being strictly professional, I took great pride in not destroying the personal lives of my clients.

That unwavering desire to keep things as discrete and private as possible was partly what made married guys so ideal. Because of the fear of discovery, they wouldn't give me any problems. They couldn't risk bringing any kind of attention to what they were doing and as a result, they wouldn't hassle me and didn't pressure me for my personal phone number. They had families to take care of, and reputations to uphold. Risking damage to either of those was not an option, so things were as hush-hush as possible.

As a bonus, since this was such a rare treat for them, married men were prepared to pay whatever it took to finally scratch their itch. How long would it be until the wife and kids were out of town again? It could be years, or never, and they knew it. With such a narrow window of opportunity to explore their infidelity, they didn't waste time arguing over cost. They accepted my prices, no matter how inflated, to sate their lust while they still had the chance.

The only downside to being the other woman was having to play therapist for strangers' relationships. I had heard every story imaginable as an excuse to justify being unfaithful, and I was tired of it. The usual story was that their wives were cold, prudish bitches who never put out anymore, who neither appreciated nor respected them.

The unifying element to virtually all these stories was that it was always the wives' fault for forcing them into a position where they *had no other choice*. Being a woman myself, I knew this was bullshit; I could agree that women were undoubtedly awful at times and shared equal blame for a disintegrating relationship, but there was also the undeniable fact that sometimes people just wanted to cheat.

After a couple of years of hearing the same sob story in countless variations, I started stopping men before they even got started; I wasn't interested in hearing a woeful tale where they were victimized and forced tragically into infidelity. It honestly disgusted me that so many husbands demanded validation from me prior to committing the damning act itself; they wanted to offload their sense of guilt on me for betraying their spouse and expected me to take their side. I wanted nothing to do with reinforcing their self-preserving internal narrative and found the behavior almost as reprehensible as the cheating itself.

After years of watching men from every walk of life imaginable cheat on their partners, I viewed marriage as a farce. Having firsthand knowledge of how badly men treated their women both before and after the wedding, I considered tying the knot an expensive joke.

Pretending that formalizing a romantic union made men more inclined to be faithful was nothing short of a lie; I saw time and time again that men would cheat if given the opportunity, and it disgusted me. Over time, I started telling my clients that not only did I not care about the *why* behind their choice to be unfaithful, but that I also didn't care. I cut them off before they could get started, forcing them to bear the weight of their decision all on their own.

For miserable marriages, the cheating mostly made sense, but there was another group of attached men who called me on a regular basis. They didn't have wandering eyes, or even feel unheard or unwanted. Instead, they harbored secrets.

An otherwise happy man would call me because he had a fetish that he was too scared/ashamed/nervous about to openly share with his spouse. I often heard this scenario explained as giving in to a long-standing, burning hunger that had been festering away for years. After breaking down and finally deciding to explore the forbidden fruit, the husband would seek out creative ways to turn his ultimate fantasy into a reality. Cue the escort, the nonjudgmental flesh-vessel ready to explore any desire with no objections or questions asked.

Admittedly, as far as the fetish stuff went, all the secrecy was practical. It was not unheard of for marriages to become irreparably damaged after a wife accidentally uncovered a husband's closeted kinks, freaking out and shaming him in the process. The resulting pandemonium that ensued ended in relationship counseling, divorce, financial strain, and ultimately a feeling of guilt and humiliation instead of sexual satisfaction.

I was reflecting on this in the bathroom and mulling over which category my client fit into. It was clear that he had a loving relationship with his wife, so I doubted this was another case of *she is so terrible, feel bad for me*. All my experience told me that this guy was probably a freak and wanted something special that his wife simply couldn't provide. I sighed, looked down at my feet, and regretted not getting a pedicure recently.

Foot fetishes were incredibly common, and by far the most common secret kink I encountered. Men would pay top dollar to lick, suck, or even stuff my whole foot in their mouths. It was weird, but easy, and who was I to judge. A few times I was even paid to give a foot-job, which was basically jerking a guy off with nothing but my feet. Compared to other requests, it was fairly benign and low effort, so I never said no.

The prospect of a bizarre and possibly amusing admission of taboo debauchery was enough to help calm my brooding. My mindset floated away from my persistent angry internal dialogue and pleasantly settled on my current environment.

The client lived in a fairly standard middle-class home, and his wife was a lovely decorator. The bathroom was color-coordinated, with the hand towels even matching the shower curtain. It was very cozy, and I admired the warmth all the subtle efforts sprinkled throughout the bathroom provided. The scent of lavender drifting lazily from a candlelit diffuser soothed my nerves, the cushioned mat beneath my feet rested my spirit, and the immaculate cleanliness cleared my head.

I took a deep, cleansing breath, spritzed myself with body spray, and walked gingerly out of the bathroom, ready to dive into the evening. The first thing I noticed when I left the bathroom was that the client dimmed all the lights. Other than the occasional nightlight, the house was dark.

In other circumstances, I would have been afraid and anxious about the prospect of being murdered at any moment. Knowing that this was a married guy in his family home, I calmed my nerves and instead rationalized the sudden darkness.

The darkness was probably to minimize the risk of nosy neighbors catching a glimpse of another woman while his wife was away. I had some annoying neighbors of my own, so it made sense to obscure visibility through the windows.

Unfazed, I tiptoed down the hall, wanting to avoid stubbing my toe or bumping into walls. As I made my way down the hall, I could see flickering light emanating out from underneath the far door, beckoning me forward and teasing my curiosity.

Once inside, the room contained the standard queen-sized bedroom furniture setup, with the eye-catching addition of a gigantic flat-screen television mounted on the wall opposite to the bed. Like the house, the room was dim, with only the running light from the TV illuminating the space. As my eyes adjusted, I could see that the client was sitting on the bed, fully dressed, and fiddling with the remote.

So far, I hadn't been able to get a grasp on what this guy's deal was, so before I negotiated a tipping price for him, I wanted to feel him out a little. My foremost goal with a married guy was to squeeze every dollar I could out of him, and seeing how nice his house was, he likely had a healthy relationship with the bank. Experience told me that if I played my cards right, getting a fat tip from him was almost guaranteed.

Studying him silently, he tested buttons on the remote, seemingly unaccustomed to operating this particular television. He was focused on his task, but his excitement was tangible; instead of the nervous apprehension I expected from a married man, he seemed… giddy. In fact, he was positively buzzing with energy and had a huge grin on his face. This was no ordinary client, and this was not his first rodeo.

Before I could break the ice and start my slew of subtle manipulations, he cut straight to the point. He reached into the bedside table, dug around for a few moments, and produced a seven-inch dildo. He then pulled out a black leather strap-on harness and tossed it onto the bed in front of me.

210

"You ever seen one of these before?" he asked, his smile broadening.

The question was obviously meant to gauge my reaction and willingness to use it on him, so I kept up my poker face, not wanting to betray my hand just yet.

I picked up the harness and examined it closely. The harness, and the dildo, were both brand new, which was a requirement for me when using any sex toys with clients. I passed the dildo between my hands, pretending to contemplate my willingness to use it.

Unbeknownst to my client, I was over the moon. At the time, I hadn't even had the luxury of pegging a personal lover at home. Sure, I had brought it up plenty of times with some of the guys I fucked around with, but none were ever interested. The usual *I'm not gay* bullshit always ended the conversation before it ever got started. Explaining to a man that being sexually attracted to men is what makes you gay, not sticking things up your butt, was a losing battle nine times out of ten.

Feeling the soft, cool sensation of the dark leather on my skin, I smiled; I had been waiting so long to fuck a man in the ass, and now I was about to get paid for it. I realized that I needed to play it cool, and not give away my interest, or my lack of experience.

"Of course, I love pegging," I said slyly, matching my client's excited energy.

My choice of words was actually quite intentional. In the business, knowing the right terms made you sound more professional, and legitimacy translated to higher bargaining power. I was not some street walker that bumbled into his house after a meth binge, I was a classy call girl, which carried the unspoken connotation that I knew my shit.

In practice, however, I was never good at integrating slang with conversational language. It didn't make sense to me why I should substitute a perfectly good word for a made up one, and I found the whole business rather odd.

To make up for my lack of naturally occurring understanding, I kept a log of all the modern colloquialisms that I heard from my classmates at school. Each day after class, I would spend a few moments looking up each word using *Urban Dictionary*, an online dictionary for modernized language, and do my best to memorize them. It was a bit of a running joke on campus that I possessed such a document at all, and had more than one amused request to see it.

For work, however, I mostly picked up my sexualized vernacular from other escorts; I observed them closely and gleaned as much useful information as possible. Socially, I was incredibly inept and had historically struggled to comprehend the emotions and motives of others my entire life. It took dedicated effort and consistent practice to execute the casual behaviors I learned from my coworkers, and over time, no one was the wiser.

My client that night, seeing that I was unfazed by the strap-on and ready to play, sprang up in bed and grabbed the harness. He then paused for a moment, shifting his gaze to the dildo and fiddling with it absentmindedly before speaking.

"I haven't done something like this before... I don't know how much this costs...?" he said, unsure.

Jackpot.

"One thousand dollars an hour," I answered without missing a beat.

This, of course, was a lie, but he didn't know that.

Having never pegged a man at work, I had no established price point. I figured that this guy really wanted to get fucked, and wouldn't get another chance any time soon, so he would likely pay whatever I wanted.

And I was right.

He didn't even flinch at my words, and immediately reached into the same nightstand and pulled ten crisp one-hundred-dollar bills out of a bank envelope and handed them to me.

Damn!

The envelope was thickly padded with more cash, and in my urgency, I sold myself short. I could have easily demanded a higher price, but it was too late; we had already struck a bargain, and there was no going back now.

Even though I lost a chance to make more, I was thrilled; I had always wanted to peg someone, and it was actually kind of cool that I was getting paid for it. I had the benefit of knowing I'd probably never see this guy again, which meant I could let loose with no repercussions or worry. My usual hang ups with a loved one were that I would accidentally hurt him or otherwise have to deal with long term emotional consequences associated with pounding his ass into oblivion. Without any worries holding me back, I was ecstatic. The client, equally excited, handed over the harness with a huge grin on his face.

As I figured out how to put it on, he started a porno on the television. At first, I thought it was your typical Asian fetish stuff; there was a petite, tanned woman prancing around outside of a beach-style bungalow. Clad in a skimpy pink vinyl bikini, she posed for the camera, making kissy faces and rubbing her hands all over her body suggestively.

The camera zoomed in on her tits while she rubbed tiny circles on pointy, hard nipples through the bikini top. As far as porn went, it was fairly mild, and even kind of boring; having watched quite a bit of raunchy X-rated videos at work, this was the tamest I had seen.

The camera then panned down to the lady's crotch, and there it was. A big ol' Asian sausage poking from behind bright pink panties to say hello.

Ah.

The puzzle pieces clicked together, and I realized what was happening; this guy had a thing for Asian transexuals and wanted to watch 'tranny porn' while I pounded his butthole. I mean, as far as secret kinks go, it wasn't too bad. I actually found the client's excitement over getting pegged erotic and was delighted for the opportunity.

After adjusting the straps and ensuring everything fit snugly around my waist and thighs, I was ready to go. I wobbled the dildo around with my hips, savoring the unique sensation of having a cock-shaped object protruding from my body. I giggled, not caring that I was being watched, and did my best to get the dildo to swirl around like a windmill. My client laughed, seemingly pleased with my enthusiasm.

I then grabbed the dildo in my hand, inspecting it carefully and enjoying the heft. Based on the size of the dildo, I could tell he was only prepared to take a few inches, but I was about to give him a whole mile.

Glancing at my client, I could tell he was waiting for me to take the initiative. I grinned devilishly, not believing my good fortune; not only was he willing, but he was also submissive. This meant he would follow orders and let me take the lead, no questions asked.

Instead of climbing onto the bed and getting right to it, I walked over to the edge and beckoned him towards me. He crawled to me on his hands and knees with all the eagerness of an obedient puppy dog, happily awaiting further instruction while I looked down at him with sadistic glee.

Without warning, I grabbed his hair and rammed the dildo deep into his mouth. The sudden movement disrupted his balance, and he struggled to keep from tumbling over as I pummeled his face. I could feel his greasy hair weaving between my fingers as I used his throat, mercilessly banging my hips into his jaw.

He resisted some and gagged a lot, but I ignored it. I knew that at any time, he could easily put a stop to what was happening, and he never did. His willingness to tolerate my abuse indicated that he enjoyed the roughness and being told what to do. When I was through with my fun, I pushed him down onto the bed.

Being a higher-end escort, I was dedicated to providing a five-star experience. If all I offered was a boring romp that he could get anywhere, I was doing it wrong. With this in mind, I carefully positioned him on his hands and knees such that he was facing the television and couldn't easily divert his gaze. We fumbled for a moment, steadying ourselves on the soft, fluffy blankets, and then it was game time. I lubed him up and let all my years of pent-up sexual desire to fuck a man in the ass guide me.

The dildo slid into his anus with less resistance than I expected, and I realized this was definitely not his first time inserting phallic shaped objects into his butt. Since he was more physically prepared than I thought, I took off the kid gloves and didn't hold back.

It was glorious fun and everything I ever wanted it to be. The backdrop of niche pornography was a nice touch, and I found that the foreign moans and titters enhanced the overall mood of raw sexuality.

When I had my fill, and was ready to wrap things up, I decided to check off another long-awaited item on my sexual bucket list: a reach-around. I easily navigated my hand around his hips, locating his rock-hard penis. He was very worked up, and it didn't take much for him to empty his load all over the bed beneath us. After he came, he collapsed limply onto the bed, landing in the puddle of his own spunk.

After a brief moment of silence, we both started laughing. At this point, we were still connected like a pair of just-mated dogs, and sort of heaped onto each other in the bed.

Suddenly, he made an urgent, nervous sound, and said he had to get up *right now*. He jumped out of bed, holding his hands over his butt, and a gooey trail of liquid shit followed him out of the bedroom. I could see that some of the poop had dribbled down the back of his legs and onto his heel, leaving brown footprints in his wake. Before I had a chance to laugh, the smell hit me, overwhelming me with its horrendous stink.

Pinching my nose, I quickly slipped off the harness, leaving it on top of the sheets in plain sight. I could see a smear of poop on the tip of the dildo and decided to cover that part with a sheet. Now, to be clear, the feces was gross, but didn't particularly bother me; anal sex involved a person's butt, and part of exploring the brown eye was accepting that things could get a little messy.

I had the feeling this guy wanted me out of his house pronto, so he could clean up without feeling embarrassed. I figured that if I had just shit all over myself in front of a total stranger, I would probably want some privacy, too. I walked over to the bathroom, where the client was still hiding, and knocked. Through the door, I told him that I had a great time and that I was leaving now, and he sounded relieved.

*

So, it's worth discussing the fat envelope full of cash in the nightstand drawer. My client had ran, cheeks clenched and oozing shit, hurriedly out of the bedroom without taking it with him.

I was alone and unsupervised and had every opportunity to take it, but I did not. It would have been extremely easy to steal the money, and it's not like the client would have reported the missing cash to the police, either. What would he say? *The woman I hired to fuck me in the ass while I watched tranny porn stole money from me?* Yeah, right.

This kind of predicament wasn't unusual for me, either. I often had plentiful opportunities to steal from my clients; medications, cash, jewelry, pricey cosmetics, illicit drugs, etc., were all left unattended and up for grabs in my presence.

But, even though I could, I never did. Stealing went against my moral principles, and since I had so few to begin with, I did what I could to maintain them.

For the most part, since my way of life was illegal, and morally corrupt depending on who you asked, I had to create my own morality. Living my day-to-day life constantly telling myself I was an awful, piece of shit human being wasn't an option; things were hard enough, and I didn't need my internal dialogue reminding me that I was human trash.

It helped that I had a hard time wrapping my head around what society deemed 'right' and 'wrong' in the first place. Since I was not religious, following moral guidelines based on faith didn't make sense either; why should I live my life based on the beliefs of another person?

They certainly were not living their life based on mine, and there was no concrete, logical evidence to support that their belief system was more right than mine. Moreover, every religious person I encountered at work was ethically corrupt and morally incorrigible. I did not want to be associated with them.

I considered stealing as one of the things that was a clear ethical violation of others. I lived life in a very Kantian way, mostly treating others how I wanted to be treated. I definitely didn't want people stealing from me, so I didn't do it to other people. The way I saw it, if a client had money left over or some valuable possession that I wanted after negotiations, it was a failure on my part, and I needed to do better next time.

A big part of this attitude also had to do with ego. As an escort, I prided myself on my ability to obtain all kinds of interesting gifts from my clients. I got iPads, clothes, perfume, expensive tools, etc. When it came to getting gifts, there was no dividing line for me; if a client had it and I wanted it, I usually got it.

Because of this, I accumulated quite a few unique items over the years. One of my favorite items was a four-foot-tall Rastafarian *Bob Marley* banana plushie, complete with a giant doobie in its mouth. It was very silly, and I held onto it for a long time before eventually donating it to a local thrift shop.

Another item I was particularly fond of was a one-of-a-kind, hand crafted art sculpture of a spooky wooden tree. It was a gorgeous, eclectic piece comprised mostly of wooden strands woven intricately together, completed with an assortment of hand crafted fabric decorations. The detail and overall craftsmanship were divine, and I was so thrilled to bring it home. It was obvious that whoever had made it had put quite a lot of time into their artwork, and I couldn't believe how lucky I was to have it.

Another more practical item I acquired was the metal bell from a hotel check-in counter. My client, who I presumed drunkenly stole it from the front desk, gave it to me during a booking. It looked like it was very old and was made of solid metal and premier quality. To this day, it sits on my counter and guests who stop by get a kick out of pressing it and hearing a reverberating *DING* fill the air.

CHAPTER EIGHTEEN

You Can Only Go Up

Things were not always so great, and when it rained, it poured.

I had recently been discharged from the psychiatric ward for another suicide attempt, had failed out of my classes due to my absence, and was on the verge of being evicted due to non-payment. My charming boyfriend had also left me, so I was even more mentally fragile, and completely alone. The only constant that remained in my life was the thing that had driven me to suicide: my job.

I had been discharged into a life that was ostensibly worse than when I decided it wasn't worth living anymore. I was broke, about to have my car repossessed, and couldn't even lean on education to mask my depression anymore.

To complicate things, my employer informed me that we were in the midst of a dry spell, and that no one had been out for weeks. I was living in my car, showering at the local twenty-four hour gym and subsisting off caffeine and cigarettes. My desperation would peak, and I would spend my evenings restlessly driving around, aching for the familiar chime that indicated work. To pass the time, I would watch sappy romantic comedies, or painstakingly do my makeup and hair in the gym locker room, ensuring that I looked perfect just in case.

As the days passed by, the little I had turned to nothing. My membership was almost up at the gym, and I didn't have much left to fuel my car. Things were looking bleak, and I needed a change.

The problem with desperation is that it makes a person willing to do things they would never consider in a million years. The more time that went by without work, the more I mused that I might be okay with lowering my standards. The strict list of disqualifying factors for sleeping with clients dwindled as the days passed by, and before I knew it, all I could think of was surviving.

I remember during that dark period that I was on a movie kick and was systematically watching all the critically acclaimed films of the modern era. I was bored and depressed, and anything was a welcome distraction.

There was one movie in particular, called *Requiem for A Dream* about a group of three drug addicts struggling with their addictions, which affected me deeply. I watched the film unfold, soaking up the broken lives and shattered dreams portrayed on screen. The message of tragedy was relatable to me, which made the movie more impactful, more real.

At one point during the film, the helplessly addicted female protagonist has no choice but to have sex with her dealer to avoid going into heroin withdrawals. I watched, wide-eyed, as the character stood in front of a mirror applying her darker-than-normal makeup in preparation for selling herself.

It was a ritual I myself had done before, and felt a pain deep within my heart awaken; the movie echoed the helplessness and emotional numbness that I felt so acutely within my own life. It was an invisible pain too raw for outsiders to understand.

As far as I knew, none of my peers could relate to my struggles, and as a result, it left me socially isolated. Watching the actress on screen go through the same numb motions brought me to tears; there, plain as day, was my suffering painted on the screen for all to see, and for the first time in a long time, I felt heard.

Client Mike

When my phone went off that night, I rushed to it, double-checking the screen in disbelief to confirm that I had indeed received a booking. There, undoubtedly, was a text from my boss, but as I scanned the details, my heart sank. I sat in my car, shaking slightly, staring in disbelief at my misfortune. The name on my phone screen was familiar, and I read it over and over.

Mike X.

I had seen this client before, multiple times, and each time was the same. He would book a room at the same hotel and get absolutely coked out of his mind. He was a bald-headed, middle-aged physician with a potbelly and pale skin, with wild, animalistic eyes. It was normal that by the time I arrived, both his nostrils oozed with blood from excessive drug use. His shifting eyes and sudden movements scared me, and he always smelled of cigarette smoke and old booze.

For whatever reason, when he went on his drug bingers he would call the company looking for me. He had been calling the agency doing this for over a decade, and by chance I took the place of another worker one night and got stuck with him. After meeting me once, he refused to see anyone else and demanded that the company send me or that he would take his business elsewhere.

So, to appease my boss, I would sit in a small hotel room with him while he snorted lines and incessantly harassed me for sex. I always said no, but he never stopped trying.

He would tip me the going rate for a nude show and spend the entire hour pushing my boundaries and ignoring my requests to stop sticking his fingers into my vagina or licking my nipples. In all respects, he was creepy with a capital 'C', and I hated him.

That night, I looked at my phone again, letting the name carve its way into my psyche. I could already feel myself dying a little on the inside, sadly aware of what awaited me.

The client had told me over the countless rejections that *one day* he would get to have me, and I always laughed defiantly in his face. I was haughty and sneered that I had standards, and that for him there was no price.

Through all those encounters, I was okay, and things were okay. I had been in a position of power, fully capable of exercising discretion and my right to choose.

Now, standing somberly in front of the mirror, I saw in my eyes defeat. My finances, or lack thereof, spoke for themselves, and based on the recent climate, I couldn't count on another booking coming in anytime soon.

As much as it boiled my blood, I had no choice. I stared at myself, weighing the truth of my situation, and started sobbing.

Big, soggy droplets rolled freely down my cheeks, speckling the counter beneath me with tiny, salty pools of uninhibited sorrow. I watched the tears stream down my expressionless face, choking back my wails in the gym locker room. I couldn't bring attention to myself, and I had to get ready.

And so, I watched as the sad, broken girl robotically applied her makeup in the mirror. She was someone I did not know, and I always feared I would become; a person who lost any remaining illusions of free will, dignity, and self-respect. I swallowed a hard knot in my throat as it dawned on me that I had become the red-headed woman from the motel parking lot so long ago.

Eventually, the tears ran dry, and all that remained was the vacant, reddened face of a stranger staring hollow-eyed back at me. She was sad. She was broken. She was me.

Mechanically, I washed my face and reapplied my makeup, ensuring that all evidence of despair was meticulously concealed under a veil of cosmetics. Beautiful again, I smiled and watched as my face contorted into a caricature of happiness, leaving only my eyes untouched. No matter how much I smiled, my eyes, windows into the world that was eating me alive, betrayed me.

Once I was satisfied with my appearance, I functioned as more of a passenger in my own body. The stranger packed my bag, the stranger drove me to the hotel, and the stranger knocked on the familiar door.

As I knocked, I felt the final reigns of control slip like a ribbon from my fingertips. I could no longer tell myself that I was not like the other women, and that I had standards that I lived by no matter what. The painful, dehumanizing words I heard used to describe prostitutes suddenly felt applicable to me; I was no different than anyone else, and I was no longer capable of executing the mental gymnastics that separated *me* from *them*.

While I stood at the door, who I was, and who I thought I was, came face to face with one another, and reconciling the difference between the two was equivalent to wringing the last bits of humanity from my tattered, thread-bare soul.

When the client opened the door with his characteristic blood stains dripping from his nose and trailing disgustingly into his mouth, I said nothing and walked inside. I think he saw that I was not my usual, cocky self, and was no fool; he immediately asked for the credit card slip to sign for the booking fee, and for another to add a tip.

I handed them over and stared at him in stony silence. It had been a battle of attrition, and he won. With a glint in his eye, he asked me how much of a tip to write in. It was clear that he knew; no amount of makeup could hide my dejection, and it sustained him. I told him a number, an amount that would solve my problems, and he nodded, quickly jotting it down on the slip and signing it with great zest. Then, he asked me to take off my clothes.

He was triumphant as I wordlessly complied and followed his directions. Laughing, he proceeded to snort several lines of white powder off the hotel desk before getting undressed himself.

The thing about drugs is that they make men last a very, very long time. I had all the time in the world to contemplate my life and decisions while I was bent over the bed, being pounded into oblivion, waiting for him to finish. He never seemed to be done, and when he got close, he would slow down and laugh evilly in my ear. He was sick and twisted, something I had always known, and was sadistically getting off on my suffering.

The only time he stopped was to snort more drugs, and I politely reassumed the position for him to continue. I was trapped within my

222

circumstances and at the mercy of a person I despised; I couldn't leave, or he could contest the payment with the bank. I had to do my due diligence and tolerate the ordeal in order to ensure I could cover my financial obligations.

I died a little inside with each thrust of his penis into my body, shutting my eyes tight and going to another place in my mind. I refused to cry, even when he hurt me, because I didn't want to give him the satisfaction. He already had taken away what little amount of dignity and pride I had left, and not letting him see me fully unravel was all that kept me going.

Numb, I dissociated from the moment; I was there, but also far away within my thoughts. I found a happy place where I was not forced to compromise my values and lived there, only being pulled back into reality by an unexpected painful sensation or loud, derogatory comment.

Eventually, after almost an entire hour, the sweet sound of my timer penetrated my thoughts and set me free.

His time was up, and I had no intention or obligation to let him renew it. He had not finished and demanded that I stay longer so he could ejaculate. Now, normally this seemed fair, and I would have complied, but he had made a game of stopping in order to keep tormenting me.

I told him that I had already been there for an entire hour and that he had plenty of chances to blow his load. Livid, he pushed me back onto the bed and demanded I stay another hour and offered another tip of twice the amount. I stared up at him, his skin moist from exertion and his eyes animalistic, and said *no*.

The first thing I did was head to the gym and take a shower. I did the best I could to wash the stink of sex and his sweat off my skin in the hot water. No matter how much I scrubbed and cleaned myself, I could not rid myself of his sickening stench. My body ached, inside and out, a constant reminder of him ravaging me. After I dried off, I curled up in my car and cried myself to sleep.

That night, as I lay awake and stared at the night sky through my windshield, something broke. I had crossed a line, and there was no going back. I could almost feel it as my heart hardened, and the spark in my eyes faded completely away. I was wholly disillusioned and irrevocably broken;

the last remnants of my childish optimism were pushed from my mind, and in its place settled a cloying shroud of cynicism.

Nothing left to lose, I abandoned my values and embraced a despondent existence of gloom, functioning as little more than a plaything for whoever was willing to pay the right price.

NINETEEN

Dry Mouth

Marriage, and relationships, as far as I know, are built upon a solid foundation of mutual trust and acceptance of the other person, flaws and all. When it came to my personal life, a healthy relationship also meant complete sexual openness and freedom to explore with each other, judgment free and without consequence. If I wasn't free to enjoy my partner physically, it didn't make sense for me to stay with particular person for very long.

Feeling comfortable discussing my various fantasies and kinks as they came up was a key element in order for my romantic attachments to be meaningful, and it was something I was unwilling to compromise on. I discovered as an escort, the sexual communication and boundaries needed to guarantee a sexually gratifying relationship were quite uncommon within most relationships.

The vast majority of my clientele were married or otherwise in a committed partnership. This was so pervasive within my client population that I doubted the veracity when told anything otherwise. Before working in the sex industry, I remember hearing the stereotype of the middle-aged, balding husband on a business trip, getting drunk and having an affair. As it turns out, it was a stereotype for a reason and heavily based in fact, with the exception of one minor detail: the business trip.

Men, it turns out, would cheat on their partners whenever the opportunity presented itself and they believed they could get away with it. Mentally, I grew to accept that I made my living off of infidelity, and over time viewed marriage as a total sham. Happily ever after seemed like a story sold to the populace in movies to convince couples to waste money on fancy weddings. After all, why get married when your husband would cheat the second he got a chance?

My feelings about marriage were further complicated by society's views on what was appropriate for the marital home. Women were supposed to be faithful, devoted, doting partners whether they worked or not, and were heavily shamed for not being perfect mothers or for wandering astray. The bar for a woman's baseline was indeed quite high: go to work, manage and raise the children, keep the household running smoothly, and attend to the every need of your husband while somehow also remaining in shape and keeping up with your looks.

In comparison, American society operated under the assumption that men go to work and provide. Anything else was extra, or asking too much. There was also the prevailing view that men are animals, helpless to their impulses, and as a result, society at large seemingly *expected* them to be unfaithful. Being an unfaithful husband carried far less negative connotations and judgment than if a woman did the same thing, and it bothered me.

All of this made me incredibly distrustful of male romantic partners. I was extremely paranoid that if I did have a boyfriend, he would be out cheating any chance he got, and since I was an adult entertainer, I was constantly creating the opportunity for ample infidelity.

The work required me to be gone most of the night and made me virtually unavailable for nighttime cuddles and cozy evenings in. After a few failed relationships that validated my skewed worldview, wherein my job was the centerpiece of blame for any wrongdoings on their part, I resigned myself to a life of casual encounters only.

As I became more comfortable and accepted my role as the unintended other woman in many American households, I started to wonder why. I stopped judging, and began listening more closely, trying to ascertain a motive that could possibly shed some light on the behavior.

Surely not all men go into legal, long-term commitments with someone they loved with the intent of cheating, and the idea of men being helpless sex animals, slaves to their hormonal drives and unable to say *No* seemed equally implausible. I started asking questions, probing the men I saw to open up, and it was illuminating.

There was a common, overarching theme amongst my clients looking to cheat on their partners: fear of judgment, and an overall lack of openness sexually with their partners. While I took the stories with a grain of salt, hearing man after man open their hearts to me and share the intimate, or rather lack of intimate, details of their relationships was eye-opening. Often, I was privy to secretive details about so-called 'dead bedrooms', where their wives hadn't touched them in ten years, and tales of hidden fantasies too dark and lewd to share with their traditional, vanilla wives.

While some of the men were unabashedly just cheaters, I found that after exploring the topic deeper, many clients preferred their spouse, if it was an option. I was told that there was nothing they wanted more than to enjoy their kinky desires with their spouse, but that they were too afraid to begin the dialogue about it due to crippling fears of divorce and familial disruption. Concerns about *losing everything* and *the kids* were part and parcel of these discussions, and the lack of openness in other parts of the marriage cultivated a crushing uncertainty that made these men paralyzed at the prospect of approaching their wives. After hearing the same stories iterated over and over again, I started to consider that there was likely some truth to what they were saying.

The thing that baffled me the most was the aspect of risk: they were unwilling to have an open, candid discussion about their sexual desires with their wives due to fear of losing them, but they had no concerns about the consequences of cheating. In my mind, infidelity would be a surefire way to guarantee disrupting their family if ever discovered, whereas a discussion only held the possibility of causing problems.

The desires at the center of the issue were often innocuous and benign in nature. I often found myself playing therapist and listening to the insecure ramblings of married men, terrified of being judged for wanting something as mainstream and commonplace as anal sex, or a woman who swallowed.

The whole situation was depressing, particularly when a man was bawling his eyes out because he was scared his wife would leave him if she ever found out he harbored something as harmless as a foot fetish.

Of course, like everything in life, desires and fantasies existed on a spectrum, with some being more extreme and niche than others.

Client Howard

I knocked on the hotel door and waited impatiently, checking my phone repeatedly as I waited for my client to hurry up. The sun was still out, and I was called to visit a client in a hotel a few cities over. I wasn't a huge fan of the area itself, because the buildings were old and run down; graffiti was scrawled across boarded up windows, and many shops were long since shut down. Bus stops were everywhere, and people could be seen sleeping on the covered benches.

The residential areas were equally run down, with trash and debris along the sidewalks and with car parts from previous accidents brushed sloppily into the curb. Vagrants were shambling around, pushing shopping carts of their belongings, and looking very much like they had seen better days. The city gave off an oppressive feeling of poverty and hopelessness, and this was worn plainly on the faces of the people I could see passing by.

This hotel was situated right off the interstate, so I didn't have to venture too far into the city itself. For this, I was grateful, because I didn't want to attract attention or get hassled by anyone. The problem was how I looked; I did my best to look like a walking billboard of feminine sexuality, and I was conspicuously out of place in impoverished areas.

Needing gas was a common issue, and whenever I stopped at the pump, men would cat-call and approach. In the seedier areas, groups of men drinking outdoors and sitting on milk crates at the entrance of convenience stores was typical, and having them stand up and walk towards me while fueling was terrifying.

They would talk to me as they got closer and usually surrounded my car; I was afraid of being raped, or even kidnapped, so I always immediately stopped fueling and drove off the second they noticed me.

In general, I disliked the attention; stares, catcalls, and the attention of strange men made me nervous and uncomfortable. Some of my coworkers encouraged it, finding clients wherever they went, but that wasn't me. Acquiring clients in public felt too much like solicitation, and since these uncomfortable moments were pointless, they were a waste of time.

To help minimize interactions with men, when I wasn't on the clock, I was virtually unrecognizable. A far cry from the persona I presented at my shows, I didn't wear makeup, flattering clothing, style my hair, or otherwise put any effort into my appearance at all. I completely transformed myself into a plain, frumpy, nerd girl with no discernable body shape beneath the baggy, loose-fitting clothing and a mop of unkempt hair. With this style, which more closely resembled my true personality anyway, I was free to live my daily life without unwanted attention from men.

But back to the booking. Since I was called to a lower quality hotel for the booking, dodging the watchful gaze of hotel staff and the bums shuffling around was impossible. Not only was I clean and well groomed, but I also wore stylish clothes and drove a nice car. In comparison, the man bumbling around in the hotel parking lot looked like he just crawled his way out of a dumpster.

The hotel clerk was another problem. For whatever reason, the front desk staff in the crappier places liked to give me a hard time and try to pump me for information about why I was in the hotel in the first place. I found it very invasive and made it a habit to brusquely walk past them without even glancing in their direction. They seldom spoke if I strode confidently past in a hurry, but their judgmental glares said enough.

Upstairs, I waited quietly at the door as the client on the other side took what he thought was an inconspicuous look at me through the peephole. When Mr. Guy on the other side was satisfied with what he saw, I heard the door unlatch, and the knob turn. He was middle-aged, very short, and of Asian descent. He had a tiny, delicate looking frame, but somehow still appeared wiry and unpredictable. Seeing that he was an Asian guy, I instantly became intrigued.

I get it. It is wrong to profile people, casting judgments about individual people based on stereotypes. As a discriminated minority due to my profession, I knew this more than anyone, and knew how ignorant it was to assume before having all the facts. Even so, a huge part of me had to admit that whenever it was an Asian guy, weird shit was about to go down.

It could have been a coincidence, or the way my boss marketed my services, but when it came to my bookings these guys never had normal requests. There was always some completely off the wall, unexpected, and more often than not, kinky as hell excuse for requesting my services.

As an anime fan, these clients often reminded me of the weird, perverted character trope commonly depicted in the shows I watched. Just like the anime, my customers had odd requests and their reactions were exaggerated, generally over the top, and kind of silly.

Granted, I had no issue with this, and found it amusing, especially in the shows I watched. Who didn't love the awkward perverted goofball in their favorite show? There were entire genres that were devoted to that character archetype and his multiple foibles with the opposite sex. Coincidence or not, all of my Asian clients mostly fit this heavily portrayed stereotype, or at least were not vanilla.

Also worth mentioning, they were all married. I wondered if they were too afraid to do these odd, sexy things with their wives. Asian guy or not, whenever a guy was married and he confided in me that he could never talk to his wife about [insert fetish here], it made me sad; communication is an integral part of a healthy relationship, and a person should feel comfortable being vulnerable with their partner.

I felt bad for both them and their wives. I often wondered if the unusual proclivities of my eastern clients were a cultural difference, but I had no idea. Did their culture not support sexual freedom and the exploration of feminine pleasure? I didn't know, and in keeping with my standard personal policy, I never asked. What I *did* know is that the client standing in front of me was paying via credit card, and I intended to max it out.

Once we settled into the room, I collected the booking fee and changed into my outfit. Right away, I knew my hunch was right: this guy was... different.

He had a penchant for dirty talk, and while his English was good, his accent was thick and the combination sounded absurd. He put a great deal of effort into clearly enunciating each word, with sharp emphasis on final consonant sounds. He also integrated a good deal of slang and casual language into his speech, and while it wasn't technically incorrect, it was hysterical due to the accent and almost clinical precision when pronouncing each word.

He was also very direct and straight to the point about negotiations and wanted to get down to the nitty gritty immediately. He asked straight up how much I cost, what kind of kinky things I had done before, do I like black guys, etc. He sounded so sure of himself, came off as slightly domineering, and kept calling me baby, but pronouncing it as 'Behb-hee' due to his accent.

The brazen display of confidence from the tiny man in front of me while he rambled incessantly about what a *sexy sex man* he was and how he *liked the sex* and was going to *plow through my pussy hole* was as exhausting as it was hilarious. I knew I couldn't keep listening to him without laughing in his face and kissing my chances at a good tip goodbye.

Funny thing, it turns out that people don't like it when a person they consider beneath them is ridiculing them, and they tend to not tip if they feel their ego has been slighted.

Fortunately for me, a certain amount of egregious cuntiness was expected of people in my profession, so I could get away with being rude if I toed the line carefully. Since he made it clear he didn't want to dance around the point, I took his cue and told him to cut the crap and tell me what he wanted me to do so I could get on with it.

Then, there was a moment of silence.

My single firm interjection was enough for me to re-establish control of the dynamic between us, and his cocky rambling subsided. Taking full advantage of the power shift in the room, I let him know I

231

would only watch him jerk off, and that's all he was getting. He agreed, got undressed, laid down uncovered on the hotel bed, and beckoned me over to him.

His dick was pretty small, but it matched his small hands and small body. For his frame, he was fairly proportionate. I sat beside him and stroked his inner thigh while playing with one of my tits as he went to town on his little weenie. It was routine and boring enough for me to start zoning out; I couldn't count the times I had sat beside a stranger in a hotel room while they masturbated.

There was nothing interesting or sexual about a man touching himself in front of me, and I knew from experience there was no sexual payoff for me, so it felt like a chore that I just wanted to hurry up and be done with. I would mindlessly go through the motions and pretend to be aroused by a dude's erection while thinking about my grocery list or if it was time for my pet's monthly flea pill.

The more convincing my acting, the quicker they would be done, and I could move on with my life. As far as I could tell, no one had been the wiser, or at least no one had complained to me or my boss about a lack of enthusiasm. I was doing exactly this, contemplating the finer details of if I had sorted my laundry correctly before loading the washing machine, when he started getting really into it.

"Are you a sweaty girl, Behb-hee?" he breathed huskily while beating his meat furiously and staring me dead in the eyes.

Caught off guard, I blinked, my mind scrambling to catch up to the present moment. I was confused, not sure that I had heard him correctly.

"Are you sweaty, Behb-hee?" he repeated, "I bet you have hairy armpits. Dirty, smelly armpits."

Fully focused, I realized that I did not mishear. This guy was a freak, and it was time to do my job. Without wasting a moment, I lifted my arm up and pretended to smell my armpit, recoiling dramatically as if the smell was atrocious. This display nearly pushed him over the edge, and he had to slow down his ham-handed meat hammering for a few moments to keep from climaxing.

"Oh yeah, Behb-hee, you need to shave. You so hairy. Nasty girl," he moaned, his breathing getting faster.

I wanted him to hurry the hell up so I could leave, so even though it was weird, I played the part so he could finish.

"SO hairy, SO sweaty," I said, matching his energy as I pretended to smell myself again, "eww so smelly, I need to shave."

He was groaning and pumping his cock, barely able to contain himself.

"Let me lick it," he gasped, "let me taste your sweaty pits, Behb-bee!"

His tone was pleading, like nothing mattered more at that moment than tonguing the fuck out of my armpit. This was a first for me, but since it was so weird and harmless (and because I wanted him to finish), I went along with it.

There I was, hunched over next to this little Asian guy while he frantically licked and mouthed my armpit while intermittently moaning things like *so sweaty* and *mmm hairy*.

He was really going for it, and I decided to switch armpits in case the flavor ran out on the first one. This seemed to help, because he redoubled his excitement when he tasted the fresh one. The whole time he was edging himself, working himself up closer and closer to busting and then stopping just in time to prolong the moment.

It was at this point that things took a turn.

"Spit in my mouth, Behb-hee, I'm going to cum."

I paused, questioning my grip on reality.

"You want me to do *what?*" I asked incredulously.

"Come on, Behb-hee, spit in my mouth!" he insisted, moaning between words.

He was red, his skin moist from exertion, his body tensed and barely holding on while he maintained a death grip on his cock. Internally, I sighed, but at that point I was committed. After some intense armpit licking, what harm was a little spitting?

So, there I was, spitting in his mouth as he throttled his meat stick. Now, if you have ever had to spit repeatedly for some reason, you'd know that your mouth dries out pretty quickly. I was struggling to produce enough saliva to keep up with his demands. As quickly as I could get it in his mouth, he would swallow it and hungrily beg for more.

Mouth dry and running out of options, I ended up gagging myself to produce gag spit to keep him satisfied, which was helpful, because he moved onto wanting me to also spit on his face as he came.

By the time he climaxed, his face was splattered with my saliva and he had consumed every bit of spit I could muster during our session. He had a dazed look on his face, and he mumbled unintelligibly for a moment before brusquely requesting a towel.

Talk about post-nut clarity.

I cannot fathom the oppressive silence that smothers a person on the drive home after paying a presumably disease-riddled hooker to let you lick her armpits and spit into your mouth while you jerked off.

Of course, like my other clients with uncommon kinks, I would see him many more times during my career. The last time I saw him, he felt comfortable enough to invite me to his actual home. Seeing the photos of his wife and children decorating the walls added a layer of humor I wasn't ready for, and I wondered again why he couldn't share these fantasies with his wife.

She looked like a natural beauty, and judging by the upper-middle-class home they lived in, she probably had a really impressive job or was at least very accomplished. If he worried she would divorce him over a fetish, I'm positive the risk was even higher if she found out he was hiring people to spit in his mouth.

The last time I ever saw him was when he jerked off and aimed his spunk at me; I had explicitly stated that I would only watch and that he better not get that shit on me. I was always clear, and for whatever reason, he ignored me that time and sprayed me down with his man mayo.

Livid, I yelled at him. Since I was in his home, he did his best to calm me down and escort me outside without incident. Needless to say, I wasn't invited back and never saw him again.

Honestly, I was kind of glad. After the novelty wore off from doing it the first time, it was a real pain having to put up with a man slobbering in your armpits for thirty minutes followed by a marathon spitting session.

CHAPTER TWENTY

Unicorn

In the entire span of my career, I could count the number of passionate sexual encounters I had with a client on one hand. It just didn't happen, and it wasn't a realistic expectation to have it happen, either. My role was of the eager plaything, fulling fantasies and desires of others. There was simply no room for my own needs, not that the clients were interested in that, anyway.

Even if a client was particularly attractive or tempting, knowing I was at work made it nearly impossible to enjoy myself. The charming blonde haired man with a six pack was cute, but my primary objective was financial and it detracted from the fun. There was no genuine connection with clients; the witty, flirtatious banter was all part of the act, superficial at best and targeted for maximizing profits.

There was also my personal life to contend with; sex was one of my hobbies, and getting paid always risked a loss of intrinsic value. It did not help that I wasn't a party girl, either, and found the whole free-drugs-and-alcohol scene inexplicably dull.

Even so, with every reason to find my job boring, it would be inaccurate to paint a picture that was all work and no play. For one, I loved the flexible schedule; I could take any number of days off in a row I wanted, at any time, for any reason.

If I was sick, or if I had a doctor's appointment, or if I simply wanted to take a vacation, I could do it with zero advance notice. I didn't have quotas, and I didn't have to walk the streets if my boss wasn't making enough money. I had no penalties for wanting to quit halfway through a shift, or for wanting to start working at three a.m. if I felt so inclined.

And while I mentioned more than once that I was nervous about refusing bookings, the reality was that I was never *truly* forced to do anything against my will. Sure, I had real financial consequences if I refused work, but I was a free moral agent, and I always maintained the ability to say *no*. There was no dirtbag pimp waiting to beat me, as commonly seen portrayed in the movies, and no house madam enacting cruel punishments on her boarders. There was only me, usually in PJ's drinking a cup of warm tea while cuddled up with a book, deciding whether or not I felt like working that day.

A caveat to this freedom was that it was true that once I was *at* a booking, I was committed to finishing it, but that was a reasonable standard I could live with. It would be bad for business if the girls came and went from a show willy-nilly, so how could I argue with a practical requirement?

I took full advantage of this freedom, too. I only worked if I absolutely had to, generally making just enough money to get by. I knew that some of the other escorts worked every night, no exceptions, and made a killing doing it. They lived in excess, drove fancy cars, wore designer clothing, and got cosmetic surgery. Unlike me, they were truly committed to the lifestyle.

Sure, I had my moments, but it was not a constant way of life for me. My employer reminded me that the possibility of living a lavish, glamorous lifestyle was at my fingertips, but respected my reticence and unpredictable schedule; I needed an equal amount of mental health days to balance the time I spent at work, or I risked the inherent pressures of the job causing me to unravel.

A big part of the reason for this was that I never knew in advance what I was walking into when I arrived at a booking. Sometimes it was chill, and other times it was not. Too many unexpected run-ins with crazies had left me mentally wounded and apprehensive.

More than once, a hotel door would open and a bug-eyed man on drugs would be standing there, staring at me like a piece of meat. It was jarring in the middle of the night, and even the sleepy high-class hotels were not immune to this. As a result, I was constantly on guard, always wary of what awaited on the other side of the door.

In the circumstances where clients more closely resembled rabid animals as opposed to adult men, I didn't bother trying to collect the booking fee. They would look at me, eyes like saucers and nostrils flaring, and I turned the other way without so much as a word. Generally, I didn't encounter issues with this strategy; it's not like they would chase me down the hallway, most of the time they were naked, and besides that, all their drugs were inside.

I know the prevailing stereotype is that a sex worker's boss beats her up, but I never encountered this even once during my five and half years on the job. My employer granted me remarkable grace and emotional support on my harder days, and always checked in to make sure I was doing okay. I was treated with kindness, dignity, and respect at all times, which was a stark contrast to my normal life. The unwavering support and a phone call asking if I was doing okay meant a lot to me when I was functionally alone in the world. And like I said earlier, the job wasn't all work and no play.

Client Pierre

During a beautiful summer afternoon, I received an unexpected call for a job around two in the afternoon. Usually, the bookings didn't start coming in until after eight or nine p.m., so I was intrigued. My boss, enjoying the weather herself, asked if I could take it, even though I wasn't on shift. At the time I was aimlessly wandering around my city shopping to kill time before nightfall anyway, so I agreed.

It was gorgeous outside and I was soaking up the sun, clad in a sundress and flip-flops, using any excuse to be outside. What made this day particularly different was that I was restless and horny; I had been hoping to find a hookup while I was out shopping but didn't find any adequate contenders.

It was one of those rare days where I was looking forward to the constant admiration I received from clients; they were always complimenting me and making me feel like the most desirable woman in the world. Of course, I knew it was total bullshit, but it still stroked my ego anyway.

A series of failed relationships and lackluster hookups had left my personal life wanting, leaving me hungry for the lust-filled validation of an eager client. I was itching for a little excitement, and if I couldn't find the perfect stranger in the wild, I was willing to settle for the slim chance I could get lucky at work.

Optimism aside, I was no fool. Admiration was an easy ask, but anything beyond that was a tad farfetched. Dates with clients were not what I would classify as 'a good time'. Clients tended to be selfish lovers and often used their time with me as a chance to fully explore their deepest desires without the burden of worrying about the other party involved. This never bothered me, because it was what they were paying for, but it resulted in a staggering amount of personal dissatisfaction.

I observed over the years that many men talked a big game in front of their friends about how good they were in bed, but in all reality, they flopped around awkwardly and moaned for two minutes before blowing their load. Now, I know my opinion is biased because I am speaking from a perspective that doesn't lend itself to requiring effort from men, but I experienced this in my personal life as well.

There never seemed to be a shortage of men who boasted about their prowess, but in reality, had no idea what they were doing. These encounters with inexperienced braggarts left more than a little to be desired.

When I arrived at the motel that summer day, I was greeted by a middle-aged foreigner with a friendly smile. His English was not bad at all, and I found his accent delicious when he did his best to politely say hello. He invited me into the room, and from what I could gather, he was on a business trip and would only be in town for a couple of days.

I thought he was kind of handsome, and instead of requesting the usual nude lap dance show, he wanted to sit with me and chat. I listened as he shared his world with me in fragmented English, his eyes captivating me as much as his words. He was very charming, and we ended up talking for the entire hour. Before I knew it, it was time to leave. I was a bit reticent, not having done any true entertaining, but he didn't seem to mind and walked me to my car. It was very strange, and nothing like what I expected. He had tipped me to have a pleasant conversation with him, and nothing more.

I reflected on my enjoyable time with him that evening and was still savoring it the next night when I received another text from my boss about a booking. To my delight, it was the same man, and he was requesting to see me again. I was still brimming with unspent sexual energy from the day before and looking forward to another rousing afternoon with the affable foreigner.

When I arrived, he opened the door and greeted me in nothing but a towel. His skin looked pink from the warmth of the shower, and he smelled faintly of soap. This time, after I got inside, I changed into my lingerie in the bathroom and joined him in bed where he waiting for me.

His English wasn't the best, but he could communicate well enough and did his best to explain to me how he had dreamed of me the night before. He used his hands to gesture and indicate that he had seen my face in his sleep. The tone of his voice and the way he caressed my cheek while he told me this indicated to me that this was meant to be a romantic sentiment, or at least flattering. It was incredibly erotic, and I felt myself swooning. I had heard many lines before, but this one was particularly cute and for whatever reason, it tickled my brain.

He motioned that he wanted to pay me and used his credit card to give me a relatively decent tip, without any kind of negotiating with me about what it was for. I accepted and decided that I would have fun with my customer. That afternoon, I let my passions run wild and fully embraced the experience. Holding nothing back, we tangled together in a torrent of hot sex as he used me, and I used him.

My run-in with the foreigner may have been the only time during my career that I was sexually satisfied by a client, but it wasn't the only time I enjoyed a shift at work.

E. S. Silversmith

Client Gregory

One evening, I found myself in the company of a middle-aged man in a classy hotel. Nothing about this was out of the ordinary; he was gross, overweight, and married. He was lying on his back on the hotel bed, sans pants (of course), while being a fat, disgusting bastard. He had been trying to convince me to polish his shriveled knob for the past twenty minutes, and I wasn't buying it. It was pretty straight forward as far as bookings go, when my client hit me with an unexpected curve ball.

"Oooh baby, you know how much daddy likes it when you use his credit card," he moaned while stroking his penis.

In an instant, he had my complete, undivided attention. Without missing a beat, I played along.

"Yes, daddy. Your baby girl loves spending your money," I purred, sliding closer to him on the bed.

As I spoke, I lightly traced his inner thigh with my fingertips, stopping just shy of his penis.

"Oooh, I know, I know. You have been such a good, good girl," he was breathing heavier now, "didn't you say you needed Daddy to buy you a new iPad?"

Internally, I screamed in delight; I couldn't believe my luck and figured I had nothing to lose by playing along.

"Yes, I'm tired of waiting. I *need* it, Daddy. Call them. Buy it for me. Now. Right now," I said pouting my lower lip and putting forth my best entitled brat impression.

Whatever hang-ups this dude had were frankly none of my business, and I put aside all judgments in order to exploit him.

When my client proceeded to call *Apple* to place an order, I was shocked. He wasn't joking, and his penis was oozing pre-cum.

When the sales lady answered the phone, he explained to her that his daughter needed a new iPad for college, and that only the best model would do.

"You need it for college, right sweetheart?" he asked, his ear to the phone.
240

"Yes. College," I answered automatically, still stroking his inner thigh and cuddling closer to him.

With the saleswoman on the phone, he accepted every single upgrade offer presented to him after asking me if *his baby* needed it. Of course, I said yes, and when she told him the price and asked where his daughter could pick it up, I gave him my real name and he used his credit card to finalize the sale.

After the purchase went through, he hung up the phone and was sporting a huge erection. I tittered in delight, and he asked me what else his baby needed. He opened up his wallet and flashed several gift cards in front of my face from popular clothing stores at the mall.

"Does my baby need to go shopping?" he asked, stroking his dick faster.

"Yes, Daddy," I purred at him as he handed over a two hundred and fifty dollar gift card for *Abercrombie and Fitch*.

The more gifts he gave me, the hornier he got. I talked him into emptying all the cash out of his wallet, tipping me on his credit card, and then let him masturbate while he watched me use his credit card to shop online for sexy lingerie and clothes from Victoria's Secret. I even purchased a five hundred dollar cardiac-grade *Littman* stethoscope for myself, telling him I needed it for college.

It was ridiculous, but I was about it. Did he have deep-seated issues about his step-daughter in college? Undeniably. Did he go as far as showing me a picture of the aforementioned stepdaughter? Of course he did, the man clearly had problems. But was I about to let an opportunity like this pass me by? Not in a million years.

For an escort, a man who was aroused by spending money was the stuff of dreams and the call-girl equivalent of a mythical unicorn. I wasn't selfish either, so when I was satisfied with what I had received, I texted one of the other escorts and told her to get her ass there pronto.

When she arrived, I told him I had to go, and that my bestie was also struggling in college and needed help from daddy. He was so excited at this that he started oozing pre-cum from his dick again. He really had a thing for helping college girls in need, and fortunately for him, my agency had a seemingly never-ending supply.

E. S. Silversmith

As I was walking out the door, the other woman was going through the same motions, squeezing every dollar she could out of him while he was lost in the ecstasy that only spending money on young ladies could provide him.

The next morning, I was still marveling at my luck and trying to prepare myself for the real possibility of disappointment when I went to pick up the iPad. I truly expected that he would have canceled the order by now, considering it was a fifteen-hundred-dollar purchase, and arrived at the store the minute it opened with my fingers crossed.

Life is full of surprises, and I was indeed surprised when the lady behind the counter handed me a brand-new iPad, no strings attached. It was the biggest, nicest model they had with every upgrade imaginable. Walking out of the store, I felt like I was in a dream; people like me simply did not get this lucky, yet here I was with brand new merchandise still in the package.

Since I used my laptop for school, I had no use for it, so it stayed in the box for months. Every time one of the items I ordered online that night arrived at my doorstep in the weeks to come, I experienced a renewed sense of disbelief. I had never had a client like that before, and during my career, I never encountered another. Truth be told, he really was the mythical unicorn in a sea of braying donkeys.

CHAPTER TWENTY ONE

Yes, Master

Within the first year of starting work as an escort, I was offered multiple opportunities to expand my income potential in ways I was not anticipating. When I started, I was under the impression that my work would consist entirely of one-on-one dates with older men. Granted, that wasn't far from the truth, but the job consisted of more unique paid experiences than I had originally thought.

After I had been working with the company for long enough and had shown I was committed to being a long-term employee, I was approached by management about the prospect of doing pornography on the side to boost my income. At the time, I was appalled that they had even asked me; I hadn't had sex with any of my clients and considered truly jumping into the pool of sex work as somewhat taboo, off-limits, and entirely beneath me.

At that time, I was still operating under the assumption that I was too good for straight up sex work, and secretly looked down on the women who engaged in it openly. I was reassured about the legality of the offer and told that I was guaranteed to make a few thousand dollars over a weekend for what amounted to minimal work. As an escort, our work was entirely unpredictable, so the appeal of making regular income on a fixed schedule sounded like a dream come true.

I wasn't pushed into the offer and was told I could take my time and think the idea over carefully. At the time, I was essentially a broody teenager, not yet old enough to drink alcohol and incredibly naïve. My main concerns about being involved in pornography revolved around the lack of choice; I knew I wouldn't be able to choose who I was having sex with, and this bothered me. I didn't want to feel obligated to have sex with someone I had a personal dislike of, and I knew if I signed a contract to do a video, I would have no choice. As an escort, I always retained the ability to leave a booking if I truly wanted to. Once I signed my name on the dotted line, my freedom vanished.

I was afraid, too, of catching a disease. I was an anxious person by nature, and terrified of catching a sexually transmitted disease. I had seen pornographic videos before and had never seen a video where the actors wore condoms.

Safe sex was essential to decreasing the probability of catching something, and I got the impression that the actors didn't get the luxury of being safe. I remembered that I read a brief autobiographical note from a former porn star around that time, and that she mentioned how everyone in the business got herpes. It was an unavoidable fact of life, and sooner or later, it happened to everyone.

The idea of a when, not if, for catching an STD was scary to me. Even as a younger person, I knew that being an escort was temporary. I knew that one day I would move on to bigger and better things and being left with a constant reminder of my former life was not in my best interest. I considered, too, how I would have to explain to every future potential sexual partner that I had a venereal disease, and how uncomfortable that would make me feel.

In the end, after weighing the pros and cons, I politely declined their offer. I was told the offer would remain open to me if I ever changed my mind in the future, and that they didn't harbor any negative feelings about my refusal. I was relieved when they dropped it and focused their efforts on my regular work, but it wasn't long before they approached me with another unique proposition.

"Have you ever done any domination before?"

My boss had called me out of the blue one evening, inquiring about my personal sexual history. I wasn't sure how to answer because I wasn't entirely sure what she was talking about.

"It's where you spank them, and you know, slap them around a little bit. They like it. It's easy."

She went on to explain that this kind of client did not involve sex at all and that instead it was entirely a power thing for them. I had a lot of pent-up anger towards the male gender in general at that point, so it didn't seem like such a bad idea.

Beat up a guy for money? Count me in.

I didn't get a crash course in BDSM before I was sent off to my first client, a member of a local church who had requested a young, beautiful woman to explore his dark desires with. I remember being surprised that it was a member of the clergy when I arrived, and feeling somewhat uncomfortable seeing all the pictures of Jesus on the wall as I spanked a naked, gagged man with a belt.

Something about it felt sacrilegious, and I was mildly terrified of being struck down by lightning from some all-knowing deity for what I had done.

As I completed each niche booking, I started collecting knowledge and experience about what I was expected to do, and what I needed in order to complete my job effectively. I learned that the clients varied in their specific desires, but as a whole wanted a beautiful woman to humiliate and/or physically harm them.

I began routinely packing things like rope, candles, and clothes pins in my dance bag to help satisfy the darker, more painful desires of my new clientele. BDSM calls also meant becoming resourceful; sometimes I had to think on my feet and use whatever was immediately available to get the job done. This meant using neckties, shoelaces, phone cords, or whatever else I could get my hands on.

The more I did it, the more I began to notice predictable patterns in my domination clients. For one, almost every one of them was a member of the local church in some capacity. I didn't pay much attention to which religion specifically, but the clients either told me directly or I surmised it from work attire and photographs.

Dehumanizing kinks and organized religion was a bizarre combination, but I didn't ask questions. I wasn't a very religious person to begin with, and after my experiences with multiple church leaders, I definitely wasn't at all; they wanted to explore lewd, kinky fantasies, and then lecture me about saving my soul afterward. The idea of these men preaching about purity, abstinence, and being a faithful husband struck me as incredibly hypocritical, and it made me sick.

I never asked where the money was coming from, but I often wondered if it was somehow funneled from the church offerings; the cash was usually in an odd cluster of cash denominations, which wasn't typical for ATM or bank distributions.

I didn't think it was right to take advantage of struggling people's strife and ask for tithes, promising a solution to their worldly problems *if only they believed or gave enough.* Perhaps I was in no position to judge as a person employed in the sex industry, but at least I wasn't hiding behind a veil of righteousness; I was transparent about what I was doing, and aside from teasing, I wasn't in the business of exploiting false hope for financial gains.

Seeing members of the clergy at work made me particularly wary of religious types, and I avoided them like the plague in my off time. If I saw them in public, I would go the other way, because I had more than a hunch that they were perverted creeps.

Sometimes a well-meaning neighbor woman heavily involved with the local church would invite me to join her the following Sunday. My policy was to smile, but politely decline, and definitely not mention how her pastor had spent the weekend with me licking dog food off my feet.

Client John

It was one a.m., and I had just arrived at a booking for one of my regular clients. I had seen him many times before and sighed to myself as I parked my car, knowing the evening would soon demand a large quantity of mental fortitude. This was no ordinary client, and I expected to spend several hours draining my social battery to keep him entertained.

Standing on his porch step, I knocked, barely visible in the dim glow of the streetlamps. The house was in a sleepy middle-class suburban neighborhood full of mature trees and evidence of children playing during the daytime. Here, in the wee hours of the night, the streets were eerily empty and quiet. The only thing I could hear was the rustling of leaves and the occasional vocalization of a stray cat.

Eventually, my client opened his front door, creaking it open slightly to verify it was me standing on his porch before pulling it all the way open and inviting me inside.

My client was a tall man, slightly pudgy around the middle, with a short, conservative haircut. His face was clean-shaven, with recent nick marks indicating he shaved in anticipation of my arrival. Judging by the deep creases on his face when he smiled, I judged the client to be early to mid-fifties, possibly older.

This client was a pastor and ran one of the local churches. Photos of him smiling, dressed in his religious attire with numerous church-going patrons were plastered all over the walls of his home. I also saw the neatly framed photos of his wife and children through the years, dressed conservatively, looking both happy and well-adjusted.

The home itself gave every semblance of being firmly middle class, with its budget furnishing choices and occasional evidence of splurging on a nicer item. Breathing in deeply, it smelled like old people, and I frowned. Judging by the latest family photos on display, I guessed that the children were long since grown and possibly off at college. All that remained was the stale scent of the older couple that resided inside.

The carpets, having a particularly garish pattern, made me wonder if he got the carpeting done for free by a contractor who attends his church and happened to have extra material one day. I thought about it, certain that no sane person would choose something so hideous if any other option was available. I loathed the idea that this man got free help and contributions from his church when I knew for a fact there was nothing godly or saintly about him.

I watch him mosey to the kitchen, producing a bottle of hard liquor from a hidden cabinet, and pour himself a stiff drink. He downed it in one gulp and offered me one while pouring himself another.

Ick.

I declined his offer, like I always did, and told him to stop wasting my time with pleasantries. Every time I saw this man, he would start drinking, offer me alcohol, and attempt some semblance of bullshit small talk. I found it incredibly annoying, and pointless. I had zero interest in hearing the condescending, hypocritical advice on how I should be living my life more in line with God's principles from this man.

The first time he began his religious tirade, I was confused. After that, I told him to shut the fuck up and save it for the church. I couldn't fathom why he thought it was the appropriate time to try to save my soul from eternal damnation, because he sure as hell wasn't calling me out to his private home at one in the morning to convert me.

I watched silently as the client downed another couple of glasses of booze before he sequestered the bottle back into its secret kitchen compartment.

What a joke.

After he finished imbibing, my client headed off to the bedroom to get comfortable, leaving me free to take my time getting changed and prepared for him. Having been there many times before, I suspected he knew that I wouldn't steal anything, so he didn't feel compelled to follow me around the house anymore.

Grumbling internally, I showed myself to the bathroom to get changed into my work attire. I noticed right away that the toilet looked dirty, like it hadn't been cleaned in well over a month or more.

I frowned, lost in how appallingly unlikeable this man was. His bathroom was a clear reflection of who he was on the inside; filthy, unclean, and in desperate need of help. The room was fitted with outdated furnishings and decades of water stains decorated the interior of the sink and tub.

My eyes caught sight of the bone-dry bar of soap resting on the counter and I grit my teeth; this mother fucker was the type to not even wash his hands after he took a shit. Hot rage boiled inside me as I recalled a photo in the entryway where he had his hand on a baby's head while he blessed it. My disgust was acid on my tongue, and I embraced this revulsion, letting it wash through me in waves.

248

I hated dealing with this client, and little details like not washing his hands made me hate him even more. Knowing what was to come, my lips curled sardonically.

Once I had joined him in the bedroom, the ritual between us began.

"How much is it again?" he asked, reaching into his back pocket for his wallet and pausing to hear my response before pulling it out.

He stalled, hand clutching his wallet, not wanting me to see how much cash he had available before I answered. In response, I said nothing and stared a hole into him, expressionless. This was a game we played, the first of many.

Every time I visited him, I gave him the same price for the same blanket of services. It had never changed, not once in the whole span of our visits. The only exception was when he inquired about a particularly unusual request on top of his usual crap, but I could already tell today he wanted his regular.

Instead of telling him to fuck off, I decided to go through the motions and play along, humoring him more than he deserved; I made an obviously over-the-top annoyed sounding sigh and then started playing games idly on my cell phone.

After a few moments of him watching me, really letting him soak in the indifference he desperately craved, I spoke.

"Your time started the second I walked in the door," I said matter-of-factly, before examining my nails with disinterest.

I let every ounce of boredom and loathing I could muster seep into my expression from the depths of my soul and hammered it home when I made eye contact with him. He needed to know that I detested these stupid games, and that every moment I spent with him was a waste of my precious time.

I stared at him, unyielding, until he started laughing nervously and handed me a wad of cash.

I knew that he would start coming up with excuses about why he tried to dupe me, but I cut him off before he could get started. Like most of my clients, he was always trying to get away with paying as little as possible for my services. Clients were always waiting for me to slip up to save a few extra bucks, often asking me quizzically how much it was last time. When I was feeling particularly bitchy, I would respond to the question by offering a drastically higher price, just to watch their faces twist into panic before they demanded to know why it was more than last time.

With the money squared away, it was time to move on. This client, like the rest of my BDSM clients, didn't get the standard sexy lingerie. I didn't need to dance around or perform a strip tease, so I could wear more complex, visually appealing ensembles. That night, I chose my staple: a black and purple corset, elbow-length black gloves, thigh highs, heels, and a pair of black, skin-tight latex shorts.

For whatever reason, going to a domination booking and dressing in the dark, shiny clothing made me feel incredibly sexy and powerful. I loved the way the black material clung to my skin and secretly enjoyed the sensation of running my hands over my breasts while wearing the clothing.

After the payment was squared away, the client got undressed and laid himself out on the bed, waiting for me to do my thing and restrain him. He had helpfully set up a few items for me to use for this purpose before I arrived, which I appreciated, and I also brought along a few special items I reserved just for him in my bag.

Our history together taught me there were no limits with him, and I intended to push that to the extreme. The only requirement he ever had of me was that I use and abuse him for my own personal amusement and show no mercy. This was something I had no issues with.

Before getting into the more sadistic side of things, it was crucial to ensure that I restrained him both safely and thoroughly to the bed; while I liked to play rough, I had zero intention of inflicting any true lasting harm. Executing a safe, secure rope knot was not as simple as it seemed. In my free time, I had to study proper knot techniques and practice at home. Learning to tie aesthetically pleasing knots that were both safe and secure took time and dedication.

I meticulously checked all my restraint points and tested the safety by having him wriggle around. After that, my norm was to observe for any signs of poor circulation before moving on. Another part of my safety precautions entailed ensuring a pair of scissors was within easy reach on the nightstand; if there was a sudden problem that required his immediate release, I didn't want to waste time fumbling around.

When I was finally content with my handiwork, I took a step back, admiring what I had accomplished. I took pride in my work and treated it like an art form when I was able; I treated my clients like a canvas, using the ropes as my brush and paints. I couldn't help but appreciate the look of a meticulously bound man wriggling in front of me.

I stepped away, looking through my bag, trying to decide how to start the evening. I was keenly aware of his eyes on me; he watched my every movement closely, buzzing with silent anticipation. I had fully bound his nude body to the four corners of the bed, and he was splayed out like a pale, fleshy starfish. I suppressed a gag when I noticed the feeling of powerlessness was already getting to him; he had an erection and was dribbling pre-cum from the tip of his penis.

His abundance of body hair and excess body fat was revolting to me, and I did my best to avoid letting my eyes linger too long on his naked form. I hated the feeling of his eyes on me, burning a hole in my back as I looked through my things. A benefit of BDSM clients was that I could easily remedy that problem.

Without saying a word, I pulled a plastic grocery sack out of my dance bag, along with a roll of duct tape. Very carefully, I pulled the sack over his head, making sure to strategically poke holes by his nose and mouth to facilitate breathing. The idea was to make sure he wouldn't suffocate from the plastic bag, so I was liberal in the size and shape of my holes. The bag itself was actually only used to protect his skin from the duct tape; once in place, I wrapped the tape around the bag where his eyes would be, effectively blindfolding him.

I took my time securing the bag with the tape, having him make test movements so I could be sure he wouldn't accidentally shift the position of the bag and cut off his ability to breathe. I also checked his vision; I had him squirm and move around, correcting blind spots with more tape as I went, resulting in him becoming completely visually deprived.

At this point, only his nose and mouth were completely exposed. He was trembling lightly now, his skin flushing as a thin layer of moisture accumulated on his skin. He was nervous, but excited. The fear aroused him, but it made me want to puke.

Watching him begin to truly squirm under the pressure, I felt myself relax. Since he couldn't see me, I no longer had to stand with perfect posture or suck in my stomach. I pulled up a chair from the corner of the room and sat down for a moment, enjoying the freedom. I rifled through my bag and pulled out a cigarette, not particularly caring that I wasn't supposed to smoke inside.

He wriggled, protesting against the smell of the smoke now filling the room, knowing better than to speak to me without permission. I could see his fat lips, quivering slightly, wanting to say something, anything to me about it.

"Shut the fuck up," I growled, lazily jabbing him with my heeled toe.

He stiffened for a moment in fear, before his muscles visibly relaxed and his body began to tremble. I rolled my eyes and sighed, closing my eyes as I took another drag off my cigarette.

Usually, I had to be constantly 'on' when I was with a client. Being completely blindfolded and restrained meant I could take my time; sometimes I played on my phone, read a book, or even wrote a grocery list. The idea was to let the client stew in silent anticipation for as long as possible, to build up his excitement and burn down the clock. I considered this to be working smarter, not harder, and I never received any complaints. All I had to do was occasionally run a fingernail along their body, and they would redouble their excitement, remaining completely oblivious to my abject boredom.

That night, I was delaying my start longer than usual. I lit another smoke as I contemplated what I was about to do. I knew that my client had been waiting for a special occasion to request my services, and my employer had helpfully facilitated the arrangement.

I was dreading it, trying to find ways to convince myself that it would be fun, and wished I could go home instead. Sometimes at work, I would hold the money in my hands, looking at it wistfully and wishing I could magically teleport to the part where I was finished. It was a fantasy I often returned to since I needed the money but hated the work.

I sat waiting, mustering the willpower to continue, knowing that once I got started, I was committed to maintaining the false persona and following through until the booking was finished. It wasn't that I was incapable of being cruel and demeaning, it was that it took a colossal amount of mental energy to creatively deliver a steady stream of kink, especially when you weren't personally invested in the experience.

The money motivated me, but not in the same way having kinky fun with a loved one would. Without mutual enjoyment, it was a huge chore. Gazing over at his pasty form, all I could think about was getting things over with.

"I have something for you," I trilled sweetly, letting just the smallest hint of sadistic delight trickle into my voice.

His body shuddered slightly and tensed in response to my voice. He was breathing heavier now, his body shaking as a silent whimper escaped his lips.

I left him in bed and skipped off to the kitchen to search for what I needed. I poked around, opening random cabinets until I found what I was looking for: an oversized, plastic tumbler. After considering the cup thoughtfully for a few moments, I also grabbed a phone charging cable from the wall and a few candles from the counter. Satisfied, I headed back to the bedroom and placed everything on the nightstand beside the bed.

At the nightstand, I took careful stock of the items before me. I wanted to make sure I had everything I needed before I got started; having to stop halfway through to find an item interrupted the flow and decreased the mounting sexual tension. I nodded to myself, adding a handful of wooden clothespins to the assortment, and felt quite pleased with my selections. For good measure, I cut a few small strips of duct tape and stuck them on the edge of the nightstand, ready to go just in case.

I sighed again, having trouble believing I was about to do what I was about to do. I lit the candles to get them burning, and then reluctantly slid off my bottoms. A short white string, slightly stained with blood, was dangling from my vagina. I groaned with disgust internally, not daring to betray my true feelings outwardly, and pulled it out. My period had recently started and was at its heaviest point in my cycle. I stared at the freshly removed tampon for a moment, reflecting on how saturated it was with my menstrual blood; large clots were clinging to the sides, and the tampon itself was swollen and misshapen. It was a disgusting red, gooey mess.

I didn't like holding it, and my first impulse was to toss it in the trash and be rid of it forever. I suppressed a gag, once again thankful for the blindfold.

Remembering my client, I gulped, resisting the urge to leave. I knew what I had to do, and wasn't excited about it.

"Open your mouth," I demanded calmly.

My words were not a request, and he obliged immediately, opening wide and awaiting further instruction.

The tampon, red and goopy, dangled freely as I stalled. I could see him, his tongue waiting impatiently for me, drying out in the open air. There was no turning back now, so I did what I was there to do: I put the entire tampon, string and all, into his mouth and quickly snapped his jaw shut, and finished him off by slapping a strip of duct tape across his lips.

He struggled, recoiling and gagging, but I ignored him. He could throw up in his own mouth and swallow it for all I cared. It wouldn't have been the first time, and I doubted it would be the last.

Watching him gag through the duct tape, I couldn't get the image of chunky blood clots dissolving and moving freely on his tongue out of my head. Despite his muffled groans of displeasure, his penis oozed pre-cum. He loved having that nasty shit in his mouth, and it made me want to hurl. Instead of giving in to the urge, I composed myself; I couldn't destroy the fantasy and risk him wanting a refund.

I watched obliquely as he squirmed, thrashing against the restraints, knowing I had to correct him. This was part of the game we played, and if I didn't discipline him, I wasn't doing my job.

I grabbed the charging cable from the nightstand, hesitating for the briefest of moments before unleashing a torrent of swift reprimand onto his quivering flesh. He winced and tensed up with each strike, making a panoply of pained groans that faded into soft, pleading whimpers. His breathing became rapid, his skin bright pink.

Finished, I investigated the spots where I had hit him. Red, looped-shaped welts were rising all over his thighs. I wondered for a

254

moment if I had been too rough, but then I saw his erection; he was rock hard. I frowned, grossed out at the sight of an old man's dick. His groans and whimpers were now turning into gentle moans, and it bothered me. Something about him enjoying having a used tampon in his mouth filled me with contempt.

"Do you like that...?" I teased him, stroking my hand gently across his face before abruptly slapping the crap out of him.

He froze, stunned, before whimpering again.

"Shut up! You think I want to hear your whiney bullshit? Do you?!" I snapped, smacking him again for good measure.

It was so hard not to laugh at times like that. I looked away, fighting back my giggle with a hand firmly clamped over my mouth. While I did my best to sound cruel, I imagined that I sounded very much like an angry kitten instead: harmless and not fooling anyone.

He continued to whimper in between his rapid, shallow breaths, so I whipped him again, this time harder.

"Shut up!" I yelled, flinging the phone cord down onto his body with every bit of strength I possessed.

He cried out, his muffled scream falling on deaf ears. His body shook, and I could hear him trying to stifle his groans. Just like every other time, it took him a few 'lessons' until he understood that he needed to remain silent, no matter what.

When it came to having to listen to his whining, I wasn't just enforcing his silence as part of my domination act. In all honestly, the real reason I demanded quiet was that I didn't want to listen to his pathetic whining while I did my job; it was so annoying, and the last thing I wanted to deal with was hearing a creepy old man moaning and crying.

He was shaking slightly in the bed, and I could see the glisten of sweat building on the surface of his skin. I rolled my eyes again and I plopped back down into the chair, looking at my phone. I still had about forty-five minutes to kill, and I was already bored. I glanced over at the nightstand, and decided to give the clothes pins a go. When I was packing them, I figured I could easily kill ten minutes slowly placing them on him one by one.

I picked up a clothespin, pinching the end so the other side opened up like the bill of a duck.

Quack quack quack.

I giggled, making no effort to conceal it. I had fun opening and closing it for a few moments before letting it clamp firmly into place on one of his nipples.

He groaned, arching his back at the unexpected pain, and began wriggling around.

"Fucking stop already," I muttered, brusquely smacking his inner thigh with my bare hand until he complied.

I looked at his nipples thoughtfully. I had about twenty pins, so I knew I couldn't conceivably fit them all on his nipples. After I clamped another into place on the other side, I set to work on his scrotum.

One at a time, giggling as I went, I placed the wooden pins onto his ball sack. I had to get creative to get them all to fit, and having so many in one place caused the skin to stretch and contort into a funny shape. Partway through, I began to forget I was at work and enjoyed myself. He was miserable, and I loved it.

"...And one riiiight here." I mused, letting another clothespin snap into place.

He inhaled sharply, his body tensing in pain. I was losing my sense of disgust, becoming lost in the absurdity of what I was doing. I started to enjoy the sudden flinches from the client and delighted in punishing him when he didn't comply with my impossible demands.

I still hated the man lying in front of me, but I loved the freedom I had to make him suffer. I felt strangely sexy and powerful knowing a grown man was completely at my mercy and eagerly willing to follow any directions I gave him.

I got up from beside him on the bed and took an inventory of where I was at with the client: he had several red, painful looking welts on his thighs, his nut sack was flayed out in a fan shape with gobs of wood sticking off it, and the clothespins attached to his nipple were barely hanging on. I could see him shaking ever so slightly as he tried to avoid screaming in pain, and it pleased me.

Now that I had passed my initial disgust, I was determined to give this guy his money's worth. Even while he struggled to keep himself from shaking, his penis was oozing; he was loving every minute of the torment, and that meant I wasn't doing my job correctly. I wanted him to have fun, but it felt like an affront to my abilities if I couldn't truly make him suffer at all. Wasn't that part of why I was there, after all?

I took one of the burning candles from the nightstand and began dripping the melted wax directly onto his exposed genitalia. The second the hot wax touched his skin, he lurched against his restraints in agony.

"No," I said firmly, akin to scolding a puppy.

He continued to struggle, so I whipped him a few times to keep him in line. Once I set boundaries, it was my job to enforce them to keep the fantasy going. Once subdued, I liberally dribbled the wax all over his penis, and then his balls.

I was giggling sadistically, savoring the moment as each hot drop burned his skin. Once I had covered his penile area, I moved onto his nipples. The candle was burning too slowly to produce enough wax, so I kept having to switch between the candles to have enough for my torment. By the time I was done, he had pinkish-red patches growing around all the spots where the wax had landed on his skin.

He was trembling constantly, and his skin was slick with nervous sweat. I could smell his nervousness thick in the air and hear his subdued pleas for mercy. He looked positively miserable, but I still had ample time before it was time to go.

At that point, I decided that removing the clothespins was probably the safest choice. I didn't want to risk any lasting physical damage from cutting off his circulation. With each removal, he exhaled sharply through his nostrils. I let him continue a few more times before I started whipping him with the phone cord again. He needed to be quiet, and if I didn't make him, I knew he would never shut up.

I needed to reinforce the idea that I was fully in charge during these shows; it was a game of power and control and letting him get away with even tiny things ruined the experience. It always surprised me how effective a phone charging cable could be for those kinds of scenarios, and after discovering its effectiveness by accident one day, it became my go-to choice for an on-the-spot corrective tool.

With the clothespins gone, the wax began cracking on his genitals, and it looked kind of neat. I peeled some of it off, revealing a swollen patch of reddened, inflamed skin underneath. It looked painful, and tender to the touch. I felt bad for a few moments until I realized his penis was growing erect in my hands as I moved it around to remove the wax.

Son of a bitch!

I let go of it immediately and smacked his shaft with my bare hand as hard as I could. The client's entire body jerked away from me, hunching itself up in a ball as much as it could with the limited mobility the restraints offered.

I had accidentally struck him in the testicles, and he was writhing in agony. I sat down and watched him, listening to the stifled groans of pain beneath his duct-taped lips. After a couple of minutes, I was bored, so I whipped him once and told him that if he didn't stop, I would keep going until he shut the fuck up. My words, sharp and cruel, turned the client into a quivering, blubbery mess. I grinned, pleased with his suffering.

After watching how miserable he was, a lightbulb went off in my head. Using his nuts was an easy way to inflict maximum suffering with minimal effort. Fully ready to capitalize on my newfound wisdom, I scanned the room for anything I could use. In the corner, I found the perfect item for the job: a pair of beat-up, old tennis shoes.

I gingerly grabbed them, removed the laces, and tied them together to create a single, extra-long string. Climbing back onto the bed beside him, I tied one end of the string securely around the base of his scrotum. I smiled, pleased with how quickly my idea came together. With the shoelace in place, I had effectively given myself the ability to yank it and inflict serious pain if he gave me sass.

I tittered with delight at how clever I was; whipping him with the phone cord was a real pain, and my arm was growing tired. This would be so much easier *and* cause him more physical pain.

Testing my idea, I gave the string a hard, sudden yank, and the client clenched his whole body in response and moaned in pain through

258

his taped lips. Immediately, I grabbed the phone cord and whipped him again in his torso and told him he better *shut the fuck up* and to *be still or else.* He made a few pathetic whimpering sounds of agreement and attempted to be as still as possible. His entire body was vibrating slightly, a mess of sweat and agony. He couldn't keep himself from whimpering barely above a whisper, and this time I allowed it.

I loved my newfound sense of raw power. I could now gently tug the string and force him into submission if he did even the slightest thing to annoy me. Even the tiniest pull made him break into panic, and I found it incredibly amusing. I would pretend like I was going to yank it as hard as I could, grabbing the string and cackling maniacally just to watch him crumble into desperate pleas. It was great fun, and I felt like a cat with a trapped mouse.

While playing my games with him, he started making some noises indicating he wanted the tampon removed from his mouth. This was a new request from him, and one I took seriously; if there was any chance something could be involved in blocking an airway, I stopped whatever I was doing to investigate immediately.

After I verified that his breathing was unaffected, I smacked him in the face and told him to shut up. I did intend to remove the tampon since he wanted a break, but I wasn't convinced he was truly ready. I had seen this client before, and if he had serious concerns, his entire demeanor would change.

Instead of giving him a break, I decided instead to take things up a notch. The client did not call me back to his home again and again because I did exactly what he said. On the contrary, I did whatever I wanted, and pushing limits was what I was all about. I grabbed the cup from the nightstand, took it to the bathroom, and filled it with my urine. I opened a couple of new tampons from my purse and dunked them into the cup, letting them fully swell with my warm piss.

Chuckling darkly, I returned to the bedroom, dangling the piss-soaked tampons above the cup to catch any stray droplets.

"You want me to take the tape off your mouth?" I purred.

My words were kind and sweet, a far cry from the tone of utter cruelty I had used earlier.

He nodded fervently, perhaps thinking my time was almost up and that I was about to let him go. Letting him get his hopes up, I carefully removed the tape from his lips, careful to avoid damage to the skin in a highly visible area.

It is worth noting that before I ever tied up my client for the first time, we had a discussion and agreed that there would be no visible marks from our playtime together that couldn't be covered up by a suit. Because he paid well, I did my best to honor his wishes. This consideration meant being very conscientious about anything on his face, neck, wrists, or hands.

With the tape gone, he opened his mouth, waiting for me to remove the tampon. I could see that his mouth had become very dry due to the highly absorbent nature of the cotton. Instead of removing it, I quickly added the two urine-soaked tampons and re-taped his mouth shut.

It was disgusting; the addition of the two saturated tampons was a bit too much, and I could see his Adam's apple bobbing as he swallowed the excess fluid. Small trails of urine were also forcing their way through the duct tape, so I cut another piece and doubled it up.

The client wasn't exactly thrilled by the new development and made angry noises at me in protest. I saw this as the perfect opportunity to utilize my new punishment method and forced him into submission by yanking on the string attached to his balls. His muffled wails filled the room, and I laughed.

"What did we learn?" I teased, tugging the line again gently.

His face was twisted into a strained mask of despair, and his body was covered in beads of sweat. He was shaking, ever so slightly, and whimpering through the tape. Even so, he was getting hard again, and it annoyed me.

Seriously? Is nothing I do good enough?

I glowered, suddenly angry; I had put serious thought and effort into being egregiously gross and cruel, and he was loving every second of it. Sure, he was into this kind of thing and had obviously called me here for this very reason, but it felt like a bit of a personal failure that I couldn't make him at least marginally regret his decision to bring me out here.

I yanked the string attached to his balls again, harder than last time, and his body stiffened, struggling against the pain. His breathing intensified sharply, and his limbs stiffened like a board. While he was trying to regain his composure, I untied his restraints.

Confused and still blindfolded, he seemed unsure what to think of his newfound freedom. He hesitantly tried moving a leg, so I whipped him again.

"You don't move unless I tell you to, understand?"

He nodded quickly and assumed the same position he was in while restrained just moments before. I needed to maintain control at all times, so I grabbed the string tied to his nuts. I didn't think he would suddenly turn on me in a violent rage, but I couldn't rule it out, either.

Whenever I did bookings like this, I did my best to avoid the nagging psychological fear that at any moment, my client could snap and exact horrible, horrible revenge on me. My BDSM clients enjoyed being physically harmed and humiliated, but I did not.

One of the fears I contended with was the possibility that a client would overpower me when I wasn't expecting it and reverse the roles. I never wanted to imagine what horrendous things a client would do to me if I was completely at their mercy, so I did my best to avoid letting those thoughts get to me.

With a firm grip on the string attached to his scrotum, I instructed the client to climb out of bed and get on all fours like a dog. He nodded and followed my touch-led guidance to maneuver himself out of the bed and onto the floor. I enjoyed the fact that he followed my instructions without question, and it renewed my confidence. I felt less afraid that the client would attack me since he was obviously still very invested in the game we were playing. Keeping the string taught, I playfully tugged and informed him in my sweetest voice that if he so much as moved a single inch without my permission, he would regret it.

Giggling, I sat on his back, my legs straddling him on either side like a human horse. Pudgy and out of shape, he struggled to hold me up without wobbling or shaking. I gave a firm warning tug, reminding him of the consequences of not following directions.

"You are my doggy now, yes?" I asked breathily, increasing the tension on the string until he nodded.

"Bark for me, Dog."

These moments weren't technically necessary, but I found them amusing. His mouth was full to bursting with the tampons, and talking, let alone barking, was out of the question. He managed to make a muffled grunting noise, and I laughed heartily.

"Okay puppy, take me to the bathroom."

At this, I tightened the string again, to ensure immediate compliance with my orders. Yes, he was blindfolded, but it was his house, and I reasoned that he surely had a vague idea of how to locate his own bathroom across the hall.

Surprisingly, he was quite clumsy despite being in his own space and had a poor sense of direction. He would crawl forward, with me sitting on his back, and bump into the door frame or the wall and grunt. In response to each bump, I would yell *bad dog!* and spank his bare bottom.

The punishment only seemed to incite him further. Each time I smacked his bottom, he redoubled his efforts to please me. Since he remained blindfolded, the excitement led to near constant bumping into the wall.

Once I grew bored of spanking him, I determined that the only way to efficiently move the process along was to up the ante. The next time he bumped into the wall, I punished him swiftly by yanking the string attached to his testicles. His body went limp as he collapsed beneath me, groaning in pain.

He was moaning, his legs shaking slightly, but I was at work, and it was not the time to develop a conscience. Naturally, the only thing I could do was to keep torturing him until he regained his composure.

I had been toying with him for over an hour by this point, and I was becoming bored of the game. I could feel his moist bare skin touching mine, and I reflexively recoiled away in disgust. I could smell his exertion, and taste salty sweat in my mouth. I was disgusted by the repulsive heap of quivering flesh beneath me, and it took considerable mental effort to keep myself from walking away.

I watched as my client moved at a snail's pace, slowly recovering from the testicular assault. I wanted to yell at him to hurry up, to get up, and to force him to his knees, but I knew I couldn't rush him through the experience and do it half-assed. If I did, I risked losing a regular client who paid well, which was out of the question.

When I wasn't personally invested in what was happening, it was both boring and mentally taxing to keep up the charade of being a total bitch, especially for stretches of over an hour or more. It wasn't sexual for me, and after doing it for years, the novelty had faded.

I was often afraid I would slip up and break character, ruining the experience for the client by showing compassion or saying something in the wrong tone of voice. I was not paid top dollar to be kind and considerate, so I had to go to great lengths to exaggerate cruelty. It might seem ridiculous, but thinking up new ways to beat someone up in a sexually charged situation was not as easy as it sounds.

After waiting on his back for a few minutes with no results, I climbed off to find other ways to motivate him. I tried tugging gently on the string, but it only resulted in more groans. I didn't want to spend the next half hour standing in a hallway watching some gross old man choke back tears, so I needed a plan.

I tried yelling demeaning phrases at him with no luck, and the whipping also was of little help. Eventually, I started kicking him in the ribs, calling him variations of a 'pathetic, useless dog', until he started stirring around. Eventually, the beating mixed with berating him worked, and he managed to make it into the bathroom.

"Good dog," I said, patting him on the head, "now sit."

When he didn't sit in the manner a dog would, I kicked him again, repeating my command calmy, but firmly.

Now, I'm not going to lie, at this point he looked pretty rough around the edges. Still, the tip of his cock was moist and drippy; a long, sticky tendril of pre-cum had oozed from the head of his penis and was now making contact with the ground, like a disgusting sexual tether. It was pretty gross, and it was also a clear indicator that this sick fuck liked every minute of his abuse.

I grimaced, and looked around the bathroom, wondering idly what kind of nasty shit I could do to him. Eventually, my eyes settled on the toilet. I inspected it, and it looked like the toilet needed cleaning. There was black, goopy dust around the base touching the floor, and yellow and brown spots speckling the toilet rim beneath the seat.

Fuck it.

Without warning, I leaned down and ripped the tape off his mouth. The surprise almost caused him to expel the contents in his mouth, but he knew better, and tried as best he could to keep the clump of tampons from spilling out. One of the tampons was halfway sticking out of his mouth, and the yellow urine it contained was dripping down his chin as he squeezed it tightly with his lips. I admired his dedication, but it was revolting and made my stomach turn.

"Drop it," I commanded.

He opened his mouth wide, and the three tampons fell onto the bathroom tile. I could see bits of the coagulated blood stuck to the inside of his cheek and lips. It was incredibly disgusting, and I barely kept myself from vomiting when I saw the client lick a piece of chunky blood off his lip and swallow it. Just looking at him made me want to take a shower and scrub all the nasty, grimy feeling off my body.

I wanted nothing more than to get up and leave at that very moment and never have to see that disgusting man again, but that was not my life. I had to push on and continue the twisted game so I could make a living and pay my bills.

He sat obediently, waiting for further instructions. I could see that his mouth looked pretty dried out, so I followed the only natural, logical choice available: I forced him to drink from the toilet.

Forcing his head down into the bowl, I could see the urine and specks of feces smearing onto his neck and chin from the rim of the dirty bowl. There was a ring of filth present in the bowl itself, and I had to look away while he lapped water out of it with his tongue like a dog. He struggled against me at first, not wanting to drink the toilet water, but kicking him in the ribs and tugging on the ball string convinced him to comply.

Even for me, it was pretty nasty. I hated watching a human being doing something so disgusting, and knowing that it aroused him somehow made it ten times worse. The client ended up vomiting part way through his drinking but kept lapping away anyway. I had to turn my face the other way to avoid vomiting myself.

I hated myself in that moment for what I had been reduced to for money. Watching my client gag and vomit repeatedly into a toilet that he was drinking out of made me question how things had gotten that far in the first place. I certainly did not wake up one day and say *hey, I want to force people to do disgusting things for money*. I didn't like doing it, and I wanted to stop.

Knowing that I only had a short time left before I could finally leave, I kicked him in the ribs and roughly dragged him into the shower. There he lay, curled up in the fetal position, with feces and vomit running down his neck and chin. He smelled like he looked, and I had to clean him off before I added a couple more touches of humiliation to finish him off.

I grabbed the tumbler from the bedroom, which still contained a good deal of urine from before, and emptied my bladder into it. Sighing again, I splashed him with it, degrading him all the while and telling him what a *filthy, nasty boy* he was for being covered in piss.

So, at this point, I was standing in a bathroom, mentally spent, and had to wrap things up with a very smelly, strangely aroused man. Setting the dial to the maximum cold setting, I turned on the shower. He was sweaty and stank to high heaven of vomity-toilet water and piss and needed to be rinsed if I was going to touch him again. I used the detachable shower head to clean him as best I could without soap, and without actually physically touching him. Once he was clean enough, I brusquely toweled him off, trying to be rough while I did it.

He was cold and shivering and looked pretty bad from the various beatings and punishments he had endured. Miscellaneous markings decorated his body, and I sincerely hoped his wife wouldn't be back in town anytime soon, because explaining away such a bizarre collection of bruises would be damn near impossible. No one would ever believe these kinds of marks were from falling down the stairs.

I wondered if, being the hypocritical piece of crap he was, there was a possibility that he would show up to his congregation, take off his shirt, and tell the whole church community how he self-flagellated himself to strengthen his resolve in Christ. It seemed like the only excuse that he could possibly get away with, but also incredibly sacrilegious. I frowned, hating him even more, angry at how plausible the idea was.

Ready to wrap things up and head home for some well-earned rest, I pushed things into the final stretch. My wrap-up routine for all my fem-dom sessions was the same; I would securely restrain the client to the bed (if he wasn't already), untie one hand, and leave.

The reason for this was that I always had a nagging fear that one of the clients would snap after an especially brutal session and possibly murder me, rape me, or worse. For this reason, I was very careful and deliberate about how I would leave them once I was done and ready to go. Getting wrapped up in a bizarre, anger fueled, horny revenge episode was not my idea of a good time.

It is also worth noting that for these types of clients, I refused to get them off, or otherwise help them achieve sexual satisfaction in any capacity. The service I offered for those clients was more about power dynamics and less about sexual gratification. They knew they were disgusting pieces of crap, and deigning to pleasure them would shatter the illusion I worked so hard to create.

There were times I did allow my domination clients to masturbate in front of me, but it was only so that I could force them to consume their own ejaculate or rub it all over their faces.

CHAPTER TWENTY TWO

Bruh

Education, as I've mentioned before, was always my sole motivation for working in the sex industry. I was not from a rich family, lived on my own, and had no other way to afford classes. Working as an escort offered me the flexibility and financial freedom needed to pursue a higher education.

Being in school full-time meant that whenever I wasn't at work, I was either studying or sleeping. Often, I had to make sacrifices, and sleep was the first to go. A typical day for me was to wake up, study, go to school, study, go to work, and catch up on sleep in between bookings if I was lucky.

At work, I received little respect, but at school, getting good grades meant that people actually looked up to me and treated me as an equal. It was a stark contrast to my work activities, and education promised me a chance at a real future.

Of course, keeping good grades meant spending lots of time with my nose in a book. Unlike being an escort, I was fully dedicated to education and invested my heart and soul in it. As a result, I only worked when I absolutely needed the money.

Working overnight and attending school during the day was a delicate balance; the cost of tuition was high, and I paid all my own bills, but rest was required to perform well academically. Balancing the two lifestyles was very challenging, and it was difficult to keep the two worlds from colliding.

At school, even though I did my best to keep my personal life private, I was unable to keep my job a secret for very long. More than once I was called out to a booking late at night that carried on until daylight, and I had to go directly from work to class. It was extremely embarrassing for me to show up for an eight a.m. test in full work attire, with my makeup smudged, and the smell of cigarettes and alcohol floating off of me.

This was complicated by how different this was from my usual get-up; normally I would be dressed in baggy, non-form-fitting clothing, with no makeup or effort to improve my appearance whatsoever.

The first time I walked into class like that, I heard hushed whispers and was peppered with probing questions from curious classmates. Even my instructor raised an eyebrow and shook their head. Physically, I had all the makings of a wild, careless party girl, but mentally I was studious and sharp witted. Socially, I remained quiet and kept to myself, and looking so ostentatious was uncomfortable for me.

Eventually, my classmates wouldn't take no for an answer and wanted details. I didn't have an excuse, so I told a half-truth: this was my work uniform. Of course, an answer like that only caused more murmurs to ripple through the classroom.

I kept things intentionally vague and let my classmates connect the dots, and it wasn't long until the entire campus thought that I was a stripper. This was a rumor that I could live with, and I neither confirmed nor denied it.

What made this especially scandalous was that I was top of my class, and I didn't match the stereotype for an exotic entertainer; I was as far from outgoing as one could possibly be, and because I lacked social skills, the idea of me dancing around clad in my underwear was utterly bizarre.

I quickly gained notoriety on campus, but I hated it. People I didn't know were either overly nice to me, or extremely cold and distant. Over time, after having no choice but to periodically show up at school dressed in my work attire, people started to care less. The novelty had worn off, and I started being approached instead by people needing help with assignments or wanting to go over test results.

Long after the infamy died down, I was still faced with a troubling problem: women at school begging for a job. Despite what I would say about the negative attributes associated with the position, there was no shortage of eager women looking to make a quick buck.

I heard a myriad of excuses when my fellow classmates asked for work, but they generally fell within two categories: women who were desperate for money, and women who wanted to live out some asinine fantasy of *being a real live stripper.*

I understood the first one, but the latter got under my skin, and I wasn't friendly about it; the way they talked about my job made it sound like a joke or a game, and it irritated me to no end. It was my day-to-day life, and to them, it was just another way to stave off boredom.

For the people desperate for money, the agency hopeful would ask me uncomfortable questions about their job readiness, such as opinions on their physical appearance or dancing skills. I quickly realized I didn't like rating the size of peers' breasts or answering questions about their weight. I had people walk up to me and ask me to fondle their fake breasts to see if they felt real enough, or ask me outright if they were sexually attractive.

I cannot express in words how uncomfortable I felt being cornered in a hallway and spontaneously subjected to a stranger's terrible erotic dancing. They would also pry me for information on what it was like to work with men drooling all over you, and how much money I made. It felt like some of my classmates romanticized my job as an escort, ignoring all my cautionary words and warnings about how awful it was.

Worker Mandy

One afternoon, I was standing in the school hallway after an exam and going through my notes. I liked to speculate about my test score, often calculating it prior to getting my exam back, so I tried to remember the harder questions in order to look them up once the test was over. While I was reviewing my material, one of the women from my class walked up to me.

"Hey E., how are you doing? Can I talk to you?"

My classmate, a moderately overweight African American woman with pretty eyes and full lips, stepped in closer to me as she spoke.

She sounded a little hesitant and nervous, which I chalked up to the test we had recently taken. It was brutal, but I had prepared for it extensively and was satisfied with my performance. Since my classmates and I regularly discussed exams while waiting for grading, I stopped what I was doing to talk with her.

"Yeah Mandy, what's up?" I said pleasantly.

"I've been having trouble lately, and I'm really behind on rent. I'm about to get evicted," she said, looking down at her feet, "you know I have a son, right?"

I was a bit taken aback by this sudden admission about her personal life; we barely spoke and were not exactly what I would call friends. Even though we shared multiple classes together, we were barely acquaintances and had previously only ever spoken to each other when school had made it a necessity.

"Okay...?" I paused, not sure what I was supposed to say.

Did I hug her? Pat her on the back? Give her words of encouragement? All of it seemed odd, and none of it was related to our classes, so it made me uncomfortable.

"That sucks," I said seriously, wanting very much to walk away, but unsure how to execute the maneuver without being rude.

Not knowing what else to do, I just looked back at her solemnly as she silently stared a hole into me. I wasn't the best with social situations and didn't know what to say or do.

I didn't know if she was looking for advice or just needed someone to listen to her cry about her sad life. We didn't know each other, so the idea of discussing such intimate details of her personal life felt inappropriate.

Not knowing what else to do, I reached over and patted her back twice, and said *there, there*, hoping the comforting gesture would be enough for her to go away and leave me alone.

On campus, I maintained a reputation of keeping to myself and minding my own business. Even though it was school, I believed that it was highly unprofessional to mingle with my colleagues socially in any regard, so I avoided it. Additionally, my lack of social skills made interactions painfully awkward for me, so I tried not to interact with people unless it was absolutely necessary.

Even outside of school, I found the tedium of small talk frustrating and took active steps to avoid it. Unless an interaction was functionally required to achieve some aspect of my daily life, I didn't do it. I utilized overnight at grocery stores, used self-checkout, and did as much shopping online as humanly possible. I did anything and everything possible I could think of to refrain from talking to people.

For this reason, the idea of voluntarily spending more time than was absolutely necessary getting to know my classmates outside of school was unthinkable. Even though I had many opportunities and offers to befriend my peers, I shied away from it as politely as possible. I enjoyed my alone time, and did not feel particularly lonely for not joining them.

Eventually, as I stared off into space lost in my own thoughts, Mandy cleared her throat and broke the silence.

"I was actually kind of hoping you could help get me a job?" the inflection in her voice rose with each syllable, sounding both unsure and hopeful, "You know, doing what you do? Maybe I could try coming to work with you so I could make some quick money to cover my rent?"

Ah, fuck.

As much as I hated people and didn't understand them, I had a heart, and a person had made themselves vulnerable to a virtual stranger in an attempt to solve their financial crisis. I definitely didn't want anything to do with her problems, but I felt deeply for her plight, especially since she had a child.

As she watched me, waiting for a response, I thought carefully about her words and wondered what would happen to her child if she got evicted. This detail was tugging at my heartstrings, forcing me to consider her proposition more with each passing moment.

I mulled over the weight of what she was asking me and sighed deeply. The idea of spending any of my precious free time with her sounded awful, but I had compassion for her situation. Reluctantly, I decided to help.

"Um... well, do you know how to dance?" I asked.

At my words, her face lit up at my words and her whole demeanor shifted.

"No, but I can learn anything."

She sounded confident about her assertion, but I knew she was anything but a quick study; her grades were mediocre at best, and the whole class knew this. Our academic rankings were not secret from one another, and she was barely passing.

I sighed again and suppressed a near insatiable urge to simply end the conversation right then and there and walk away. Thoughts like *fuck you and your problems* and *I'm busy and your problems are your own damn fault, be a better human for fuck's sake* floated to the forefront of my mind.

I didn't want to become personally involved with any of my classmates, and this budding non-school-related relationship looked like it transcended far beyond the realm of the loathsome everyday interactions I was already barely willing to tolerate.

Somehow, despite my reservations, compassion won. I gave her my information, and after a brief chat, I understood that her bind was serious enough to warrant starting work that evening. We made plans to meet up at my house later that night to review the basics before going out into the wild.

She was over the moon with irrational jubilation; even though I told her repeatedly to calm down and that I couldn't guarantee any results, she kept gushing about how becoming a dancer would solve all her financial problems. I didn't like what was happening, but I was committed at that point. After standing politely and pretending to listen for as long as I could manage, I quietly removed myself and snuck away to a quiet alcove in the library to go over what had just happened.

I had agreed to expose a virtual stranger to my terrible inner world, and I felt a pang of guilt; the job was undeniably awful in every conceivable way, and worse still for Mandy because she didn't possess the physique needed to capture the attention of generous customers.

Based on her appearance, I couldn't bring her to an actual booking, because she was far too overweight and lacked a few traditionally desirable feminine features, such as long hair. Besides her physical shortcomings, I had to consider that she lacked experience as well; she was completely green and had no idea how to talk to the men, or what to charge them. I sighed again, sadly accepting that the only place we could possibly go to was a strip club.

In a sense, it was a practical choice. She could putter around a crappy club with no harm done and get her feet wet, all while possibly making a little money. I had low expectations for either of us making any money since clubs were highly competitive and the men who frequented them were seldom high rollers, but we had no other option.

Thinking of this, I felt another pang of guilt; Mandy had been so hopeful that she would make all of her missing rent money, and instead we were about to be fighting tooth and nail with other women for one-dollar bills.

The more I thought about it, the more I remembered how much I loathed strip clubs. They smelled disgusting, the people who patronized them were cheap, and unlike my private shows, you didn't get tipped up front for a floor show. The men would make you work your ass off for their measly chump change, teasing a ten-dollar bill at the edge of the stage for an entire set.

It was absolutely awful. The mere idea of having to go back into a grimy, disgusting club rife with sleazy drunks and cigarette smoke made me shudder, and regret swept over me.

I groaned, rethinking my choice but knowing it was too late to change my mind. Strip clubs were the absolute worst, but they were still safer than bringing her to an actual booking. At private shows, anything could happen, and I frowned at the mental image of Mandy's oversized frame huffing and puffing down a flight of stairs as a crazed crackhead chased her.

Before she came over, I instructed Mandy to bring makeup, a stage outfit for dancing, and the coverup she intended to wear when she wasn't on stage. When she arrived, her jaw dropped at the sight of a *real live* stripper pole installed in my living room.

273

"You have one of these?!" she gushed.

She was a jittery ball of excitement, and I hated it.

"Yes, I practice newer moves at home and use it to work out," I answered politely, demonstrating a couple of simple routines.

This was all true. A little-known fact is that pole dancing is extremely strength-intensive, so it is a great way to stay in shape. I explained this to her as she walked past me to examine the pole and fuss over its presence in my living room.

"Can you show me how to use it?" she asked blithely.

She was out of shape, and I knew there was no way in hell she could do anything but shake her ass while she held onto it. If she tried something advanced, she could hurt herself, and the last thing I wanted was to have to explain to EMS why an overweight stranger was lying half-naked on the floor in my living room beside a dance pole.

"Mandy, the pole is harder than it looks. Doing the tricks takes a lot of athletic ability, let me show you what I mean." I removed my top and bottoms, exposing my bare skin so it could make contact with the pole. While suspended in one of my favorite poses known as *Allegra*, I explained how friction points on my bare skin contacting the pole made this possible.

As kindly as I could, I demonstrated how pole dancing required a level of fitness she did not currently possess, as well as a good deal of practice. Still, she still seemed determined to try, so I let her jump onto it and grab it with her bare thighs to suspend herself. I knew it would be extremely painful for her skin to hold up all her weight, especially since she wasn't used to the sensation, but I let her find this out the hard way.

As I suspected, the sudden pain of her skin straining against the metal ended her interest in the pole. I felt bad tricking her, but was relieved that she wouldn't get hurt trying to flip around when her body couldn't handle it.

To get her attention off what she *couldn't* do, I proceeded to show her some hip wiggling and floor work that was well within the realm of possibility for her. I taught her how to clap her ass cheeks and showed her step-by-step how to do a seductive floor routine for teasing the customers.

And I had to admit, it was kind of fun. I could see her confidence returning because this kind of stuff was very achievable for her and didn't require athletic ability. While she was on the floor practicing her gyrating, I decided it was time to give her some real-world advice.

"Listen, dancing on stage is fun, but the real money isn't made on stage. It's made on the floor talking to the men and seducing them with your wit and personality. You can be the best dancer in the world and make absolute shit if you don't apply yourself correctly to your customer. You are a fantasy and it's your job to sell yourself to these guys. Forget who you are and what you care about; all that matters is that you can shape yourself into whatever *they* want you to be."

I saw that she was listening, but I wasn't sure if she took my words to heart. Usually, newer girls didn't get this important lesson right away, and no matter how much you explained it to them, they had to learn things the hard way.

She looked thoughtful for a few moments and then stopped her booty flopping on the floor. She was sweaty, and this was probably the most exercise she'd had all year. I was glad the clubs were dark and smokey, so no one would be able to tell.

"How do you know what they want?" she asked me while catching her breath.

"You have to read them. Pay attention to their body language and what they say. Stay close to me and I'll show you how. I promise it's easier than it sounds."

This was a lie. It was in fact not easier than it sounded, and it took me a lot of practice and mistakes to get good at it. To be fair, I was bad with people in general, so it was very possible that other women picked up the skill much faster.

After I gave her a few more pointers on dancing, we did our makeup. I did my usual routine, which didn't take long, and watched as my classmate did her best to emulate it. She looked like a mess, and I took another moment to silently appreciate how hard it was to see in a club.

Before we left, I did my best to explain to her that you couldn't count on getting a certain amount of money with a job like this, but she laughed me off. Looking at her all made-up, I was feeling some misgivings.

She had many positive qualities, I'm sure, but her potential as an exotic entertainer was not one of them. My expectations for the night were appropriately low, and hers were delusionally high. I wasn't about to burst her bubble, though, so on we went.

Thinking it best we drove separately in case I was called out to a booking, I told her to meet me at one of the sketchier clubs on the far side of town. This was the kind of club that was on the other, *other* side of the railroad tracks. The sort of place where seeing a cockroach scurrying in the kitchen was no big deal because no one was under any illusions about the place not being a total shithole. It wasn't an establishment I would normally step inside of in a million years, but for Mandy, I made an exception.

I figured it made more sense for multiple reasons; they would let us just walk in and work after a brief chat with no questions asked, and also there was the matter of Mandy herself.

She had zero experience and didn't have the ideal body type for the stage. All you had to do was just look at her and it was obvious she didn't belong. She didn't have the body and lacked the soulless, thousand-yard stare that veterans in the business couldn't hide even if they wanted to. She stuck out, but in a bad way.

In my mind, if she managed to do well here despite her shortcomings, I was in no place to say she couldn't hack it. Then again, if she tried her hardest but failed spectacularly anyway and had her spirit dashed into pieces, it was probably for the best.

Sure, I wanted to be supportive of her plight, but the closer we got to actually working, the less faith I had in her. She was just not the right fit physically or mentally for what we were about to do; she had the determination but was dumb as a door-knob and just as ugly. All of which made her a likely target to be taken advantage of.

I was also harboring concerns about the very real possibility that the other dancers would eat her alive before she ever had the chance to even step on stage. In my experience, exotic dancers were notoriously catty bitches and were a colossal pain to deal with. The bullying and aggression were some of the main reasons I stayed away from the clubs and stuck to private shows.

When I was at work, I wanted to focus on making money, not dealing with high school drama from a bunch of idiots in their underwear. It was incredibly taxing to navigate the bullshit working in a club required, and in reality, the behavior wasn't baseless; no one wanted competition when funds were scarce, so pushing out new blood was the best way to ensure you earned a living. When it came to my classmate, I was banking on no one paying any attention to her due to her appearance, so however minor, perhaps there was a real chance of avoiding the drama.

I was mentally exhausted, and we hadn't even started yet. At that point, I didn't care which way it would go. I was bored of teaching her and was looking forward to getting this trainwreck over with. Maybe I would make a little cash in the process so it wouldn't be an entire waste of my time. Plus, I would have zero difficulty talking Mandy into giving me a cut of whatever she made that night because I was *training* her, after all.

Was that wrong? Yes. Did I care? No. I was taking her under my wing and showing her the ropes, so she owed me for that.

When I arrived at the club, I couldn't help myself. I laughed out loud. This was the grimiest, most ghetto shithole of a club I had ever seen in my entire life. The parking lot was littered with miscellaneous trash, used syringes, and a couple of broken-down cars. I could see used condoms around one of the parking spaces in the far corner of the lot beside the dumpster. It was awful, and I half expected to see a pack of wild dogs roaming the area.

The establishment itself was no better than the parking lot; the building was somewhat dilapidated and had clearly seen years of wear and tear with no apparent maintenance. Attached to the main club by a breezeway was a lap dance area, which was a separate building where men could get private time with their favorite entertainers for the right price.

I laughed again. This place represented everything I hated about the industry. I shuddered at the thought of what kind of women used this club as their regular haunt, and wondered to myself what they could possibly look like; good looking women crowded the higher end clubs, so who ended up working in a place like this? Maybe I was wrong in thinking Mandy would stand out here.

Outside the club, a group of men were smoking near the entrance dressed in garish, obnoxious clothing. When they saw me, they started hooting like a band of idiotic monkeys. It turned out that I was the one standing out like a sore thumb, and I was already attracting way too much attention for my liking.

What I really wanted was to stay under the radar and avoid dealing with any of the riffraff while I helped Mandy get her feet wet. The men catcalling me by the entrance were the exact sort that I wanted to avoid. I knew from my past experience working in strip clubs that they were more trouble than they were worth; they seldom had money, and what they lacked in funds they made up for with their aggressive, tough-guy attitudes.

They would watch you on stage, never tip, and then throw a fit when you shifted your attention to paying patrons. Nine times out of ten they were flat broke, pretentious, rude assholes who somehow always seemed to travel in packs.

Even though they would be extremely loud and offensive in the club, management seldom removed them because they bought drinks. What grated my nerves the most was their insistence on overly objectifying women and upholding a generalized policy of treating women like crap. I had overheard countless conversations between these types of men where women were discussed like a disposable commodity. Strangely, I got the impression that they believed treating women like dirt made them cool and manly. I considered this a fascinating feat of mental gymnastics utilized to avoid feeling inferior to women, particularly in a place where females maintained full control of the situation.

I had very little patience for rude, disrespectful men, and did not find their behavior attractive or appealing in the slightest. Even if they had money, which they usually didn't, I didn't want it. Even though I went to work to make money, I had to maintain a semblance of dignity and self-respect to avoid becoming emotionally burnt out. I couldn't handle dealing with them, and the women who did on a regular basis must have been made of sterner stuff than me.

When we got inside, I observed that the inside of the club was just as bad as the outside, and I heaved a heavy sigh. The music was extremely loud and exceedingly vulgar, even for a strip joint. Through the haze of dim lights and smoke, I could see that the club was packed with the exact type of client I tried so hard to avoid.

Women danced on stage, doing their best, and men watched from afar, cocktails in hand. There was one man seated at the stage, and he was holding a single dollar bill and making the women in front of him really work for it.

A groan escaped my lips, and I already couldn't wait to leave. This place was the pits. My expectations, which were already low, dropped further and I strongly considered accepting the night for the disaster it was and just scrapping the whole evening altogether.

I was ready to turn around and walk out when I looked over and saw the sunny disposition radiating off my classmate. She clearly had no clue just how awful this place was. Still, she needed money and seemed willing despite the nightmare in front of us, so I decided to stick it out for her sake.

"Come on, Mandy, you ready for this?" I called playfully, jabbing her with my elbow.

As the atmosphere sunk in, her confidence faded and was replaced with a terrified, unsure expression, and I laughed. I told her we were already there, and that we weren't backing down now.

Holding her arm in mine, we pushed past the group sitting closest to the door, brushing off their grabby hands off our asses as we walked by. Unlike Mandy, I had plenty of practice snapping phrases like *get your fucking hands off me, you piece of shit!* when someone touched me without my permission.

The men here weren't fazed in the slightest by my sudden outburst; instead of apologizing, all I got in response was an *oooooo, she's feisty* and a *this one's got attitude, bro, she likes you.* I gritted my teeth, a sense of dread washing over me, and silenced the better judgment that demanded I leave immediately.

Before we could get started, I had to locate the management and get them to let us work. Because it wasn't a high-end establishment, I didn't expect any pushback. Indeed, all it took was a quick chat with the man in charge and we were given permission to do whatever the hell we wanted.

The stage itself had three poles and wasn't very large. Staring at it, I couldn't understand how three women could be up there safely at the same time. How could they dance without hitting each other? There was no way to spatially accommodate the movements of three women, even if they were very small with short limbs.

My reverie was interrupted when a new set started, and three new women strutted out to do their thing. I realized then that pole dancing was not on the menu, and instead, the women here focused exclusively on floor work. All I could see was ass shaking and floor humping. It wasn't very creative, but the men here liked it. Watching them, I had to admit that one of the girls was very talented; she shimmied her entire body in a mesmerizing way while she moved in an elegant, enticing manner.

Enchanted, I watched for a few moments, appreciating the beauty and elegance of the display. The others, however, relied heavily on shaking ass and clapping cheeks.

Wanting the best chance for Mandy, I thoughtfully observed the other dancers for an entire set, gauging the competition and trying to get a handle on what the customers responded to. I wanted to formulate the best strategy for Mandy to be successful, so I used my brain as much as my body.

I could see that there was a lot of meat up on stage, but none of the men were tipping. They seemed content sitting back and observing the women, licking their lips and sipping their drinks. Even the men seated right at the stage were stingy and weren't spending any money. Watching this, I didn't understand how the women here made a living.

Why would someone continue to work at a club where men didn't tip? Something was fishy, and I knew there had to be something else going on. Otherwise, it wouldn't make sense that women came here at all. Looking around through the haze, I began to wonder what the gimmick was. When the set finally wrapped up, I grabbed Mandy, and we headed to the dressing room to get ready for the stage.

Inside the cramped space, the other women were not happy to see me. The guy in charge had told me that *girls like me* did well, but that was only if they managed to stay long enough. I didn't consider myself special, but I did have a unique look compared to the other women in the dressing room.

Mandy, on the other hand, fit right in. This was fortunate because it meant they didn't give her the stink eye or make rude comments to her. I, however, was the target of menacing glares and not-so-hushed whispers of divisive comments.

I wasn't interested in dealing with any drama, so I ignored them and focused on giving Mandy a pep talk; I wanted her to succeed, and to make her rent money if possible. It was why we were there, after all. When I heard the announcer start the next set, we bravely stepped out onto the stage and in front of a crowd of aloof onlookers.

The other dancers were undeniably pissed that I was there, and I inadvertently became public enemy number one. I was curious what kind of crap they would pull to try to get rid of me when I saw in the corner of my eye that three of them joined Mandy and I on stage.

This was irregular, and they weren't supposed to do it, but I wasn't about to stop them. Ignoring them, I started my routine, which to be fair *was* different than what I had just seen on stage from the other performers, and started making money right away. The men were tipping, and it made the other women sour.

I couldn't tell if it was because I looked unique, or if it had to do with my different dance style. Honestly, I had no idea, but I intended to give all the cash I generated to Mandy.

I thought things were going well until a few of the customers came up and sat in the seats right at the stage. This would have been fine, except that the other dancers crowded the space between the customer and myself and started twerking.

I didn't want to accidentally hurt one of them or myself by continuing my pole routine with them in such close proximity. They were very obviously forcing me off the stage and taking over my set. Since this was a hill they were willing to die on, I let it happen. I didn't give two shits about these crappy clients and their seven dollars, so they could have them. I scooped up the cash I made and walked back into the dressing room.

Inside, the women were less than pleasant. They didn't seem too keen on a random woman showing up and stealing away their potential profits. I couldn't blame them for the hostility; in all honesty, it made sense, and I would have felt the same way. They sneered at me and made snide remarks. It was like the old times at the club when I first started, and I found that definitely I didn't miss the competitive bitchiness.

I tossed on my coverup as I heard the sound of a new set starting, but didn't see Mandy. Ignoring the jeers from the other dancers, I walked out of the dressing room and onto the floor, searching for my classmate.

Mentally, I was completely done with the place; fighting tooth and nail for petty cash that wasn't even a tenth of my normal booking fees alone was not my style. I was out of my element and wasn't interested in stepping up to the challenge. I searched around, squinting through the smoke and avoiding the grabby hands of men as I walked.

Finally, I found her.

Across the room, at a table not too far from the stage, Mandy was standing next to an older man who had his arm wrapped snuggly around her waist. She looked happy, was holding some cash, and I got the impression I didn't need to intervene. She seemed to have found her footing despite the conditions, and once I made eye contact and she winked at me, I knew she was good to go.

Personally, I was done with the place and ready to leave. The club held no allure for me, and I knew I wouldn't make any decent money by hanging out. But, being a naturally inquisitive person, I had to satisfy my curiosity and investigate the mysterious happenings of the other side of the club before I left. I had to venture into the private show area.

Considering what a shit show the club was, I truly wanted to know what was going on behind closed doors. The men here were not the best stage tippers, so I had more than an inkling that some less-than-reputable happenings were going on. I wasn't about to rock the boat and put a stop to it, but I simply had to know. At the very least, it could be entertaining, and if I was lucky, it might be educational.

With mixed expectations, I walked through the door linking the main club to the secondary structure and was shocked. The mood was totally different; soft, romantic lighting permeated the space and there were comfy couches everywhere. The music was mellow and non-obtrusive, so conversations and quiet whispers were possible between dancers and patrons. It smelled nice, and overall, there was a very cozy, welcoming vibe to the place.

In the corner, I saw a few men getting slow, sensual lap dances, and nearby it appeared that another man was busy getting a hand-job. The entertainers without a customer were hanging out in a group, chatting quietly amongst themselves. A far cry from the dressing room, these women seemed friendly and approachable.

It was so… different from what I was expecting, and I was disappointed. I had psyched myself up to see some *shit*, and on all accounts, it was pretty tame. Yes, obviously, the chicks in here were fellating men for money, but that wasn't exactly a secret; in the main club area, the DJ would announce periodically how customers could check out the private dance area to get 'taken care of'.

Legally, blatant sex work was not permitted, and strictly against the law, so I wondered how a business like this managed to keep itself from getting shut down by the police. If I waited around to find out, I was taking the risk of getting caught up in whatever legal strife was waiting to implode. Because of how brazenly they were selling sex, I suspected this was a likely target for undercover officers.

Before I left, I walked around a little bit more, checking out the room a bit and giggling at some of the decorations that looked like they had been hanging on the wall for forty years. The experience wasn't an entire waste, however, because I ran into a dancer who had the nicest pair of fake tits I had ever seen in my life, and she even let me play with them.

After I satisfied my curiosity, I was ready to leave. I had to get back home and prepare for my actual job before the calls started coming in. I thought it prudent to check up on Mandy one final time before departing, just to be on the safe side.

When I found her, she was still with the same gentleman and voiced no interest in leaving anytime soon. I wasn't entirely comfortable leaving her there all night to fend for herself, but she reassured me that everything was going well and that I could go without her.

I felt conflicted about abandoning her there; sure, she had given me permission to leave, but she was too inexperienced to know any better. I didn't want anything unsavory to happen to her, but she refused to leave with me when I insisted. After accepting that she wouldn't take my advice, I got her to at least check in with me when she got home so I knew she was okay. She nodded yes, and that was the end of that.

By the time I got home, I had to get ready for work, so I didn't give Mandy and the strip club another passing thought. I was too wrapped up in my own life to notice that I never received a text from Mandy later that night. In fact, I had forgotten all about her until I was in school the next morning and my classmate was conspicuously absent.

No doubt about it, she wasn't there. I rationalized that she simply lost track of time making her rent money and ended up staying out too late. Her empty chair gave me butterflies, but I told myself that she was probably at home in bed, exhausted and asleep. When you are that tired, forgetting to send a text message wasn't unreasonable. Satisfied with my rationalization, I didn't dwell too deeply on her absence.

The following day was the same thing, and I grew concerned; she still hadn't reached out to me and my texts asking about her whereabouts went unanswered. I kept obsessively checking my phone that day, hoping that each notification was from Mandy.

I didn't know her very well, so I couldn't report her missing; I didn't know her last name, where she lived, and didn't even remember what car she drove. I couldn't ask another classmate, either, because I risked embarrassing her and exposing her crisis. Her personal life wasn't my business to share, so I kept my mouth shut. Finally, on the morning of the third day, I awoke to the sound of my phone ringing.

"Hello...?" I answered groggily, still half asleep.

"Hey E., it's me, Mandy. Can you talk for a second?"

Her voice sounded tense, and far away.

"Wha..? Mandy?" I asked, rubbing my eyes and rolling out of bed, "where have you been? I didn't see you in class. You missed a test."

I couldn't hide my relief, and the sound of her voice shook me from my sleepy stupor immediately.

Fully alert, I listened intently as Mandy recounted a story to me that ended with her being in a town about ten hours' drive away. She confided in me that she was trying to get away from her pimp and needed help.

"Um... What?" I asked incredulously.

I started laughing, knowing she was joking because the words she was saying didn't make any sense. After all, I had seen her just a few days before and everything was fine. The idea of her suddenly being trapped in another state ensnared by a cruel pimp was completely absurd, and surely the stuff of fiction.

Turns out, it was not a joke at all. Somehow in the span of just a couple of days, she had managed to get caught up with some loser who had beaten the shit out of her and driven her to some other club across the country in order to pimp her out. Following this series of unlikely events, she had already progressed to the stage where she was trying to escape her pimp because it dawned on her that he didn't really love her.

I listened, astonished as I sipped my coffee, amazed at how absolutely fucking ridiculous it was. I questioned her, having a hard time believing her story, but she insisted it was true. I stalled, not sure what to say; I didn't want to get embroiled in what could very well be a sex-trafficking operation.

"Wow Mandy, that's really something..."

I wasn't entirely certain the facts were precisely how she presented them, either. It seemed too outlandish to be this cut and dry, and I suspected there was far more to this than she let on. But there was a chance, however improbable, that her story *was* entirely true.

Sex trafficking is no joke, and is the kind of thing that people do serious prison time for. Dawning on me that perhaps her story was true, I became anxious about my connection to her. Generally speaking, I did my best to stay under the radar when it came to legal issues.

Getting involved in any way with something so potentially serious went against my personal principles. I knew I couldn't offer any real help to her, so I did the best thing I could think of: I advised her to contact local law enforcement for assistance.

285

She wasn't happy with this answer, being afraid of getting in trouble herself, and wanted me to help her. I was not about to get in my car and drive ten hours away to deal with her bullshit. I did warn her about this very thing before taking her out to the club, and I didn't think it was right for her to expect me to clean up her mess.

Considering her story, I vacillated between feeling hugely at fault, and feeling indignant; she had clearly disregarded my instructions, which I emphasized repeatedly were of the utmost importance in this profession. I was not sure how to proceed. Did I help her, risking myself in the process, and become the unwilling savior? What if I got pulled into her problems in the process? I found it hard to believe it would be as simple as picking her up from a gas station and driving off without incident.

From the outside, it may look like I am being a cold-hearted asshole for being so insensitive to her situation. Unlike what movies would have you believe, real life was dark and gritty, and I knew going down there would not turn into some humorous bonding escapade where we narrowly escape the odds and somehow come out on top.

Real life had many people ending up in prison or lying dead, half buried in the woods. After deliberating, I decided to err on the side of caution; I could not risk becoming inadvertently wrapped up in what could very well be highly dangerous, illegal activities.

"Well, that really is unfortunate, Mandy. Do let me know how that turns out for you. I gotta go."

The sound of her protests became literally and figuratively distant as I took the phone from my ear and hung up on her.

As I sipped my coffee, I sat down and stared out the patio window and watched the rain. The pitter patter from the droplets hitting the roof filled me with a sense of calm. I sighed deeply, unable to stop mulling over what had just transpired.

The whole situation was incredibly unusual; I had been an escort for nearly half a decade, and I had never *once* been approached by a pimp, let alone beaten up by one. That she had managed to fall in love with one and end up in a city across the country in such a short time was completely ridiculous.

The more I thought about it as the raindrops fell, the more confused I became. How did something like that even happen? How did she sit in a car for hours, never stopping to think that perhaps what she was doing was a bad idea?

She had her phone. She could have called the police in the bathroom at a rest stop at any time, but she didn't. Having traveled for leisure, I knew that anti sex-trafficking signs were abundant in rest-stop restrooms. It was impossible to travel along the interstate without seeing at least one of them.

Grumbling into my coffee, I felt bad. Instead of improving her financial dilemma, I had invariably made her life worse in more ways than one. It was comforting to know that she was at least reaching out for help, and I hoped her next call was to law enforcement.

Taking another sip of my warm beverage, I decided that the poor outcome was nothing but a stroke of terrible luck. Likely the unfortunate result of a series of bad choices exacerbated by my classmate's lack of practical experience as an adult entertainer. A bit of the old wrong place at the wrong time. Satisfied with my internal explanation of events, I mentally moved on, pouring myself into my studies and not giving the situation a second thought.

Perhaps it was because I considered Mandy's unfortunate destiny such a fluke, I didn't think twice when I agreed to help another woman in a similar state of utter financial desperation.

Worker Shelby

A casual acquaintance from school approached me one day begging for help. She was behind on her rent and mere days from becoming homeless. To make matters more complicated, she was going through a nasty divorce, and her dilemma was directly the result of her former spouse financially screwing her. I really felt for her; it was easy to empathize with her hatred for men. I dealt with jerks on a regular basis, so I knew just how awful they could be.

When she brought up the idea of getting a job at my agency, I balked; she was, in the kindest words I can manage, not the ideal body

287

type for this type of work. Sure, she was blonde, but she was also overweight, and was not what I would call conventionally attractive.

The idea was to be a fantasy, enticing clients with an experience they would never forget, not to offer them a woman they could easily pick up at a local gas station. With this woman, I couldn't get around the glaring fact that there wasn't much to be desired. Still, she possessed enthusiasm in spades, which was more than I could say for most of the people I worked with.

Sympathetic to her situation, I agreed to procure her employment at my agency as a call girl. After what happened with Mandy, I didn't want to take my chances stepping into another club; I still felt a little grimy from before and couldn't be bothered to waste my time in seedy strip joints. There wasn't much cash to be made, anyway, and I wanted to make some money, too. Unlike last time, I didn't have the fluid capital to sacrifice my working hours to solely focus on teaching.

The other reason I chose the agency versus a club was that even if we went to a classier establishment, she couldn't hack it due to her weight. I didn't like it, but being rail-thin was what sold.

Since the options were limited, the path forward was clear: my new would-be protégé would skip the bullshit and go straight to private parties. What she lacked in natural beauty she more than made up in confidence. It was immediately apparent during the first booking we did together that she was cut from a different cloth; she had no hang-ups about getting down and dirty to show clients a good time and would do things with them I never would.

Her sparkling, bubbly personality captivated clients and made her the life of the party wherever we went. She took shots with them, did bong hits and shared cigarettes, and overall did a great job of forging connections and showing customers a great time. Her less-than-perfect looks were irrelevant, especially with no other women around for comparison.

I only had to spend a few multi-girl shows training her, being sure to hammer home the essentials, before I felt she was capable of being on her own. I taught her how to negotiate with clients, set hard limits on what she would and would not do, and to avoid accepting drinks from anyone.

I made a point to caution against drinking alcohol or using drugs with the clients, and also communicated explicitly that she should not offer sex in exchange for money. While I was training her, she verbally agreed to my instructions, but her behavior told a different story.

She would drink and carry on with the clients without a care in the world, and it made me uneasy. I lectured her about it, and she agreed that her behavior was dangerous. She also promised me she would make better choices, but I had a feeling her promises were just as empty as the bottles of liquor littering her apartment.

I had to accept that she was her own person, and it was out of my hands what she chose to do behind closed doors. Since things were mostly okay, barring her recklessness, I felt confident stepping away and letting her out from under my wing.

*

I heard nothing from her for well over a month and honestly forgot all about her. I was busy with my own life and wasn't socially inclined. I enjoyed my solitude, and not hearing from an acquaintance was the norm, so I thought nothing of it.

My peace was interrupted one afternoon when I received an unexpected phone call from my employer. There was no text message indicating a booking, and I had not received any notice that I would be contacted in advance. This was highly irregular, so I stared at the ringing phone with growing apprehension. I had this feeling, deep in my heart, that I was about to be involved in some bullshit, and I wanted nothing to do with it.

When I answered the phone, my suspicions were confirmed: I was informed that my acquaintance would be coming to my house to drop off some money that was owed to the company. Not counting the lack of notice, this was a very odd request for multiple reasons.

The only way to owe money to the company was through booking fees. Whenever a girl was booked, the agency charged a base hourly rate and a good chunk of it went to the company. A small portion was given to the escort, and the rest of the entertainer's money was made

289

entirely through tips. The company had a firm policy on depositing their share of the booking fee at the bank the following day, so it didn't make sense why my acquaintance would owe money. Strangely, the money was being brought to me instead of the bank.

I was very confused, but I knew better than to ask questions; I wanted to stay on a need-to-know basis so I could stay out of whatever drama was going on. It was already bad enough that I had to collect owed money, and I didn't want to become any more involved than I already was.

I sat on my front porch step, waiting patiently, and speculated about what manner of train wreck was about to grace my presence. Sighing, I shook my head and gazed out into the empty parking lot. It didn't take a genius to know that things had gone wrong, but just *how* wrong was the burning question.

Before long, an older model car that roughly resembled a steaming pile of dog shit pulled into a space and parked in front of my house. I couldn't believe that pile of junk was safe to drive, let alone road legal. Vibrations from the base rattled the porch step, and I frowned, disliking the disturbance in my peaceful neighborhood.

In the passenger seat, I could see my acquaintance, and sitting beside her was a man I did not recognize. Sighing again, I stood up and casually made my way towards the car. I was in no hurry to deal with whatever bullshit this was, but the sooner I got it over with the better.

The passenger-side window rolled down when I got close, and a thick plume of smoke wafted into the open air. The smoke smelled of stale cigarettes and crappy weed. I made eye contact with her, and frowned, making a point to silently communicate my displeasure. She had a sheepish, apologetic look on her face and mouthed the words *I'm sorry*.

The man seated in the driver's seat was a shirtless African American man covered in shitty tattoos. His boxers were visible above his sagging pants, and I could see a gun tucked into his front waistband. He looked to be in his older twenties, maybe early thirties. He had a joint in the corner of his mouth and gaudy jewelry on. Overall, he looked like the living embodiment of trying too hard to be a gangster.

It was then that I noticed that my acquaintance had a cast on her left arm and was babying it carefully. Judging by the looks of it, her arm was recently broken, and I had a sneaking suspicion about who had broken it.

I stared at her, wordlessly taking in the sight in front of me, when her companion spoke up and broke the silence.

"Hey baby girl, you lookin' *real* good. You want a job?" he smiled as he spoke, not bothering to remove the joint from his lips.

I scowled, not in the mood for any bullshit from a woman beater. Men who hit women were the scum of the earth, and seeing her broken arm filled me with rage.

"Shut the fuck up and give me the money," I snapped.

I did my best to stare him down through the window; this guy was a real piece of shit and clearly wasn't afraid of taking things to violence. Fortunately, he didn't know who I was, but he did know I was collecting money for the agency. I was hoping my rude confidence would make him uneasy enough to hand over the money without a fight.

Conceptually, the agency was a nebulous idea that many people outside the business had no firm grasp of. Sure, I knew that it was a small business that paid its taxes and was run by a small, close-knit group of staff that wouldn't hurt a fly, but no one else knew that.

In the past, laymen had shared their beliefs with me that companies like mine were run by thugs, hardened criminals, or mafia types. There were fantastical assumptions that the people involved were scary and could make undesirables disappear.

To me, it all sounded silly. No one I worked with had ever told me about encountering a company like that, which meant the prevailing fantasy was nothing but baseless rumors likely generated by media-mediated misconceptions, or perhaps by the companies themselves to deter prying eyes. I was banking on this unknown, hoping the stereotype would be enough to intimidate the asshole sitting stoned in the driver's seat.

Luckily, the stars aligned, and the man was too stunned to argue. After fumbling around in the center console for a moment, he produced a wad of cash which he promptly handed to Shelby, who then handed it to me.

I glowered at him, stuffing the money into my pocket, letting my direct gaze burn a hole into him as he became increasingly uncomfortable. Underneath his tough-guy persona, he was a cowardly little bitch, and we both knew it.

For clarity, I never had a boyfriend who would beat me up, but the people I knew who did said it sucked. I always encouraged them to leave their abusers, which meant that I usually wasn't welcome at their homes; their lovers seldom approved of a friend who tried to talk some sense into their victim.

The excuse I heard a lot was that the boyfriend didn't want me around because I was a bad influence. Which, from the abuser's perspective, perhaps I was. I was confident and didn't tolerate the aggressive bullying crap that cowardly men often used to control their victims. I didn't let them push me around, physically or otherwise, and that was bad news for a person who thrived on a system of fear-based control.

Ignoring the man completely, I addressed the sad girl with the broken arm gazing up at me from the passenger seat. She looked tense but refused to get out of the car when I offered her the option. I asked her if she was okay, told the man to shut up when he tried to answer for her, and ultimately accepted her response that she would text me later. I didn't like it, but there was little I could do. What a mess.

Later that night, I got a call from her. Her voice was muffled as she explained to me that it wasn't as bad as it looked, that yes, he had broken her arm, but he was actually really sweet, and it was an accident. She claimed that he loved her, and he only broke her arm because he got too carried away.

In true victim fashion, she blamed herself for his behavior and made excuses justifying his abuse. It was hard to listen to; her once cheerful disposition was now replaced with trepidation, and it filled me with sorrow.

She went on to say that he was her manager now and had taken full control of her finances and work schedule. While she didn't state it explicitly, she alluded to him forcing her to work when she didn't want to and punishing her when she didn't make enough money.

I read between the lines and figured her broken arm was the result of her failing to satisfy his financial demands. When she went to the hospital, she lied about what happened to avoid being pushed into pressing charges against him. Apparently, the staff knew it was the result of domestic violence due to the type of fracture, but she refused to comply with requests to involve law enforcement.

All of what she was telling me painted a clear picture as to why I was collecting past-due booking fees from her. My employer had no patience for the kind of drama she was so clearly enmeshed in, so it made perfect sense that she had been terminated.

The icing on the cake was when she asked me if I wanted to come and work for her boyfriend instead of the agency. After everything she just told me, I couldn't imagine why she thought I would ever say yes to such a ridiculous request. She emphasized that he *wasn't so bad once you got to know him* and repeatedly reminded me that *he will treat you right, I promise.*

I couldn't believe what I was hearing, and suspected that trying to recruit me was her pimp's idea. I asked her again if she was okay, and then she burst into tears. Through her choked sobs, she confided in me that she was pregnant by this man, and how she wanted to keep the baby.

I said nothing, listening to the misery drifting through the phone and echoing in my mind.

Pregnant. Keeping the baby. Jesus.

She had really fucked up, no doubt about it, and there was little I could do to bail her out of her own poor judgment. Before I got off the phone, I told her she needed to get an abortion and leave the abusive relationship immediately. I even offered to pay for it and take her to the clinic. Of course, she refused.

As a final measure, I advised her to call the police and get in touch with a domestic violence shelter, encouraging her to utilize the many resources available for this exact kind of situation. I didn't know where she was staying and had no way to send the police myself, so my hands were tied when it came to reporting.

Besides, she needed to *want* to leave, and no amount of intervening on her behalf would solve the problem if she refused to accept the help.

In the end, we went back and forth about getting an abortion, which she refused to do, and she wouldn't agree to take any of my advice. I knew I couldn't become personally involved, so I wished her the best, and informed her solemnly that it was never too late to get help before hanging up the phone.

My heart was hurting for her, especially since she was pregnant, but I had to emotionally distance myself from what had happened. As tragic as it was, I couldn't hold myself personally accountable for the choices of another adult. I had made a concerted effort to educate her on the dangers of the industry, so the fallout from mismanaging her life was not my burden to bear.

That night in bed, I couldn't help but marvel at the similarities between what had happened to Mandy and the now-pregnant Shelby. Just like Mandy, she had rapidly spiraled out of control and encountered situations I hadn't seen once during the entire span of my employment.

I was astounded that both of them had managed to so thoroughly fuck things up at such an unprecedented pace. Staring up at the ceiling, I wondered how I had never run into the same problems. Considering that I wasn't particularly special or intelligent, I attributed my success to not using drugs and a general distrust of others.

It was around this time that I began to understand that not everyone is cut out for being an escort and that it took a special type of person to avoid falling victim to the ever-present pitfalls associated with the profession.

Not long after, and against my better judgment, I helped yet another desperate woman into the business and things took a similarly disastrous turn. I tried so hard to prevent history from repeating itself but failed miserably. I had convinced myself that if I did a more thorough job preparing a person, they wouldn't end up like the other two. Sadly, this just wasn't the case, and another poor woman ended up pregnant with a physically abusive boyfriend.

After watching my fourth trainee end up in jail, I made an oath to never help another person into the industry. I had enough objective evidence at that point to know for certain that even if I educated a person as best I could, there was a high probability that they would make catastrophic choices anyway, ultimately leading them to ruin.

For reasons I did not understand, it seemed that most women were simply incapable of avoiding terrible situations. Since I couldn't sleep at night thinking I was irreparably ruining lives, leading one woman after another to terrible destinies, I resolved to maintain my stance no matter what.

Additionally, just saying no to hopeful inquirers wasn't enough. My conscience demanded that I make a concerted effort to talk people out of getting into the industry in the first place; if a woman approached me asking me questions about getting a job at my agency, I would do my best to dissuade her.

I wouldn't sugarcoat anything and painted a bleak, and sadly accurate, picture detailing how awful and soul crushing the job was. I explained the dangers, the moral compromises, and the frequent sleepless nights.

No woman who spoke to me was under the impression that the job was financially stable or lucrative, either. I made it clear that it was unpredictable and by no means an end-all solution to their problems.

Once the harsh reality of it was laid bare, many would-be escorts had second thoughts. I know that a few of them chose to pursue regular jobs or an education instead, and I was grateful for that. Even if my influence was small, it made me feel like I was making a difference by preventing disasters.

Of course, some people could not be dissuaded; try as I might, some women ignored my advice and still sought out the job anyway. Since I had done my due diligence and refused to offer assistance of any kind to get them started, I no longer harbored any guilt or a sense of responsibility for what happened to them.

Afterword

So, you're probably wondering, *how does it end?*

Did I eventually find a wealthy client a la *Pretty Woman* and have all my problems whisked away by a limitless bank account?

Did I finally say *enough is enough* and tell my boss off once and for all, before quitting in a brilliant, unforgettable blaze of glory?

Did I encounter some unspeakable tragedy, barely escaping with my life, and then swear off the industry out of abject terror?

Well, no.

Real life is not a fairy tale, and often does not have penultimate moments that end things with a bang any more than it has beautiful, happy endings that can be tied up with a neat little bow. What I can say is that I did not meet my prince charming at work, and that I never told my boss how much I hated the job and that she could shove it up her ass.

What actually happened was far more mundane than could be believed; after I graduated from school top of my class and started a respectable job, my interest in escorting slowly petered out. That is to say, I didn't stop immediately. I carefully phased out my financial safety net before saying goodbye to the industry forever.

After I left the job, though, I was left with a parting gift I never anticipated: a unique perspective on society that has flavored my every interaction since.

Even today, well over a decade later, I still struggle with the way being an escort fundamentally changed me. Events that are considered tragic or terrifying to others are viewed instead with an objective, almost factual indifference. Sometimes, I find inappropriate, awful things amusing, much to the horror and confusion of those around me.

I am also plagued with a sensitivity to situations that others find equally confusing and strange. The most obvious example is that I still cannot stand the smell of alcohol on a person's breath and find large social gatherings and bars intolerable. I find no joy or entertainment value in parties, and do not understand the appeal of getting drunk, using drugs, or anything of the sort.

The very thought of older men looking at me fills me with instant revulsion and disgust, and I can't help but find the unsolicited kindness of male strangers under any circumstances to be anything more than an excuse to try and have sex with me.

Romantically, my ruthlessly ingrained belief that men cheat has fostered an intense distrust in my relationships. This spilled over into my platonic relationships as well, where I have inadvertently become sexist, questioning the motives of men and preferring women by default.

Physically, once I was free of all ties to the industry, I did a major overhaul of my appearance. Because I no longer required admiration from men to get by, I stopped wasting time and effort on beauty. As true now as it was then, I am a huge nerd, and prefer video games and anime over skirts and high heels nine times out of ten.

The first thing I did was go on a no-shaving strike and let my body hair grow wild and free for months on end. I also stopped wearing makeup and dressing provocatively, instead adopting a comfortable style somewhat reminiscent of a sleepy homeless person. I wore messy buns, mismatched socks, and seldom brushed my hair. I polished my appearance to professional standards during business hours at my new post-graduation career, but nothing more.

As a whole, when I began interacting with more people in what I call 'the real world', I started to understand that my experiences and perceptions of society were not relatable to those around me; I couldn't discuss what I had been through in casual conversation, and many people view what I did to get by as immoral.

Some of my opinions, like how sex work should be legal and unionized so the workers are safe and have proper medical care, are not popular and elicit negative reactions even from close friends. Because of this, even today years later, my former life remains very much a secret. Speaking to me, you would never guess in a million years the truth about my past.

I think it is very important to note that as a person, I don't consider myself particularly good, or bad. I am just a person, not on a journey to make amends for past faults, and not self-righteous operating under the assumption that I am superior to others for possessing resilience. I am simply a person, not different from any other sex worker, former or current.

None of the women I met, myself included, wanted to work as an escort. We only did it because we had no other choice. After working for five and a half years seeing the darker side of humanity, my heart overflowed with compassion for the misfits. I often pause and ponder the *why* behind people living tough lives. What is the story? I know that pervasive homelessness, debilitating mental illness, and drug addiction don't happen overnight. Judging a person based on a mere snapshot of their existence ignores so much of the bigger picture, of the rich, colorful human experience that flavors life itself.

I was fortunate to find a way out, fighting for it every step of the way, but not every person is so lucky. Overdoses happen. Abusive boyfriends and pimps beat people to death. A woman is murdered, and the body is dumped in a ditch. These were all possible realities for me and are the tragic futures waiting for many women in the business today.

About The Author

Long since retired from her days moonlighting as an entertainer, E. can be found in the sleepy pine forests of the Pacific Northwest enjoying the solitude of the mossy greenery. Having fully embraced her inner nerd, when she isn't working her dream job, E. spends her time watching anime, playing *Magic the Gathering*, and playing video games.

Connect on Social Media

You can find scene readings, interviews, Q & A sessions, and more on YouTube under E. S. Silversmith's handle *bcdmemoir*.

www.ingramcontent.com/pod-product-compliance
Lightning Source LLC
Chambersburg PA
CBHW011213120626
46545CB00008B/2980